SYLLOGE OF COINS
OF THE BRITISH ISLES

SYLLOGE OF COINS OF THE BRITISH ISLES

Published by the British Academy, except Nos. 8 and 34 published by the Trustees of the British Museum, and Nos. 16, 31, and 33 published by Spink & Son Ltd.

All quarto, cloth bound

SYLLOGE OF COINS OF THE BRITISH ISLES

36

STATE MUSEUM BERLIN COIN CABINET

Anglo-Saxon, Anglo-Norman, and
Hiberno-Norse Coins

BY

BERND KLUGE

Dr. phil., Keeper of medieval coins

PUBLISHED FOR THE BRITISH ACADEMY AND
THE STATE MUSEUM BERLIN, CAPITAL OF THE GDR

by the OXFORD UNIVERSITY PRESS
and SPINK & SON LIMITED
5-7 KING STREET, ST JAMES'S, LONDON S.W.I
1987

Oxford University Press, Walton Street Oxford OX2 6DP

Oxford New York Toronto
Delhi Bombay Calcutta Madras Karachi
Petaling Jaya Singapore Hong Kong Tokyo
Nairobi Dar es Salaam Cape Town
Melbourne Auckland

and associated companies in
Beirut Berlin Ibadan Nicosia

Oxford is a trade mark of Oxford University Press

British Library Cataloguing in Publication Data
Sylloge of coins of the British Isles.
36, State Museum Berlin, coin cabinet:
Anglo-Saxon, Anglo-Norman, and Hiberno-
Norse coins.
1. coins, British—Catalogs
I. Kluge, Bernd II. British Academy
III. State Museum. Berlin
737.4941'074 CJ2476
ISBN 0-19-726048-9

Printed in Great Britain
at the University Printing House, Oxford
by David Stanford
Printer to the University

CONTENTS

CONTENTS

FOREWORD

THIS fascicule of the *Sylloge of Coins of the British Isles* is the result of collaboration between the State Museum Berlin, capital of the German Democratic Republic, and the British Academy. It was the late Professor Michael Dolley who in 1978 invited the coin cabinet of the State Museum to publish their stock of Anglo-Saxon coins in British Academy's *Sylloge* series. The Generaldirector of the State Museum and the Ministry of Culture of the German Democratic Republic gave their consent and support to this undertaking which was initiated by a visit of two of the editors to Berlin, Professor Dolley and Mr Mark Blackburn in 1979.

The present volume is the work of Dr Bernd Kluge, Keeper of the collection of medieval coins in the Berlin coin cabinet. We hope that it will provide a useful contribution to the study of Anglo-Saxon numismatics as well as that of German medieval monetary history, and set an example for the development of numismatic research through international collaboration.

We wish to extend our formal thanks to the British Academy and the editors of *SCBI*, as well as to the Generaldirector of the State Museum Berlin and the Ministry of Culture of the German Democratic Republic.

DR HEINZ FENGLER
Director of the Berlin coin cabinet

ACKNOWLEDGEMENTS

THIS fascicule owes its conception to the late Professor Michael Dolley. His summary listing of the Anglo-Saxon coins in Berlin prepared in 1979 was the first step towards the realization of this volume and he maintained a warm interest in its progress. Unfortunately he did not live to see its publication, but this volume will always be intimately connected with his name.

Besides Michael Dolley I give my warm thanks to the other editors, Mr Christopher Blunt and Mr Mark Blackburn, for their invaluable help in reading and correcting earlier drafts of the manuscript. Many other individuals have also contributed substantially to its final form. Particular mention should be made of five scholars who gave specialist advice, Dr Michael Metcalf on the sceattas, Miss Elizabeth Pirie on the stycas, Mr Hugh Pagan on the early East Anglian coins, Mrs Yvonne Harvey on coins of Winchester, and Dr Veronica Smart the normalized forms of the moneyers' names. The late Mr Herwig Leonhardt made the majority of the casts on which the plates are based; the rest were produced by Mrs Regina Boreck. To all concerned I am most grateful for their kind and efficient help.

I wish to extend my formal thanks to the British Academy, the British Council, the State Museum Berlin, and the Ministry of Culture of the German Democratic Republic which enabled me to make two study visits to England in connection with the *Sylloge* in 1981 and 1985. Last but not least, I must express my special thanks to my friend Mark Blackburn who has been unstinting of his time and help in the translation of the text and preparation of the manuscript for the press; and to him and his wife Fiona for their amicable hospitality during my visits to England.

Cambridge, September 1985   B. K.

THE COIN CABINET OF THE STATE MUSEUM BERLIN

HISTORY AND DEVELOPMENT

THE coin cabinet is one of the oldest departments of the State Museum in Berlin (GDR). As the coin collection of the electors of Brandenburg, later kings of Prussia, its origins probably go back to the sixteenth century, although its virtual founder may be regarded as Elector Friedrich Wilhelm (1640–88), the Great Elector. In 1649 he initiated the first inventory of the collection, which records 4,900 coins, predominantly ancient ones in the prevailing taste. Friedrich Wilhelm and his son Friedrich III (1688–1713, from 1701 King Friedrich I of Prussia) were both personally interested in the collection and its progress, and for a time the coins were housed in their own appartments in the castle of Berlin. A monument to the collection as it was around 1700 is provided by the *Thesaurus Brandenburgicus* published in three lavish volumes (1696–1701), which included illustrations of a large number of coins. The author, Lorenz Beger (1653–1705), the first outstanding and professional numismatist in Berlin, arrived in 1686 with the coin collection of the evangelic electors of the Palatinate which had been bequeathed to the electors of Brandenburg. Until his death in 1705 Beger had the whole collection under his care and this was the first flourishing period in the history of the cabinet; though it was to be followed by a century of stagnation. The coin cabinet became part of the collection of antiquities and was supervised by librarians or other scholars without any special numismatic interest or knowledge. When Napoleon captured Berlin in 1806 the greater part of the collection was evacuated to Memel in East Prussia, but another part was taken by the French troops to Paris and this was not intact when returned in 1815.

In 1830 the Royal (later State) Museum was founded and the Royal collection of antiquities and art was exhibited in a newly erected building (the 'Altes Museum') opposite the castle at the Lustgarten, designed for the purpose by Friedrich Schinkel. The coin cabinet also moved to the new building and became part of the department of Antiquities ('Antiquarium'). The medieval and modern coins were separated from the ancient coins and were independently administered until 1868 by Heinrich Bolzenthal (1797–1870) their first keeper. In 1840 Julius Friedlaender (1813–84) became assistant and later keeper of ancient coins. When Bolzenthal

Note: A more detailed description of the history of the Berlin cabinet is given in: J. Friedlaender and A. v. Sallet, *Das Königliche Münzkabinet. Geschichte und Übersicht der Sammlung nebst erklärender Beschreibung der auf Schautischen ausgelegten Auswahl*, 2nd edn. (Berlin 1877) and J. Menadier, *Die Schausammlung des Münzkabinetts im Kaiser Friedrich Museum. Eine Münzgeschichte der europäischen Staaten* (Berlin 1919).

retired in 1868 the ancient and the medieval and modern coins were reunited and the coin cabinet became a new department of the Museum, of which Friedlaender was the first director. Under his administration the Berlin coin cabinet established an international reputation. Even before this, acquisitions such as the collections of Adler 1821 (*c*.28,000 coins), Ruehle von Lilienstern 1842 (*c*.6,000 coins) and Benoni Friedlaender (Julius' father) 1861 (*c*.18,000 coins) were not unimportant, but Friedlaender succeeded in organizing a rapid series of major purchases: 1870 Dannenberg (*c*.3,000 medieval coins), 1873 Gansauge (*c*.6,000 medieval and ancient coins), 1873 Prokesch-Osten (*c*.11,000 ancient Greek coins), 1876 Guthrie (*c*.15,000 oriental coins), 1879 Grote (*c*.9,500 medieval coins). Such enormous acquisitions were only possible because in addition to the very substantial Museum budget, Friedlaender was able to obtain further grants of public money from the Prussian Provincial Diet and the Prussian Ministry of Public Workmanship and Education. In 1840 the cabinet possessed 26,341 ancient and 46,770 medieval and modern coins. When Friedlaender died in 1884 he had enlarged the collection to 90,000 ancient coins, 79,000 medieval and modern coins, and 22,500 oriental coins.

Under Friedlaender's successors, Alfred von Sallet (1842–97) who was director 1884–97 and Julius Menadier (1854–1939) who was director 1898–1921, the rise and growth of the collection continued, and the following important collections were acquired: 1892 Dannenberg (*c*.5,000 highly important medieval coins), 1896 Fikentscher (*c*.15,000 German late medieval coins), 1900 Imhoof-Blumer (*c*.22,000 ancient Greek coins), 1906 Loebbecke (*c*.28,000 ancient Greek coins), 1911 Gariel-Ferrari (*c*.1,000 Carolingian coins). Apart from these rich collections many further acquisitions were made with the aim of achieving as complete a representation as possible in all series, special regard being paid to the ancient and medieval German coins.

In 1904 the cabinet moved to the newly built Kaiser-Friedrich-Museum, now the Bode Museum, where it was given rooms constructed with special regard to the requirements of a coin cabinet. In these functional rooms the collection could for the first time be systematically spread out and be given a completely new arrangement.

With World War I and the following period of inflation, and particularly during the Third Reich, the growth of the cabinet was brought to a halt. At the beginning of World War II the Museum was closed and when the bombing of Berlin commenced the collection was packed up and deposited in secure basements. By the end of the war in 1945 the museums in Berlin on the 'Museums' island' were heavily damaged, some lay in ruins. They no longer provided adequate security and the collections were therefore taken to the Soviet Union where they were well accommodated and carefully restored. In 1958 they were brought back to the GDR and the coins returned to their old rooms where the coin cabinet is still situated today. The collection lost only a very small number of pieces during the war; just one from the Anglo-Saxon series (*Sylloge* no. **155**). Its total stock is at the moment about half a million coins, medals, jetons, seals, and payments in non-coin forms. The medieval and modern coins presently number *c.*160,000 specimens, of which *c.*2,600 are English (including 10 'Tealby', 46 Short Cross, 104 Long Cross, 47 Edwardian sterlings, 98 later medieval to 1509, 479 Tudor and Stuart, 890 modern and 1,054 tokens), 179 Scottish (66 medieval to 1542, 113 post-medieval), and 295 Irish (81 medieval to 1509, 214 post-medieval).

THE COLLECTION OF ANGLO-SAXON COINS

English coins have never been well to the fore of the cabinet's interest. The main emphasis of the collection was and still is the ancient and the German coinages, but scholars like Julius Friedlaender and Julius Menadier were also interested in the development of all European series with special regard to coins of the Middle Ages. The Anglo-Saxon element of the collection benefitted particularly from the influx of English coins of the late tenth and the eleventh century into the Slav lands, since much of the West Slav region until World War I and II belonged to the territory of Prussia, from 1871 that of the German Reich. Many of the hoards discovered during the nineteenth and early twentieth century were acquired in whole or in part by the Berlin cabinet, either directly or via private collections. No less than 48 hoards from the Slav region are represented in the *Sylloge* and nearly half of the coins recorded here have specific hoard provenances. This is perhaps the most important aspect of the present volume, especially since this material is illustrated here for the first time and it can in many cases be used to refine the published accounts of the Anglo-Saxon element of these hoards (see the following section of hoard listings).

For the great majority of the hoards only a selection of coins were acquired. It was never intended to have a separate collection of hoards such as that which exists in the Stockholm coin cabinet. The coins were all integrated in the systematic collection and badly preserved or fragmented material was not normally retained. Providing the type and the mint were represented, the cabinet did not go out of its way to obtain coins of different moneyers or exhibiting variants in the legends. This in part explains why the number of coins in the Berlin collection cannot compete with those in the cabinets of Stockholm, Copenhagen, or even Leningrad, though it must also be borne in mind that the Anglo-Saxon element in the West Slav hoards is very much smaller than in the Scandinavian or Russian ones. Furthermore the local museums had an interest in the hoard material so that it was often shared between them and the Berlin coin cabinet. In these cases Berlin normally identified the coins and selected those which it required for the systematic collection (mostly German ones) before sending the rest, usually the greater part, back to the provincial museums. This was the normal routine especially under the administration of Julius Menadier when during the 1880s and 1890s numerous hoards were sent to Berlin. It should also be remembered that until after World War II Germany had no treasure trove law (the 'Bodendenkmalpflegegesetz' relating to antiquities including coins and coin

hoards prior to 1500 was enacted in the GDR in 1954) and hoards were often sold
privately to collectors or dealers, some even going directly into the melting pot.

Those hoards of which the Anglo-Saxon element is preserved intact in the Berlin
coin cabinet are: 'Frankfurt 1840' (no. 29), Stolp/Słupsk 1846 (no. 4), Althoefchen/
Starydworek 1872 (no. 12), Witzmitz/Wicimice 1878 (no. 7), Klein-Roscharden II
1886 (no. 6), and Juura/Odenpäh 1888 (no. 46). The richest of these is Althoefchen/
Starydworek with 77 English coins. Those of which quite large portions, i.e. more
than half of the English coins, are preserved are: Ciechanow 1868 (no. 13), Mgowo
1893 (no. 23), Kinno 1900 (no. 17), and two hoards for which the findspots are
unknown (nos. 39, 40). The remaining 37 finds are represented by a small selection
or contained only a very few Anglo-Saxon, Hiberno-Norse, or imitative coins. One
outstanding exception is the hoard from Lupow/Łupawa 1888 (no. 34), which
consisted almost entirely of crude imitations of German, Anglo-Saxon, and Danish
types and of which 68 specimens displaying Anglo-Saxon influence in their designs
are represented here.

The beginning of the collection of Anglo-Saxon coins can be traced back to the
early nineteenth century. The inventory of c.1825 is the first which records Anglo-
Saxon coins, six of Æthelred II and two of Cnut,[1] besides those in the Adler
collection (see p. 6 below). This small number may be explained by the fact that
when in 1806 the collection was evacuated in the face of the French troops to Memel,
one barrel containing the largest part of the English coins was lost. With the
acquisition of the Adler collection in 1821 the number of Anglo-Saxon coins
increased to 61. During the next 20 years the collection made slow progress; 19 coins
were obtained, 13 of Æthelred II, five of Cnut, and one of Edward the Confessor,
though they cannot now be individually identified. The purchase of the Ruehle von
Lilienstern collection in 1842 (see p. 7 below) then brought a further 192 Anglo-
Saxon coins to the cabinet. Occasional purchases during the years 1842–68 added
another 23 coins (ten of Æthelred II, seven of Cnut, four of Harold I, and two of
Edward the Confessor) as well as the 22 coins from the Benoni Friedlaender
collection acquired in 1861 (p. 8 below).

Thus in 1868, according to the handwritten inventories, the Anglo-Saxon
collection stood at 336 coins. Of these 71 were varied acquisitions, not from the three
major private collections, and these are recorded here as 'Old collection'. Their
provenances are only known in a few cases, for instance the coins from the hoards
from Stolp/Słupsk 1846, Ploetzig/Płocko 1850, Grapzow 1856, and Wielowies 1856.
For the bulk of the coins in the 'Old collection' we can only say that they were
acquired before 1868. Most probably all the coins came from hoards found in
Prussia, which at that time included Pomerania and a part of Poland (the province
of Posen), and this is supported by two factors. The 'Acquisitions Journal' which

---

[1] Sylloge nos. **207**, **212**, **427**, **530**, **587**, **617**, **1000**. The eighth coin was the same as no. **274** (Friedlaender coll.) and
probably was disposed of when the Friedlaender collection was acquired in 1861.

lists all coins *bought* after 1825, together with the prices paid, makes no mention of Anglo-Saxon coins. On the other hand we know that several eleventh-century hoards which could have contained Anglo-Saxon coins were received by the Museum, but their contents are only very summarily described; an example is the find from the Posen region (no. 28). The three 'porcupine' sceattas in the 'Old collection' could perhaps come from the Barthe hoard (no. 1).

The year 1868 was a decisive one in the history of the Berlin coin cabinet. As mentioned above the cabinet became an independent department of the Museum and Julius Friedlaender its first director. The collection of ancient coins and that of medieval and modern coins were united and a new joint 'Acquisitions Journal' established. It recorded all acquisitions with a sequential numbering, from 1870 onwards with an annual current number (e.g. 556/1872), and these numbers were noted on the ticket given to each coin. Thus, after 1868 the provenance of all coins can normally be determined from the acquisition number; this system is still in use.

The stock of Anglo-Saxon, Anglo-Norman, and Hiberno-Norse coins in the collection today was largely built up under the direction of Friedlaender and Menadier, scholars of exceptional ability and wide range, who pursued any opportunity that arose to develop the medieval collection. Between 1868 and 1890, 363 Anglo-Saxon coins were purchased. The most important acquisitions were the collections of Dannenberg 1870 (42 coins), Gansauge 1873 (72 coins), Grote 1879 (94 coins), the Anglo-Saxon element of the Althoefchen/Starydworek hoard 1872 (77 coins), and 11 mainly ninth-century Anglo-Saxon coins bought in 1872 from the London coin dealer William Webster. The period 1891–1900, when the medieval coins were under the keepership of Menadier, saw the purchase of the highest number of Anglo-Saxon coins in any decade, 226 specimens. They came mostly from hoards, notably Mgowo 1893, Juura 1888 (acquired in 1897), Birglau/Bierzgłowo 1898, and two unknown hoards from Poland and Russia, though complemented by numerous acquisitions in sales or by private treaty. From the beginning of the twentieth century the inflow of Anglo-Saxon coins declined. Two significant acquisitions were made early in the century. In 1905, 15 ninth- and early tenth-century Anglo-Saxon coins from the Murdoch sale were bought in London from Spinks, their quality and importance being a tribute to Menadier's judgement even in a series with which he was unfamiliar. These were followed in 1911 by 28 coins of the Vikings of Northumbria, part of the great Gariel-Ferrari collection of Carolingian coins; in the nineteenth century these coins were often attributed to Frankish Viking mints. It has already been said that World War I brought an end to the remarkable growth of the collection in general as well as of the Anglo-Saxon series. Between the two Wars only 68 coins relevant to the Sylloge were acquired, 57 of them degraded imitations from the 1930 Hoffmann collection which originally derive from the Lupow/Łupawa hoard. Since 1945, 28 Anglo-Saxon coins have been acquired for the collection, and only one Viking-Age hoard containing a small number of fragments of Anglo-Saxon coins has been discovered in the GDR, that from Dorow 1975 now deposited in the Museum fur Ur- und Frühgeschichte in Schwerin.[2]

A more detailed account of the major private collections which have contributed Anglo-Saxon coins to the Berlin cabinet is given below in chronological order of their acquisition.

ADLER COLLECTION 1821

The collection of the Berlin merchant Peter Philipp Adler (1726–1814) was purchased in 1821 after protracted negotiations. It was an enormous, universal collection of 28,000 coins, of which Adler himself wrote a manuscript catalogue in three folio volumes entitled *Numophylacium Adlerianum* which was passed to the Berlin cabinet with his coins. For the medieval series there are numerous mis-attributions reflecting the state of numismatic knowledge at the beginning of the nineteenth century, but since Adler for the most part reproduced the legends we are able to identify many of his coins in the trays today. For the English coins, described in vol. I, pp. 95–115, he listed 287 specimens from the ninth to the eighteenth century. They start with one coin of Eadmund of East Anglia (855–69), followed by those of Æthelred II (978–1016) which he attributed quite well.

In this Sylloge, 51 coins from the Adler collection are recorded. Two further coins are described in his catalogue but are no longer present in the collection, having probably been disposed of by sale or exchange in the nineteenth century. One is a coin of Æthelred II, *Last Small Cross* type (Winchester, uncertain moneyer) and the second is Harold I, *Fleur-de-Lis* type (probably trefoil of pellets variety, mint and moneyer not specified). Some others described as English are in fact Danish or badly preserved German types or Slav imitations.

As a collector Adler did not specialize in any particular series, but took whatever he was able to obtaïn. English coins were not prominent in his collection; he had bought those that came his way without hunting them out. Since we know from his letters that he had had the opportunity to acquire hoard material, it is very probable that his coins from Æthelred II to Edward the Confessor came from West Slav finds, even if we have no specific hoard provenances. Moreover, the dominance of coins of Æthelred II (22 specimens) compared with those of Cnut (17 specimens), and later Anglo-Saxon rulers (5 specimens), and the presence of imitations, are typical of the general composition of the West Slav finds. By contrast he had only 12 later medieval English coins from 1066 to 1422, mostly sterlings.

---

[2] B. Kluge, 'Die europäischen Münzen des Schatzfundes von Dorow, Kr. Grimmen', *Jahrbuch Bodendenkmal-pflege in Mecklenburg* 1977 (Berlin 1978), pp. 181–206.

RUEHLE VON LILIENSTERN COLLECTION 1842

The collection of the Prussian Lieutenant-General August Ruehle von Lilienstern purchased in 1842 was at the time a highly important acquisition for the cabinet's medieval European series, which could admittedly be enlarged considerably. It is probably not an exaggeration to say that this was then the most important collection of medieval European coins from the sixth to the twelfth century in Germany.

Johann Jakob Otto August Ruehle von Lilienstern (1780–1847) was a many-sided, talented personality. As a Major in the Prussian army during the Napoleonic wars, he served at German headquarters. In 1815 he was appointed Colonel, with military functions in the ministry in Berlin, rising to Lieutenant-General in 1835. Besides his career in the army he was a productive writer on military matters, the founder and editor of several journals, a poet, painter and collector of coins and plants. He published only one paper on a numismatic subject in which he wrote about unattributed and unpublished medieval, mostly German, coins.[3]

Ruehle began to collect coins when, after the demobilization of the Prussian army in 1807, he became chamberlain to the Duke of Saxony-Weimar where he had time to follow his interests. He preferred the medieval series which was unusual at this time. He collected with passion and built up a highly important collection of 6,028 coins (1,396 ancient and 4,632 medieval coins) which he offered to the Museum in 1837. The price of 3,500 Talers was not high having regard to the value of the collection, but it was beyond the budget of the Museum so that the purchase could not be completed for some years, until it received approval by an order in council of the Prussian king Friedrich Wilhelm IV. The collection was incorporated into the cabinet in 1842, although it had been deposited there since 1837 in twenty separate boxes.

The strength the Ruehle collection lay in the coins of the early and high Middle Ages, and while in the German series it was later to be exceeded by the Grote and Dannenberg collections, for Anglo-Saxon coins it remains in quantity and quality the most important acquisition the Berlin cabinet has made. After German bracteates and coins of the Dark Ages, Anglo-Saxon coins seem to have held a special interest for Ruehle. Unfortunately no catalogue of his collection exists, only his own manuscript summary, in which the Anglo-Saxon coins appear in second position after the Carolingian ones. No details are recorded, only the number of specimens of Æthelred II (97). When the Ruehle collection was incorporated in the cabinet the coins were distinguished by separate tickets, sometimes noting the mint, moneyer, or weight, and it is on these tickets that we rely for identifying the coins in the trays today.

The present volume records 192 coins from Ruehle von Lilienstern and gives an impression of the importance of his collection. No earlier provenances are recorded

---

[3] 'Beiträge zur Münzkunde des Mittelalters', an appendix to G. B. Loos, *Über die Königlich-Preussische neue Scheidemünze* (Berlin/Posen 1823), pp. 1–32.

for the coins, and it cannot be stated, as in the case of the Adler collection, that they came only from Slav hoards. Those hoards are just one possible source, for it is likely that he bought coins at sales, possibly even in England. The coins of Æthelred II and Cnut for the most part probably derive from Slav hoards, though there is nothing to prove this. Of special interest are ten coins of Æthelstan (924–39) which have a similar green patination and must come from the same hoard (**163–5, 167–72**). This may be an early Pomeranian rather than an English hoard. The coins show no particular regional bias, and the absence of peck marks does not necessarily exclude a Southern Baltic origin for it is not clear that the Slavs were pecking coins in this period. The only Slav hoard containing coins of Æthelstan is the shadowy Pomeranian one from an uncertain findspot (no. 2); may there perhaps be some connection? The next oldest finds with Anglo-Saxon coins from the Slav Lands contain no coins earlier than Edmund (939–46); cf. Blackburn and Jonsson, p. 235, W 2–3;[4] Kluge 1981, pp. 262 and 287.

BENONI FRIEDLAENDER COLLECTION 1861

Benoni Friedlaender (1773–1858), the father of the well known numismatist and first director of the Berlin coin cabinet Julius Friedlaender, became a dedicated amateur scholar and collector of wide knowledge. He was in contact with all the important numismatists of his day, although he never published anything, and it was his son Julius who made the name Friedlaender well known in numismatics.[5] Friedlaender's collection of about 18,000 coins and medals (*c*.6,000 ancient and *c*.12,000 medieval and modern) was purchased by the cabinet in 1861 at his own request. Its most important series was the coins and medals of the Italian Renaissance. The European coins of the Middle Ages were only slightly represented because Friedlaender had come to an agreement with Ruehle von Lilienstern about collecting medieval coins; Friedlaender would concentrate on the Italian ones which Ruehle renounced, and Ruehle would specialize in the European medieval series, especially the German and English, which Friedlaender would in turn avoid. It is not surprising, therefore, that Anglo-Saxon coins were weakly represented in Friedlaender's collection and of the 22 specimens recorded here, 16 come from the so-called 'Frankfurt' hoard (no. 29) of which Friedlaender had a free selection. If the Slav provenance is certain for these coins, so it may be assumed for the other six Anglo-Saxon coins in his collection.

GANSAUGE COLLECTION 1873

Hermann von Gansauge (1799–1871) was an officer in the Prussian army, from 1861

[4] The hoard of Dransau 1902 in Schleswig-Holstein recorded as no. W1 in Blackburn and Jonsson consequently does not belong to the Slav region hoards. It contained one coin of the Vikings of Northumbria (CVNNETTI) and one of Edward the Elder (899–924).

[5] The biography of Benoni Friedlaender by his son Julius is published in *ZfN* 24 (1904), pp. 1–16.

a Lieutenant-General, and like Ruehle von Lilienstern he enjoyed wide interests outside his military career. He was interested in science, wrote about military history and had a deep numismatic interest, although he never published anything in this field. His collection of *c*.3,200 ancient and *c*.2,600 medieval coins was acquired in 1873 from his widow. The collection was of high quality, the coins of the Middle Ages being particularly well selected for their fine condition and interest.

The Anglo-Saxon element of the collection reflects Gansauge's desire to build up a representative collection, and it is notable that 37 of the 72 Anglo-Saxon coins pre-date Æthelred II. Such a large number of quality specimens could not have been found on the German coin-market alone, and we must suppose that Gansauge as well as Ruehle acquired some of his coins in England. Others no doubt were acquired locally and must derive from Slav hoards, but these would be limited mainly to those of Æthelred II and Cnut, and there is no record of their provenances. No special catalogue of this collection exists and the identification of the coins relies on the tickets accompanying them in the trays.

GROTE COLLECTION 1879

Hermann Grote (1802–95) is one of the greatest German numismatists and with Hermann Dannenberg (see below) he may be regarded as one of the founders of scholarly medieval numismatics in Germany. His numerous works, written in a brilliant style, had an enormous influence on German numismatics. He was also the founder and editor of such numismatic journals as *Blätter für Münzkunde* (Hannover 1834–44), *Münzstudien* (Leipzig 1855–77), *Numismatischer Anzeiger* (Hannover 1868–73), and *Blätter für Münzfreunde* (Leipzig 1874–81).[6]

By profession Grote was a lawyer, but his private means allowed him to live for his studies of numismatics and heraldry. He was in constant contact with many coin dealers and collectors through whom he built up his collection. It was initially one of universal range, but he soon specialized in medieval coins though with special regard to Lower Saxony and Westphalia. Grote sold his collection in 1876, during his lifetime, to the merchant and collector Hermann Jungk (1834–1902) of Bremen.[7] Three years later Jungk offered the Grote collection to Berlin and it was acquired *en bloc*, with the exception of the relatively small byzantine and oriental elements. Most of the 9,560 coins were of the German Middle Ages. Grote was not greatly interested in other European medieval coins though he would acquire them if a good opportunity arose, usually when he had the choice of local hoards. Of the 94 coins of Grote in this volume, ten are sceattas from the Barthe hoard 1838 (no. 1) and 16 of the 32 coins of Æthelred II are from the Ciechanow hoard 1868 (no. 13) of which he

---

[6] Grote published a lively and elegant autobiography in his journal *Münzstudien* 7 (1871), pp. 145–70. For an appreciation of Grote see P. Berghaus, 'Hermann Grote als Sammler und Gelehrter', *Festschrift Hermann Grote aus Anlass der 150. Wiederkehr seines Geburtstages* (Münster 1952), pp. 7–15.

[7] Jungk is known as a numismatist mainly for his book *Die Bremischen Münzen* (Berlin 1875).

acquired a substantial parcel from the Polish collector Karol Beyer in Warsaw (d. 1877). Peter Berghaus published this parcel based on papers left by Grote (Berghaus 1954), and from this it has been possible to identify all the coins of Æthelred II in this collection from the Ciechanow hoard. Unfortunately the coins of Cnut from this hoard are not specified; we only know that there were 12 specimens, and these are probably among the 16 Cnut coins in the Grote collection recorded here. It has been possible to identify other coins of the Grote collection as coming from the Polish hoards of Baranow/Baranowo (no. 20) and Richnau/Rychnowo 1854 (no. 30), so that for the bulk of his coins from Æthelred II onwards Slav origins may be presumed. Grote himself paid no attention to the provenances of his coins so that today they can be identified only by chance, for example from the papers published by Berghaus.

DANNENBERG COLLECTIONS 1870 AND 1892

Hermann Dannenberg (1824–1905) is probably the best known German scholar of medieval numismatics from his main work *Die deutschen Münzen der sächsischen und fränkischen Kaiserzeit* (4 vols., 1876–1905). He was born in Berlin, and lived there all his lifetime. His profession was that of a judge, working finally, before his retirement in 1889, as a Landgerichtsrat at the Zivilkammer of the county court in Berlin. Between 1848 and 1905 he wrote several monographs and about one hundred articles. Particularly through his numerous hoard reports he laid the foundations of German medieval numismatics. The majority of Viking-Age coin hoards discovered in Germany and Poland during the nineteenth century passed through his hands and were mostly attributed and published by him.[8]

The Berlin cabinet acquired Dannenberg's collection of medieval coins in 1870, after which he began forming a second one which was in turn acquired in 1892. He then concentrated mainly on Greek coins and these, together with some medieval ones not taken by the cabinet in 1892 and some acquired subsequently, were auctioned after his death in 1905 (A. Hess sale, 6 November 1905). The first collection consisted of 3,077 coins and the second of *c*.5,000 coins. Both were of broadly similar scope and range, and reflected Dannenberg's predominant interest in the German series. These were the most important acquisitions made by the cabinet of German coins of the tenth and eleventh centuries, though they were also rich in later medieval coins.

The Anglo-Saxon elements of the collections—42 specimens in the first and 38 in the second—are small considering the many hoards of which he had the first selection and from which he built up his unrivalled collection of tenth- and eleventh-century German denars. He had, for instance, the opportunity to go through the enormously rich Lübeck hoard (no. 26), and acquired nearly all the important

---

[8] An appreciation of Dannenberg is given by the present writer in his edition of selected studies by Dannenberg (Dannenberg *Studien*, pp. viii–xxxviii).

German coins, but no more than one Anglo-Saxon coin. It was similar with the hoards of Plonsk 1854 (no. 35) and Vossberg 1883, which are two of the largest finds from the West Slav region with a relatively high proportion of Anglo-Saxon coins, yet Dannenberg acquired only three Anglo-Saxon coins from the Plonsk hoard and none from the Vossberg hoard. None the less, among Dannenberg's Anglo-Saxon coins are some of outstanding interest, including for example the unique coin of Edward the Martyr from the mint of Horncastle (**194**).

The Dannenberg coins can be identified only by their tickets in the trays, and these unfortunately record no hoard provenances. By comparing the coins in the *Sylloge* with the descriptions of hoards from which we positively know that he acquired coins, it has been possible in some cases to restore the find provenances. For many this could not be done, but it is very likely that most if not all the coins from Æthelred II to William II in his collection come from Slav hoards.

FINDS REPRESENTED IN THE BERLIN COIN CABINET

ANGLO-SAXON, Anglo-Norman, and Hiberno-Norse coins or their imitations from the following finds are represented in the MKB; in most cases the hoards are preserved only in part. The finds are arranged in the order of the *terminus post quem* (*tpq*).

The findspot is first given in the form, usually German, current at the time of discovery and which was used in the original publication of the find. This is followed, where relevant, by the modern Polish form as recorded in the *PSW Atlas*, with in parentheses the name of the old districts (pow., i.e. powiaty) as previously used in *PSW* I–IV. The date of discovery is then given.

The *tpq* of the whole hoard is recorded, as well as that of the Anglo-Saxon element, and in cases where the dating of the latest coin is doubtful or seems inconsistent the *tpq* of other elements is also given.

The contents of the hoards are then summarized, concentrating on the English element, with abbreviations for the ruler and type following Smart 1981 (see 'Abbreviations' and the introduction to 'Index of Mints' below). Where possible, the number of whole coins and fragments are distinguished in parentheses: (whole + fragments).

Reference is made to the most authoritative, detailed description of the find, followed by its number in the standard summary listings of the West Slav finds (*PSW*, Zak, Blackburn and Jonsson). Finally, after any special comment on the hoard, the acquisition numbers/collections are given for coins from the hoard now in the MKB and the Sylloge numbers of those specimens included in this volume.

1. Barthe, Kr. Leer, Ostfriesland, FRG
1838

*tpq: c.*730?

Uncertain number of Frisian 'porcupine' sceattas (*c.*780 preserved)

Ref. Berghaus 1958, 46, no. 16; Hill 1977.

Comment: Some 750 coins from this find are preserved in the museum at Emden. Those in MKB, from the Grote collection 1879, were identified as from the Barthe find on grounds of patination by Peter Berghaus in 1975.

MKB Grote coll. 1879, inc. **6–10**, **12**, **14–15**, **18**.

2. Pomerania, findspot unknown
Before 1897

tpq: ?   German and Arabic
924 Anglo-Saxon, Æthelstan

Uncertain number of coins (19 (7 + 12) preserved):
German 8 (3 + 5); Arabic 9 (4 + 5)
Anglo-Saxon 2 (0 + 2):
Abp Plegm (1)
Æthst viii (1)

Comment: Unpublished. The coins were acquired by exchange from the Gesellschaft für Pommersche Geschichte und Altertumskunde in Stettin/Szczecin. No information about the provenance survives, but it is probable that they come from a Pomeranian hoard since the Gesellschaft für Pommersche Geschichte only collected coins found in the province.

This appears to be the oldest hoard with Anglo-Saxon coins from the Slav region since no coins prior to Eadmund (939–46) are otherwise recorded (cf. Kluge 1981, 286–7). For the possible association with the group of ten coins of Æthelstan in the Ruehle von Lilienstern collection, see p. 8 above.

MKB 544–5/1898 (19 coins), inc. **91, 173**.

3. Belgard, Kr. Belgard, Rb. Köslin, Pomerania
Białogard (pow. Białogard), woj. Koščalin, Poland
1904

tpq: 976 Germany, Regensburg, Duke Otto (976–82), Dbg. 1065e; Hahn 17.i.1.6 (this coin)
975 Anglo-Saxon, Edward the Martyr

Uncertain number of coins (48 preserved):
German 8; Nordic 39
Anglo-Saxon 1:
Edw II   Thetford

Ref. Malmer 1966, 285, find 127.

MKB 227–33/1904, bt. Kube (48 coins), inc. **196**.

4. Stolp, Kr. Stolp, Rb. Köslin, Pomerania
Słupsk (pow. Słupsk), woj. Słupsk, Poland
1846

tpq: 991 Germany, Otto-Adelheid-Pfennige
c.979 Anglo-Saxon, Æthelred II, *First Hand*

c.3,000 coins (90 preserved), mostly German Otto-Adelheid-Pfennige:
German *c*.2,500 (49 preserved); Bohemian 21 (or 25?); Italian 2; Nordic 1; Byzantine 4;
Arabic 5 + x; Roman 3
Anglo-Saxon 5:
Edg vi (1)   Leicester
Edw II (1)   Stamford
Æth II A1 (2)   Northampton, York
Æth II B1 (1)   Rochester

Ref. Dannenberg 1848. *PSW* II 153; Zak 105; Blackburn and Jonsson W 23.

MKB 377/1846 (87 coins), inc. **189, 195, 197–8, 211**.

5. Lenz-Ilsenhof, Kr. Saatzig, Pomerania
Moskorze (pow. Stargard), woj. Szczecin, Poland
1931–2

tpq: 991 Germany, Strassburg, Bishop Widerold (991–9), Dbg. 934
        *c.*985 Anglo-Saxon, Æthelred II, *Second Hand*

293 (107 + 186) coins, hacksilver:
   German 190; Bohemian 29; Italian 1; Nordic 4; Byzantine 2; Arabic 63 + 261.54g
   fragments
   Anglo-Saxon 4:
      Edg vi (1)   Thetford
      Æth II B1 (2) London (2)
      Æth II B2 (1) London

Ref. Suhle 1954. *PSW* II 105; Zak 75; Blackburn and Jonsson W 22.

Comment: Suhle 1954 records 288 (120 + 168) coins; the numbers given above are those of
the *PSW* II 105 and Zak.

MKB 52–69/1933 (40 coins), inc. **193**.

6. Klein-Roscharden II, Kr. Cloppenburg, Oldenburg, FRG
1886, 14 July

tpq: 996 Germany, Emperor Otto III (996–1002), Cologne (Dbg. 342), Dortmund (Dbg.
           744), Mainz (Dbg. 777/779)
        *c.*979 Anglo-Saxon, Æthelred II, *First Hand*

694 coins, hacksilver:
   German 685; Bohemian 1; French 1; Arabic 3
   Anglo-Saxon 4:
      Æth II Bl (4)   Exeter, Hertford, London, Winchester.

Ref. Dannenberg 1887; Berghaus 1951. *Polabia*, p. 72, no. F.

MKB 174–205/1887 (195 coins), inc. **200**, **203**, **205**, **218**.

7. Witzmitz, Kr. Regenwalde, Rb. Stettin, Pomerania
Wicimice (pow. Gryfice), woj. Szczecin, Poland
1878, 16 June

tpq: 996 Germany, Dortmund, Emperor Otto III (996–1002), Dbg. 744b
        *c.*991 Anglo-Saxon, Æthelred II, *Crux*

*c.*500 + x coins, hacksilver:
   German *c.*450 + x; Bohemian 12 + x; Italian 2; Nordic 8 + x; Arabic 16 + x
   Anglo-Saxon 10 + x:
      Æth II B1 (4)   Leicester, London, Winchester, York
      Æth II B2 (2)   Canterbury, Lymne
      Æth II B (3)   London, Winchester, mint?
      Æth II C (1)   Bath

Ref. Friedlaender 1879. *PSW* II 197; Zak 73; Blackburn and Jonsson W 33.

MKB 923–1042/1878 (120 coins), inc. **204**, **206**, **217**, **220**, **224**, **229**, **236**.

8. Jarocin, Kr. Pleschen, Rb. Posen, Posen
Jarocin (pow. Jarocin), woj. Kalisz, Poland
1878

tpq: 1004 Bohemia, Jaromir (1004–12)
      1002 Germany, Regensburg, King Henry II (1002–14), Dbg. 1074c; Hahn 27
      *c.*991 Anglo-Saxon, Æthelred II, *Crux*

781 coins, 1,000g fragments and hacksilver:
  German 597; Bohemian 107 (or 114?); Italian 5; Nordic 3; Byzantine 2; Arabic 11
  Anglo-Saxon 4:
    Æth II C (4)   Exeter, Ilchester, Winchester, York

Ref. Dannenberg 1880; Jazdzewski 1879. *PSW* I 41; Zak 195; Blackburn and Jonsson W 52.

MKB Dannenberg coll., inc. **259**.

9. Dobra (pow. Płock), woj. Płock, Poland
1869

tpq: 1009 Germany, Regensburg, King Henry II (1002–14), second period 1009–24, Dbg.
        1075–7; Hahn 29
      *c.*1003 Anglo-Saxon, Æthelred II, *Helmet*

702 coins:
  German 676; Bohemian 3; Italian 1; Arabic 2
  Anglo-Saxon 19:
    Æth II B2 (1)   Winchester
    Æth II C (14)   Cambridge (2), Exeter (2), Hertford, Leicester (Dannenberg: as
        Chester), Lewes, Lincoln, London (4), Southwark/Sudbury, Win-
        chester
    Æth II D (2)   Leicester (Dannenberg: as Chester), London
    Æth II E (2)   London, York
  Hiberno-Norse 1: Phase I, Sihtric, '*Long Cross*', Dublin

Ref. Dannenberg 1874. *PSW* III 19; Zak 267; Blackburn and Jonsson W 59.

MKB Dannenberg coll., inc. **243**, **277**, **283**.

10. Rummelsburg, Kr. Rummelsburg, Rb. Köslin, Pomerania
Miastko (pow. Miastko), woj. Słupsk, Poland
1861

tpq: 1011? Germany, Saxony, Duke Bernhard II (1011–59), Dbg. 587
      1006 Germany, Metz, Bishop Dietrich (1006–47), Dbg. 19
      *c.*997 Anglo-Saxon, Æthelred II, *Long Cross*

*c.*1,200 coins (176 described), mostly German Otto-Adelheid-Pfennige and Sachsen-
pfennige:
  German 119 + x; Bohemian 32; Italian 3; Arabic x
  Anglo-Saxon 20:
    Æth II B1 (2)   Exeter, York
    Æth II B2 (1)   London
    Æth II C (14)   Exeter, Lincoln, London (8), Lydford, Thetford, Winchester (2)
    Æth II D (3)   Lincoln (Dannenberg: as Chichester), London, York
  Imitations of Anglo-Saxon types 2

Ref. Dannenberg 1863. *PSW* II 98; Zak 106; Blackburn and Jonsson W 65.

Comment: The hoard is usually dated after 1011, but it is possible that the type Dbg. 587 belongs to Duke Bernhard I of Saxony (973–1011) so that the *tpq* of the hoard could be 1006.

MKB Dannenberg coll., inc. **202**, **219**, **962**.

11. Leissow (Leissower Mühle), Kr. Weststernberg, Rb. Frankfurt, Brandenburg
Lisówek (pow. Rzepin), woj. Gorzów Wlkp., Poland
1894, September

tpq: 1011 Germany, Lüneburg, Duke Bernhard II (1011–59), Dbg. 589
        *c.*1003 Anglo-Saxon, Æthelred II, *Helmet*

4,816 coins, hacksilver:
   German *c.*4,652 + x; Bohemian 71; Polish 4; Italian 5; Nordic 2; Swedish 2; Norwegian 1;
   Byzantine 5; Roman 5; Arabic 78 (19 + 59)
   Anglo-Saxon 122 (112 + 10):

Edg vi (3)	Oxford, Shaftesbury, York
Æth II B1 (5)	Canterbury, London (2), Norwich, Thetford
Æth II B2 (4)	Canterbury, Exeter, London, Thetford
Æth II B2/C (1)	Rochester
Æth II C (84)	Bridport, Cambridge (2), Canterbury (7), Derby, Dover, Exeter (7), Hertford (4), Huntingdon, Lincoln (7), London (29), Lydford, Norwich, Rochester (2), Southwark/Sudbury (9), Thetford (3), Wilton, Winchester (6), York
Æth II Ca (3)	Canterbury (2), Rochester
Æth II Int A/C (4)	Exeter, London, Winchester (2)
Æth II D (16)	Chester, Lincoln (2), London (6), Romney (Æthelwine), Shrewsbury, Winchester (2), York (3)
Æth II E (2)	Norwich (2)

   Imitations of Anglo-Saxon types 4

Ref. Bahrfeldt 1896; Menadier 1898a. *PSW* I 65; Zak 220; Blackburn and Jonsson W 64.

Comment: Two of the coins of Exeter, *Crux* type, recorded by Bahrfeldt are probably Scandinavian imitations. The four imitations recorded above are Bahrfeldt 1896, nos. 104, 105 (as Eadgar), 587 (*Long Cross*, double reverses), and Menadier 1898a, p. 176, no. 48 (Æthelred II, *Helmet*, 'London', cf. Sylloge **987**).

MKB 1270/1896 (77 coins), inc. **199**, **213**, **223**, **230**, **245**, **272**, **282**, **987**.

12. Althoefchen, Kr. Birnbaum, Rb. Posen, Posen
Starydworek (pow. Miedzyrzecz), woj. Gorzow Wlkp., Poland
1872, April

*tpq: c.*1017 Anglo-Saxon, Cnut, *Quatrefoil*
        1014 Germany, Emperor Henry II (1014–24), Dinant (Dbg. 173), Trier (Dbg. 462),
            Deventer (Dbg. 562), Tiel (Dbg. 578), Strassburg (Dbg. 920)

Several thousand coins (575 preserved), mostly German Otto-Adelheid-Pfennige and Sachsenpfennige (none preserved):
   German 411 + x; Bohemian 23; Polish 14; Italian 4; Byzantine 4; Danish 1; Arabic 22

Anglo-Saxon 75:

Æth II B1 (2)	Exeter, Wilton
Æth II B2 (1)	London
Æth II C (23)	'Æsthe', Cambridge, Canterbury (2), Dover, Exeter (2), Hertford (2), Ilchester, London (5), Maldon, Rochester, Shaftesbury, Southwark/Sudbury, Stafford, Thetford, Wilton, Winchester
Æth II D (30)	Exeter, Hereford, Lincoln (4), London (17), Lydford, Oxford, Shaftesbury, Shrewsbury, Warwick, Winchester, York
Æth II E (5)	Exeter, Ipswich (Friedländer: as Cambridge), London (3)
Æth II A (8)	Canterbury, Cricklade, Dover, London (3), Lydford, Stamford
Cn E (5)	Lincoln, London, Stamford, Winchester, York

Hiberno-Norse 1: Phase I, Sithric, '*Long Cross*', Dublin
Imitations of Anglo-Saxon types 2

Ref. Friedlaender 1877. *PSW* I 125; Zak 218; Blackburn and Jonsson W 91.

Comment: In *PSW* I 125 the find is dated *c*.1025 based on coins of Boleslaw Chrobry as king of Poland (1025). These types are now attributed to his rule as duke of Poland and dated to 992–1015 (Suchodolski 1967, types 1, 13, 15, 14, 20).

MKB 556/1872 (575 coins), inc. **201, 216, 228, 239, 246–7, 260, 269, 278, 284, 291, 294, 296, 304, 306, 308, 314, 316, 328, 330, 332, 356, 358, 365–6, 371, 375, 380–1, 384, 387, 389, 395–6, 398–9, 402, 404, 408, 410, 415, 418, 421, 423, 425, 433–5, 449, 456, 461, 468, 472, 482, 484, 489, 503, 510, 534, 537, 549, 553, 562, 593, 622, 638, 654, 667, 675, 927, 961, 963**.

13. Ciechanow (pow. Ciechanow), woj. Ciechanow, Poland
1868, August

tpq: c.1017? Anglo-Saxon, Cnut, type?
    1014   Germany, Strassburg, Emperor Henry II (1014–24), Dbg. 920

c.1,300 + 3,500 coins (*c*.770 preserved)
  German *c*.617; Bohemian 43 (32 + 11); Polish 8; Nordic 12 (0 + 12); Byzantine 1; Arabic 12 (2 + 10)

Anglo-Saxon 79 (56 + 23):

Æth B1 (2)	Derby, Ipswich
Æth C (12)	Exeter, Lincoln (2), London (4), Southwark/Sudbury, Thetford, Totnes, Winchester (2)
Æth II D (14)	Canterbury, Colchester, Exeter, Lincoln (3), London (4), Northampton (Menadier: as Harwich), Wilton, Winchester, York
Æth II E (1)	London
Æth II A (8)	Lincoln (2), London (2), Thetford, Winchester, York (2)
Cn (12)	types and mints unknown
Uncertain 30 (7 + 23)	

Imitations of Anglo-Saxon types 4

Ref. Menadier 1898d; Berghaus 1954, pp. 214–18. *PSW* III 15; Zak 277; Blackburn and Jonsson W 161.

Comment: This hoard was dispersed and is known from two parts. The first parcel came into the possession of the collector Karol Beyer in Warsaw and a selection of these passed to the Grote collection. A list of the Beyer coins also passed into Grote's possession, and this was published by Peter Berghaus in 1954.

A second parcel (530 coins) belonged the Superintendent K. A. Diehl in Warsaw who in 1896 offered it, together with a detailed report, to the MKB, which bought only 30 coins (German and Bohemian). The report of Diehl was published with some corrections by Menadier as 'Fund von Ciechanow' in 1898. Both parts of the hoard are included in the summary above.

The report by Diehl/Menadier gave the hoard a *tpq* of 1047, but this appears to be too late, for three coins in the Diehl parcel (Menadier 1898d, nos. 8, 18, 40) were considerably later than the rest of the hoard and probably came from another source. The Diehl report also included a 13th-century bracteate which Menadier omitted in the published version.

MKB Grote coll. 1879 and 221–33/1896 (30 coins), inc. **267**, **310**, **334**, **342**, **357**, **364**, **368**, **416**, **459**, **514**, **524**, **544**, **548**, **575**, **588**, **591**.

14. Thurow bei Züssow, Kr. Greifswald, Bez. Rostock, GDR
1893, Autumn

tpq: 1021 Germany, Erfurt, Archbishop Aribo (1021–31), Dbg. 877
        *c.*1017 Anglo-Saxon, Cnut, *Quatrefoil*

882 coins, hacksilver:
  German 635; Bohemian 9; Italian 3; Nordic 2; Swedish 1; French 1; Arabic 28 + 60;
    Carolingian 1; Roman 2; uncertain 6 + 55
  Anglo-Saxon 37 (14 + 23):
    Æth II B2 (1)   London
    Æth II B2/B3 (0 + 1)   Winchester
    Æth II C (1 + 4)   Rochester, York, mint? (0 + 3)
    Æth II Ca (1 + 1)   London, Rochester
    Æth II D (1 + 4)   Lincoln, London, mint? (0 + 3)
    Æth II E (1 + 4)   Chester, London, York (2), mint?
    Æth II A (6 + 11)   Colchester, Dover, Huntingdon, London (2), Stamford (2),
                           Thetford, Winchester (3), mint? (0 + 6)
    Cn E (2 + 1)   Lincoln, Stamford, York
  Hiberno-Norse 1: Phase I, Sihtric, '*Long Cross*', Dublin
  Imitations of Anglo-Saxon types 4 (3 + 1): Æth II C (1), D (1 + 1), E (1)

Ref. Dannenberg 1897a; Pyl 1897; revised report in preparation (Kluge and Simon). *PSW* II 179; Zak 27; Blackburn and Jonsson W 173.

MKB 151–6/1895 (44 coins), inc. **582**.

15. Wielowies, Kr. Krotoschin, Rb. Posen, Posen
Wielowieś (pow. Krotoszyn), woj. Kalisz, Poland
1856

tpq: *c.*1023 Anglo-Saxon, Cnut, *Pointed Helmet*
        1022 Germany, Hildesheim, Bishop Gothard (1022–38), Dbg. 712

433 + x coins, hacksilver:
  German 410; Bohemian 6; Hungarian 2; Italian 1; French 2; Arabic 2
  Anglo-Saxon 4:
    Cn E (3)   Barnstaple, London, Norwich
    Cn G (1)   Lincoln
  Imitation of Hiberno-Norse coin 1: Phase I, '*Long Cross*'

Ref. Menadier 1887, p. 176. *PSW* I 144; Zak 202; Blackburn and Jonsson W 96.

Comment: The *tpq* of 1039 given in Menadier 1887 and followed by later scholars is based on two uncertain coins of King Henry III (1039–46) but they were probably struck under Henry II (1002–24).

MKB 261/1856 (433 coins), inc. **594, 643, 646, 700, 951**.

16. Birglau, Kr. Thorn, Rb. Marienwerder, West Prussia
Bierzgłowo (pow. Toruń), woj. Toruń, Poland
1898, October

tpq: 1024 Germany, Maastricht, King Konrad II (1024–7), Dbg. 2004
      *c.*1017 Anglo-Saxon, Cnut, *Quatrefoil*

539 coins, hacksilver:
  German 470; Bohemian 11; Arabic 13; French 1; uncertain 16
  Anglo-Saxon 25:

Æth II C (12)	Cambridge, Canterbury, Ipswich, Lewes, London (5), Winchester (2)
Æth II D (9)	Exeter, Lincoln (3), Thetford, Warwick, Wilton, Winchester, York
Æth II E (1)	Cambridge
Æth II A (1)	Winchester
Æth II type? (1)	mint?
Cn E (1)	Winchester

  Imitations of Anglo-Saxon types 3: Æth II C(3)

Ref. Menadier 1898b. *PSW* II 11; Blackburn and Jonsson W 97.
MKB 1170–88/1898, 190–2/1899 (51 coins), inc. **261, 268, 287–8, 317, 444, 448, 451, 953, 954–5**.

17. Kinno, near Skubarczewo, Kr. Mogilno, Rb. Bromberg, Posen
Kinno (pow. Mogilno), woj. Konin, Poland
1900, Autumn

tpq: 1025 Poland, King Boleslaw Chrobry (1025)
      1021 Germany, Erfurt, Archbishop Aribo (1021–31), Dbg. 887
      *c.*1017 Anglo-Saxon, Cnut, *Quatrefoil*

*c.*715 coins, hacksilver:
  German 663, Bohemian 6; Polish 6; Italian 1; Byzantine 2; uncertain 8
  Anglo-Saxon 24:

Æth II B2 (2)	Canterbury (2)
Æth II C (4)	Lewes, London (2), Winchester
Æth II D (10)	Bath, Colchester, London (5), Thetford, York (2)
Æth II E (2)	Bath, London
Æth II A (1)	Winchester
Cn E (5)	Cambridge, Chester (Menadier: as Leicester), London, Norwich, Peterborough/Medeshamstede

  Imitations of Anglo-Saxon types 5

Ref. Menadier 1902. *PSW* I 47; Zak 154; Blackburn and Jonsson W 104.

MKB 666–85/1901 (104 coins), inc. **262, 270, 336, 348, 382, 405, 442, 458, 481, 572, 603, 645, 650, 952, 956, 964**.

18. Parlin, Kr. Mogilno, Rb. Bromberg, Posen
Parlin (pow. Mogilno), woj. Bydgoszcz, Poland
1874, 10 June

tpq: 1027 Germany, Cologne (Andernach?), Archbishop Piligrim and Emperor Konrad II
               (1027–36), Dbg. 381a; Hävernick 224
         *c.*1023 Anglo-Saxon, Cnut, *Pointed Helmet*

297 g coins (9 preserved) and 240 g hacksilver:
   German 1; Polish 4; Hungarian 1; Arabic 1
   Anglo-Saxon 1:
      Cn G (1)   Lincoln
   Imitation of Hiberno-Norse type 1: Phase I, '*Long Cross*'

Ref. Menadier 1887, pp. 176–7. *PSW* I 93; Zak 155; Blackburn and Jonsson W 95.

MKB 343/1874 (9 coins), inc. **691**, **950**.

19. Daber, Kr. Naugard, Rb. Stettin, Pomerania
Dobra (pow. Nowogard), woj. Szczecin, Poland
1894, May

tpq: 1031 Germany, Erfurt, Archbishop Bardo (1031–51), Dbg. 878–80

807 (499 + 308) coins (71 + 11 preserved), hacksilver:
   German 47 + x; Bohemian 3; Russian 1; Arabic 4; uncertain 16; Anglo-Saxon?
   Imitations of Anglo-Saxon types 1

Ref. PSW II 23.

Comment: The coins were acquired from the Gesellschaft für Pommersche Geschichte und
Altertumskunde in Stettin/Szczecin where the find was deposited. Menadier's intention to
publish this find together with some others discovered at this time (Hornikau/Horniki 1890,
Londzyn/Ładzyn 1887, Mgowo 1893) in the *ZfN* was not realized. His manuscript is now
lost.

MKB 396–434/1894 (82 coins), inc. **1082**.

20. Baranow, Kr. Inowroclaw, Rb. Bromberg, Posen
Baranowo (pow. Inowroclaw), woj. Bydgoszcz, Poland
Before 1875

tpq: 1034 Bohemia, Bretislav I (1034–55)
         *c.*1017 Anglo-Saxon, Cnut, *Quatrefoil*

Unknown number of coins (6 preserved):
   German 2; Bohemian 2
   Anglo-Saxon 2:
      Æth II D (1)   mint?
      Cn E (1)   London

Ref. Berghaus 1954, p. 219. *PSW* I 1; Zak 148; Blackburn and Jonsson W 133.

MKB Grote coll. 1879, inc. **641**.

21. Grapzow, Kr. Altentreptow, Bez. Neubrandenburg, GDR
1856

tpq: 1034 Bohemia, Bretislav I (1034–55)
        1027 Germany, Emperor Konrad II (1027–39)
     *c.*1017 Anglo-Saxon, Cnut, *Quatrefoil*

*c.*1,800 coins (182 preserved) and fragments, mostly Sachsenpfennige:
   German 168; Bohemian 5; Hungarian 1; Italian 1; uncertain 6
   Anglo-Saxon 2:
     Æth II D (1)   London
     Cn E (1)   Dorchester

Ref. Polabia 70; Zak 29; Blackburn and Jonsson W 79.

MKB 267/1856 (182 coins), inc. **414**.

22. Rawicz, Kr. Cröben, Rb. Posen, Posen
Rawicz (pow. Rawicz), woj. Leszno, Poland
1880

tpq: 1034 Bohemia, Bretislav I (1034–55)
        1027 Germany, Strassburg, Emperor Konrad II (1027–39), Dbg. 922
     *c.*1023 Anglo-Saxon, Cnut, *Pointed Helmet*

321 + x coins:
   German 279 + x; Bohemian 18; Polish 1; Italian 3; Byzantine 1; Roman 1; Arabic 4 + x
   Anglo-Saxon 13 + x:
     Æth II B2 (1)   Canterbury
     Æth II C (3)   Lymne, Stamford, Wilton
     Æth II D (2)   Lincoln, London
     Æth II A (3)   Dover, Lincoln, uncertain mint ('BRINT . . . ORD')
     Cn E (1)   Southwark
     Cn H (3)   Gloucester, Lincoln (2)
   Imitations of Anglo-Saxon types 2

Ref. Menadier 1887, pp. 105–9; Friedlaender 1881. *PSW* I 112; Zak 207; Blackburn and
Jonsson W 137.

Comment: Friedlaender did not record the findspot. Menadier gave it as Wättrisch/
Sokolniki, but it is in fact Rawicz (Bahrfeldt 1888, p. 93).

MKB 94–106a/1880 (14 coins), inc. **289**, **519**.

23. Mgowo, Kr. Briesen, West Prussia
Mgowo (pow. Wabrzezno), woj. Torun, Poland
1893, November

tpq: 1034 Bohemia, Bretislav I (1034–55)
        1027 Germany, Cologne, Archbishop Piligrim and Emperor Konrad II (1027–36),
           Dbg. 381
     *c.*1023 Anglo-Saxon, Cnut, *Pointed Helmet*

*c.*2,000 (800 + 1,200) coins, hacksilver:
   German 674; Bohemian 26 (1 + 25); Polish 9; Hungarian 1; Nordic 7 (0 + 7); Danish 4;
   Byzantine 3; Arabic 94 (3 + 91)

Anglo-Saxon 34:

Æth II B2 (1)	Totnes
Æth II C (3)	London (2), Southwark/Sudbury
Æth II D (1)	London
Æth II E (1)	Chester
Æth II A (4)	London (2), Stamford, Winchester
Æth II type? (8)	mints?, inc. Cambridge, York
Cn E (6)	Huntingdon, Lewes, Lincoln (2), London, York
Cn G (6)	Cambridge, London (3), Southwark, Wallingford
Cn type? (4)	mints?, inc. Colchester, Taunton, York

Imitations of Anglo-Saxon types 4

Ref. Dannenberg 1906/9 (Anglo-Saxon types not specified). *PSW* II 97; Zak 136; Blackburn and Jonsson W 119.

MKB 562–90/1894 (113 coins), inc. **231, 266, 271, 302, 424, 466, 550–1, 565, 577, 610, 614, 616, 624, 626, 676, 678, 701, 705, 717, 733, 735, 1002.**

24. Zottwitz, Kr. Ohlau, Rb. Breslau, Silesia
Sobocisko (pow. Oława), woj. Wrocław, Poland
1902, March

tpq: 1034 Bohemia, Bretislav I (1034–55)
    *c.*1029 Anglo-Saxon, Cnut, *Short Cross*

264 coins:

German *c.*190; Bohemian *c.*62; Polish 2; Hungarian 2
Anglo-Saxon 6:

Æth II C (1)	Cambridge
Æth II D (1)	London
Æth II A (2)	Shaftesbury, Worcester
Cn E (1)	Bristol
Cn H (1)	London

Hiberno-Norse 1?: Phase I, Sihtric, '*Last Small Cross*', 'London'

Ref. Seger 1928, pp. 145–6, no. 16. *PSW* IVB 41; Zak 230; Blackburn and Jonsson W 138.

Comment: The coins in MKB were acquired from F. Friedensburg. It is uncertain whether the Hiberno-Norse coin acquired from him ten years later belongs to this hoard.

MKB 367–87/1903 (42 coins); 795/1914 (1 coin), inc. **238, 407, 558, 584, 598, 772, 940.**

25. Runowo, Kr. Wirsitz, Rb. Bromberg, Posen
Runowo Krajeńskie (pow. Sępólno Kraj.), woj. Bydgoszcz, Poland
1892

tpq: 1034 Bohemia, Bretislav I (1034–55)
    *c.*1017 Anglo-Saxon, Cnut

240 (107 + 133) coins:

German 98; Bohemian 12; Hungarian 1; Danish 1; Arabic 5; Roman 1; uncertain 48
Anglo-Saxon 8 (0 + 8):

Æth II (0 + 6)	type? mint?
Cn (0 + 2)	type? mint?

Imitation of Anglo-Saxon types 1

Ref. PSW II 140: Zak 143; Blackburn and Jonsson W 125.

MKB 920–6/1892 (16 coins), inc. **1015.**

26. Lübeck, FRG
1875

tpq: 1038? Germany, Breisach, Duke Henry (1038–45), Dbg. 1374
    1035 Denmark, Harthacnut (1035–42)
   *c.*1029 Anglo-Saxon, Cnut, *Short Cross*

*c.*2,850 coins, hacksilver:
  German *c.*530 (450); Bohemian 1; Italian 1; Danish *c.*200 (162); Swedish 1; Arabic 1
  Anglo-Saxon *c.*1,900:

Æth II C (3)	Canterbury, London (2)
Æth II D (18)	Exeter, Hereford, Lincoln (3), London (5), Milborne Port, Northampton (2), Norwich, Stamford, Wallingford, Worcester, mint? (1)
Æth II E (8)	Exeter, Ipswich, Hastings, Lincoln, London (2), Winchester, mint? (1)
Æth II A (15)	Hereford, London (7), Romney, Southampton, Wareham, Winchester (3), mint? (1)
Cn E (214)	Bath (7), Bedford, Bristol (1 + 3 Ed), Cambridge (7), Chester (10), Colchester (6), Cricklade (6), Exeter (4), Gloucester (3), Hertford, Huntingdon (2), Ilchester (4), Ipswich, Langport, Leicester (3), Lincoln (20), London (24), Lydford, Malmesbury (3), Northampton (2), Norwich (2), Oxford (14), Shaftesbury (2), Shrewsbury (2), Southampton (2), Southwark (2), Stamford (7), Thetford (3), Wallingford (2), Wilton, Winchester (17), York (43), mint? (6)
Cn G (810)	Barnstaple, Bath (6), Bedford, Bridport (2), Cambridge (3), Canterbury (34), Chester (20), Chichester (2), Colchester (3), Cricklade (3), Derby, Dover (30), Exeter (16), Gloucester (9), Hastings (38), Hereford (5), Huntingdon (8), Ilchester (5), Ipswich (3), Leicester (5), Lewes (6), Lincoln (78 + 1 Ga), London (310), Lymne, Maldon (2), Northampton, Norwich (10), Nottingham (3), Oxford (9), Rochester (4), Romney (4), Salisbury (6), Shaftesbury (5), Shrewsbury (3), Southwark (7), Stamford (33), Thetford (18), Totnes, Wallingford (3), Warwick, Wilton, Winchcombe, Winchester (27), Worcester (5), York (69 + 2 Gc), mint? (5)
Cn H (809)	Axbridge, Barnstaple, Bath (2), Bedford (2), Bridport, Bristol, Bruton (2), Canterbury (43), Chester (11), Chichester (4), Colchester (8), Cricklade, DENE (London?), Derby, Dover (86), Exeter (8), Gloucester, Guildford (2), Hastings (8), Hereford, Hertford (6), Huntingdon (3), Ilchester (2), Ipswich (2), Lewes (4), Lincoln (88), London (258), Lymne (4), Northampton, Norwich (23), Nottingham (3), Oxford (9), Rochester (5), Romney, Salisbury (8), Shaftesbury (7), Shrewsbury (2), Southwark, Stamford (51), Steyning (3), Thetford (32), Wallingford (7), Warminster, Warwick (2), Wilton (3), Winchester (23), Worcester (3), York (68), mint? (4)

  Hiberno-Norse 4
  Imitations of Anglo-Saxon types *c.*25(?)

Ref. Cohn 1877 (Anglo-Saxon and Scandinavian coins); Dannenberg 1877 (German coins). *Polabia* 106; Zak 9; Blackburn and Jonsson W 142.

MKB Dannenberg coll., inc. **244**.

27. Farve, Kr. Oldenburg, FRG
1848

tpq: *c.* 1038 Anglo-Saxon, Harold I, *Fleur-de-lis*
      1035 Denmark, Harthacnut (1035–42)
      1034 Bohemia, Bretislav I (1034–55)
      1027 Germany, Cologne, Archbishop Piligrim and Emperor Konrad II (1027–36),
            Dbg. 381; Hävernick 222; and Duisburg, Emperor Konrad II (1027–39), Dbg.
            311–14

*c.*3,775 (3,349 + 426) coins:
  German *c.*3,500; Bohemian 11 + x; Hungarian 242; Italian 2; French 1; Nordic 2; Danish
    2 + x; Arabic 8
  Anglo-Saxon 15 (4 + 11):
    Æth II C (0 + 2)   Southwark/Sudbury
    Æth II D (2 + 2)   Cambridge, Exeter, Lincoln, Winchester
    Æth II A (1 + 3)   Cadbury, Lincoln, London, Winchester
    Æth II ? (0 + 3)   mint uncertain
    Cn H (1)   Lincoln
    Har I B (0 + 1)   mint uncertain
  Imitation of Anglo-Saxon types 4 (2 + 2)

Ref. Friedlaender and Müllenhoff 1850. *Polabia* 50; Zak 7; Blackburn and Jonsson W 139.

Comment: Friedlaender (who described the coins, Müllenhoff the non-monetary silver) recorded 16 Anglo-Saxon coins and fragments, but his no. 79 (Sylloge **1023**) is in fact a Scandinavian imitation. The fragment (no. 81) which he gave to Harthacnut is in fact of Harold I, *Fleur-de-lis* type. His two Irish coins (nos. 88–9) are Danish.

MKB 28853/1869 (65 coins), inc. **1023**.

28. Posen/Poznan (region), Poland
*c.*1854

tpq: 1039? Germany, Duisburg, King Henry III (1039–46), Dbg. 316?
      *c.*1038 Anglo-Saxon, Harold I, *Fleur-de-Lis*
      1034   Bohemia, Bretislav I (1034–55)

Uncertain number of coins (42 preserved):
  German 27; Bohemian 4; Danish 1
  Anglo-Saxon 9:
    Æth II (2)   type? mint?
    Cn (6)   type? mint?
    Har I B (1)   London
  Imitation of Anglo-Saxon types 1

Comment: Unpublished. The coins were bought from Dr Bruns, Librarian of the Königliche Bibliothek in Berlin. Their identification is difficult because the description in the Acquisitions Journal is very summary. Among the coins in this sylloge only one of Harold I and one imitation could be identified with any certainty. It is very probable that the others, two coins of Æthelred II and six of Cnut, are among those from the 'Old collection'.

MKB 170/1855 (42 coins), inc. **809** or **810**, **1027**.

29. 'Frankfurt': Pomerania or Poland, findspot unknown
Before 1840

tpq: 1042? Germany, Regensburg, King Henry III (1039–46), Dbg. 1098; Hahn 44
    1036 Germany, Halberstadt, Bishop Burchard I (1036–59), Dbg. 628; Cologne,
        Archbishop Hermann (1036–56), Dbg. 385, Hävernick 251
    *c.*1023 Anglo-Saxon, Cnut, *Pointed Helmet*

*c.*400 coins (90 preserved), mostly German Otto-Adelheid-Pfennige (none preserved):
  German 66; Bohemian 1; Hungarian 1; Italian 2; Danish 1; uncertain 3
  Anglo-Saxon 14:
    Æth II C (3)   London (2), Wallingford
    Æth II D (3)   Exeter, Winchester, York
    Æth II E (1)   Leicester
    Æth II A (4)   Canterbury, Lincoln, York (2)
    Cn G (3)   Lincoln, London (2)
  Imitations of Anglo-Saxon types 3

Ref. Friedlaender 1843. *Polabia* 52; Zak 42; Blackburn and Jonsson W 144.

Comment: In the literature the find is known as 'Frankfurt', however it was not found but
sold in Frankfurt. Later it came to Berlin where Benoni Friedlaender had the opportunity to
select the better preserved and interesting material for his collection. He chose 90 coins, and
only these were later published by his son Julius Friedlaender.

The *tpq* of 1042 is based on a Regensburg type which Friedlaender (no. 44) gave to King
Henry II (1002–14), Dannenberg to Duke Henry VI/King Henry III (1037–46) before 1040,
and Hahn to the same ruler but post 1042. Friedlaender's *tpq* of 1040 was based on his nos.
46–50 which he gave to Duke Henry VII (1040–7), Regensburg, but these are attributed by
Dannenberg and Hahn to Duke Henry V (1017–26), Dbg. 1090, Hahn 31.

MKB Friedlaender coll. 1861, inc. **274, 276, 312, 355, 454, 464, 475, 504, 523, 589, 592, 696,
704, 718, 1029, 1045**.

30. Richnau, Kr. Thorn, Rb. Marienwerder, West Prussia
Rychnowo (pow. Golub-Dobrzyń), woj. Toruń, Poland
1854

tpq: *c.*1042? Anglo-Saxon, Edward the Confessor?
    1039? Germany, Trier, Archbishop Poppo and King Henry III (1039–46), Dbg. 466
    1034 Bohemia, Bretislav I (1034–55)

*c.*1,300 coins (42 described):
  German 34 + x; Bohemian 2; Polish 1; Swedish 1
  Anglo-Saxon 4:
    Æth II E (1)   Tamworth
    Cn E (3)   Chichester, London (2)
    Edw III?,   type? mint?

Ref. Cappe 1857, pp. 47–54, 61, 67–9; Berghaus 1954, pp. 219–20. *PSW* II 143; Zak 137;
Blackburn and Jonsson W 153.

Comment: The only reliable source for this dispersed hoard is a list of 16 coins published by
Berghaus (1954) from Grote's papers, which includes the four Anglo-Saxon coins described
here. It is probably the same hoard as that recorded by Cappe (1857) found near Thorn in
1854. Cappe saw *c.*1,300 coins from which he selected 300, but he described only some of the

types: Otto-Adelheid-Pfennige (nos. 240–54), Andernach (no. 264; Dbg. 433), Trier (no. 266; Dbg. 466), Cologne (Andernach?—no. 267; Dbg. 342i; Hävernick 83), Deventer (no. 307; Dbg. 563), Cologne (Duisburg?—no. 338; Dbg. 363; Hävernick 271), Magdeburg (nos. 339–43; Dbg. 648). Cappe also mentions that coins of Edward the Confessor were present in the hoard (pp. 50, no. 68 as 'Edmund, 1042–66'), though the types or mints are not given and Cappe's information may be wrong.

The *tpq* of 1039 given by the German type Dbg. 466 is also uncertain because this type occurred in the hoard from Årstad (Egersund) which Skaare (1976, p. 152, no. 95) dates post 1029. The presence of the type Dbg. 466 in the Rychno find is attested by Dannenberg (1857, p. 190).

MKB Grote coll. 1879, inc. **498**, **629**.

31. Ploetzig, Kr. Flatow, Rb. Marienwerder, West Prussia
Płocko (pow. Miastko), woj. Słupsk, Poland
1850, 9 May

*tpq: c.*1048 Anglo-Saxon, Edward the Confessor, *Small Flan*
1046? Germany, Strassburg, Emperor Henry III (1046–56), Dbg. 925?
1034 Bohemia, Bretislav I (1034–55)

*c.*464 coins, mostly Otto-Adelheid-Pfennige and Sachsenpfennige, plus hacksilver:
German *c.*371; Bohemian 19; Italian 1; Arabic 1?; uncertain 63 or 64
Anglo-Saxon 7 or 8:

Æth II and Cn (3 or 4)	type? mint?
Cn E (1)	Exeter
Cn G (2)	London, York
Edw III B (1)	uncertain mint
Imitations of Anglo-Saxon types 1 + x	

Ref. Flothow 1851. *PSW* II 124; Zak 107; Blackburn and Jonsson W 164.

Comment: The three or four coins of Æthelred and Cnut recorded but not identified are presumed to be among those in the Old collection without provenance.

MKB 14/1851 (264 coins), inc. **605**, **710**, **741**, **857**, **1062**.

32. 'Berlin I'. Pomerania, findspot unknown
*c.*1856

tpq: 1055 Bohemia, Spytihnev (1055–61)
*c.*1044 Anglo-Saxon, Edward the Confessor, *Radiate Small Cross*
1042 Germany, Regensburg, King Henry III (1039–46), Dbg. 1098; Hahn 44.

*c.*3,200 coins (491 described), mostly Otto-Adelheid-Pfennige and Sachsenpfennige:
German 341 + x; Bohemian 27; Hungarian 28; Italian 1; Danish 36
Anglo-Saxon 27:

Æth II C (1)	Winchester
Æth II A (3)	Chester (Dannenberg: as Leicester), London, Thetford
Cn E (2)	Hastings, York
Cn G (4)	Lincoln, London, Winchester (2)
Cn H (2)	London, York
Har I A (1)	Southwark
Har I B (6)	London (4), Thetford, York

HCn = Cn I (2)   London (2)
Edw III D/HCn A (1)   Exeter
Edw III D (2)   Lincoln, London
Edw III A (3)   London, York (2)
  Imitations of Anglo-Saxon types 27

Ref. Dannenberg 1857, pp. 147–220. *PSW* II 234; Zak 80; Blackburn and Jonsson W 170.

Comment: Dannenberg recorded 34 Anglo-Saxon coins but seven of these are Scandinavian imitations (Dannenberg 1857, nos. 138, 142, 160, 165). The *tpq* of the German coins is problematic. Those originally attributed to Emperor Henry III (1046–56) were later given by Dannenberg to Emperor Henry II (1014–24) (Dbg. 163). For the Regensburg types of King Henry III (1039–46), Hahn suggests a *tpq* 1042.

MKB Dannenberg coll. and 295/1892, ex Weyl auction 114, inc. **567**, **694**, **807**, **819**, **824**.

33. Zaborowo, Kr. Cröben, Rb. Posen, Posen
Zaborowo (pow. Wolsztyn), woj. Leszno, Poland
1871, 5 April

tpq: 1055 Bohemia, Spytihnev II (1055–61)
         c.1044 Anglo-Saxon, Edward the Confessor, *Radiate Small Cross*

702 coins (5 preserved), mostly by Sachsenpfennige:

  German 2; Bohemian 1; Hungarian 1
  Anglo-Saxon 1:
    Edw III A (1)   London

Ref. Menadier 1887, pp. 177–8. *PSW* I 147; Zak 213; Blackburn and Jonsson W 171.

MKB 536–9/1872, inc. **836**.

34. Lupow, Kr. Stolp, Rb. Köslin, Pomerania
Łupawa (pow. Słupsk), woj. Słupsk, Poland
1888, 1 October

tpq: late 11th century; latest of the *c.*100 regular coins: German, Mainz, Archbishop
   Siegfried (1060–84), Dbg. 810

*c.*15kg silver = *c.*15,000 or 7–8,000 coins?, with hacksilver:
  German x; Bohemian x; Hungarian x; Nordic x; Danish x; Arabic x
  Anglo-Saxon:
    Æth II   type? mint?
    Cn   type? mint?
    Har I   type? mint?
    HCn   type? mint?
  Imitations of Anglo-Saxon types 68 + x

Ref. Fiala 1916. *PSW* II 95; Zak 104; Blackburn and Jonsson W 166.

Comment: This very large hoard of degraded Slav imitations of German, Danish, and Anglo-Saxon types has never been properly described. Large portions came into the collection of the Gesellschaft für Pommersche Geschichte und Altertumskunde in Stettin/Szczecin, to the private collection of Emil Bahrfeldt in Berlin, and to the collection of the Duke of Cumberland (Welfencollection). The coins in the Bahrfeldt collection were auctioned at Frankfurt am Main in 1921 and *c.*400 of them were bought by Tassilo

Hoffmann. In 1930 these came to the MKB with the Hoffmann collection. The MKB already had 233 coins from the hoard purchased in the year of the discovery.

Emil Bahrfeldt often mentioned the Lupow hoard in his papers, and said that he had made many drawings of the types, but he never published it. He estimated the number of coins at *c*.7,000–8,000. Eduard Fiala, who made a survey of the types in the Welfencollection (now in the possession of the Deutsche Bank in Hannover) computed the number of coins in the hoard at 15,000 based on papers from the Museum in Stettin/Szczecin (Fiala 1916).

MKB 187/1888 (233 coins) and ex Hoffmann coll. 1930 (*c*.400 coins), inc. **(979)**, **1037–8**, **1042–4**, **1046–7**, **1049–53**, **1057–60**, **1063–72**, **1075–7**, **1079–80**, **1084–7**, **1089–94**, **1097**, **1100–7**, **1109–13**, **1115–25**, **1127**, **1132**?

35. Płonsk (pow. Płonsk), woj. Ciechanow, Poland
1854

tpq: 1061 Bohemia, Wratislaw II (1061–92)
        1051 Germany, Mainz, Archbishop Lupold (1051–9), Dbg. 807
        c.1050 Anglo-Saxon, Edward the Confessor, *Expanding Cross*

c.4,400 g (4,700 g) silver, *c*.3,300 g coins (874 described). More than half of the coins were melted down (i.e. Otto-Adelheid-Pfennige, Sachsenpfennige, denars of Cologne and badly preserved coins):

German 537 + x; Bohemian 73; Hungarian 46; Polish 2; Italian 4; Danish 23; Swedish 1
Anglo-Saxon 152:

Æth II B (3)	Exeter, Maldon, Oxford
Æth II C (17)	Cambridge, Canterbury (3), Exeter, London (7), Norwich, Southwark/Sudbury (2), Thetford, York
Æth II D (13)	Hertford, Lewes, London, Norwich, Oxford, Shrewsbury, Stamford (2), Thetford, Winchester, York (3)
Æth II E (4)	Exeter (2), London, Southwark/Sudbury
Æth II A (15)	Bath (2), Chester, Lincoln (4), London (2), Shaftesbury (2), Shrewsbury, Winchester (3)
Cn E (45)	Cambridge (3), Canterbury (3), Lincoln (9), London (14), Lydford, Norwich (3), Stamford, Taunton, Wilton (2), Winchester (3), York (5)
Cn G (13)	Canterbury, Hertford, Leicester (Chester?) (4), London (2), Thetford (3), Wallingford, York
Cn H (22)	Ipswich (2), Leicester (Chester?), Lincoln (2), London, Norwich, Shaftesbury (3), Stamford (6), Wallingford, Winchester (4), York
Har I A (7)	Cambridge, Chester, Colchester, Lincoln (2), London, York
Har I B (4)	Exeter, London, Lydford, Thetford
Edw III D (3)	Exeter, Lydford, Winchester
Edw III A (2)	Colchester, London
Edw III C (1)	London
Edw III E (2)	London, Thetford

Hiberno-Norse 2: Phase I, Sihtric, Dublin, '*Long Cross*', '*Last Small Cross*'
Imitations of Anglo-Saxon types 35

Ref. Dannenberg 1871/3. *PSW* I 77; Zak 275; Blackburn and Jonsson W 187.

Comment: The Anglo-Saxon coins are not described by Dannenberg in detail, so it is difficult to identify the coins, although we know that they were in his collection. An identification of types, mints, and specimens is given by Zak (1963, 275) which we follow here, although the source of his information is unknown.

There are only two imitations described by Dannenberg. One is a coin of the *Last Small Cross* type with CNVT REX ANGLORV / HEARDECNVT MO EOF and one is a coin of the *Agnus Dei* type. A second coin of *Last Small Cross* type with the name of Cnut and the London mint-signature is recorded by Zak, probably the same as Sylloge **1000**. The two coins of Harthacnut cited by Dannenberg are in fact Danish, not English.

MKB Dannenberg coll., inc. **290**, **1000**?, **1001**.

36. Borzecice, Kr. Krotoschin, Rb. Posen, Posen
Borzecice (pow. Krotoszyn), woj. Kalisz, Poland
1883, April

tpq: 1061 Bohemia, Wratislaw II (1061–92)
                Hungary, Bela (1061–3)
           1051 Germany, Mainz, Archbishop Lupold (1051–6), Dbg. 807
           *c.*1050 Anglo-Saxon, Edward the Confessor, *Expanding Cross*

529 coins:
   German *c.*379 + x; Bohemian 8 + x; Hungarian 4 + x; Polish 1
   Anglo-Saxon 6:
      Æth II D (1)   Chester
      Cn E (3)   Lincoln, London, York
      Cn H (1)   London
      Edw III E (1)   Exeter

Ref. Menadier 1887, pp. 174–6. *PSW* I 5; Zak 200; Blackburn and Jonsson W 183.

MKB 488–522/1883 (35 coins), inc. **344**, **623**, **636**, **674**, **763**, **858**.

37. Simoitzel, Kr. Kolberg, Rb. Köslin, Pomerania
Siemyśl (pow. Kołobrzeg), woj. Koszalin, Poland
*c.*1860

tpq: 1064 Hungary, Geza (1064–74)
           1056 Germany, Cologne, Archbishop Anno (1056–75), Dbg. 396,
                Hävernick 333; Speier, Bishop Konrad (1056–60), Dbg. 839
           *c.*1048 Anglo-Saxon, Edward the Confessor, *Short Cross*

*c.*500 coins:
   German *c.*445; Bohemian 3; Hungarian 29; Danish 10; Arabic 2; Roman 1
   Anglo-Saxon 8:
      Æth II C (2)   Canterbury, Hertford
      Cn E (1)   Lewes
      Cn H (1)   York
      HCn B (1)   Bristol
      Edw III D (1)   Oxford
      Edw III B (2)   Colchester, London
   Imitations of Anglo-Saxon types 2?

Ref. Dannenberg 1865. *PSW* II 149; Zak 87; Blackburn and Jonsson W 193.

numismatist E. Gariel was sold, by the subsequent owner Ferrari de la Renotiere, to the MKB in 1911 under mediation of the coin dealer Egger (Vienna). **67, 105–6, 108, 110–14, 116, 121–4, 126, 128, 130–32, 134, 136, 138–9, 141, 143–7**

Gesellschaft für pommersche Geschichte und Altertumskunde	Cf. Pomerania, findspot unknown (no. 2)
Grabow	Ludwig Grabow (1881–1954), coin dealer at Rostock **56, 394, 559, 632, 712, 766, 768, 908**
Grote	The collection of *c*.9,500 medieval coins of the famous numismatist Hermann Grote (1802–95) sold to the cabinet in 1879 by the merchant and numismatist Hermann Jungk (1834–1902) (see pp. 9–10 above). **31, 38, 43, 45, 48, 51, 97, 101, 104, 107, 120, 125, 127, 181, 232, 241, 292, 299, 301, 318, 323, 373, 441, 445, 474, 545, 547, 574, 578, 600, 618, 648, 652–3, 656–7, 663–4, 669, 673, 707, 720, 753, 759, 765, 787, 801, 852, 854, 873, 877–8, 889, 895, 903–4, 907, 924–5, 932, 944, 949, 989, 1022, 1040–1, 1131** Cf. also finds of Barthe, Ciechanow, Baranow, Richnau/ Rychnowo (nos. 1, 13, 20, 30)
Grunthal/Ball	Hugo Grunthal and Robert Ball, coin dealer in Berlin (Robert Ball Nachf.) **518, 923**
Hahlo	Julius Hahlo, coin dealer in Berlin **215, 692, 835, 846** Cf. also Rawicz find (no. 22)
Hamburger	L. and L. Hamburger, coin dealer at Frankfurt am Main **55, 177**
Hess	Adolph Hess, coin dealer at Frankfurt am Main **834, 850, 875** Cf. also Lodejnoe Pole I find (no. 43) and Juura/Odenpäh find (no. 46)
Heyn	Private collector at Strelitz (Silesia) **825**
Hirsch	Heinrich Hirsch, coin dealer at Munich **33, 65, 68, 84, 178**
Hoffmann	The collection of the numismatist Tassilo Hoffmann (1887–1951) acquired in 1930. It contained only coins of Pomerania among them *c*.400 imitations of German, Anglo-Saxon, and Danish types from the Lupow/Łupawa find. Cf. Lupow/Łupawa find (no. 34)
Jungfer	Robert Jungfer, coin dealer in Berlin **210, 986, 991–2, 994–6, 1030, 1061, 1108, 1114**
Kassel	All non-Hassian coins of the collection of the Hessisches Landesmuseum at Kassel were sold in 1924/5. The bulk of the ancient coins came to the MKB. The medieval coins were auctioned by A. Riechmann, Halle (auction catalogue no. 29, 25 November 1924). **13, 26**
Kirsch	Theodor Kirsch (1847–1911), Amtsgerichtsrat at Düsseldorf **359, 369, 376**
Kube	Rudolf Kube, coin dealer in Berlin, cf. finds of Belgard/Białogard and Altranft (nos. 3, 41)
Lange	Julius Lange (1825–1905), private collector at Potsdam in **999**
Lau	Dr H. Lau, private collector in Berlin **492**
Lehndorff-Steinort	Count Karl of Lehndorff-Steinort, collector of Prussian coins in **374**

Loewenstimm	State prosecutor in St Petersburg (Leningrad) cf. Russia, findspot unknown (no. 39)
Morchio and Mayer	Dealers of coins and antiquities in Venice **159, 183**
Meinardus	In 1872, 134 coins of the collection of the Hofrat H. G. Ehrentraut were bought from Prof. Meinardus at Oldenburg **50, 180**
Murdoch	John Gloag Murdoch, d. 1902, Sotheby Sale 31 March 1903. The following coins were bought from Messrs. Spink & Son Ltd., London in 1905. **71-4, 85-7, 89-90, 92, 148-150, (151), 154**
Old collection	Coins with unknown provenance acquired before 1868, mostly between 1830 and 1868 (see p. 4 above). **16, 21, 24, 207, 212, 281, 322, 326, 354, 360, 388, 393, 400, 409, 411, 427, 452, 462, 471, 480, 487-8, 491, 502, 532, 536, 552, 555, 576, 585, 587, 601, 615, 617, 647, 662, 682, 702, 713-14, 723, 745, 767, 781, 809-10, 813, 856, 864-5, 960?, 968?, 978, 1000, 1008-9, 1014, 1032, 1039, 1048, 1073, 1088, 1098, 1126, 1129-30**
Pfister	John George Pfister (d. 1883), a founder member of the Numismatic Society of London and, from 1850, on the staff of the Dept. of Coins and Medals at the British Museum **899**
Redder	Chr. Redder, coin dealer in Leipzig **102**
Reichsbank	The remnant of the former collection of the Deutsche Reichsbank was delivered up to the MKB in 1953. **3, 17, 20, 29, 242, 265, 325, 329, 440, 455, 531, 634, 957, 985, 1074, 1083, 1096**
Roemer	Professor in Breslau (Wrocław), cf. Visby find (no. 49)
Ruehle von Lilienstern	The important collection largely of medieval coins formed by the Prussian Lieutenant-General August Ruehle von Lilienstern (1780-1847) acquired in 1842 (see pp. 7-9 above). **4-5, 22-3, 25, 32, 39, 41, 69, 158, 160, 163-5, 167-72, 174, 190, 191 or 192, 221-2, 225-7, 237, 249, 254, 264, 273, 279, 285, 293, 295, 298, 305, 311, 321, 331, 333, 335, 337, 340-1, 343, 345-7, 352, 361-2, 370, 372, 378, 386, 390, 397, 401, 403, 417, 420, 426, 430, 446-7, 450, 453, 457, 460, 469, 473, 476, 496-7, 505, 507-8, 511-13, 515-16, 521-2, 526, 528-9, 541, 546, 556-7, 566, 570-1, 579-81, 583, 595-7, 604, 606, 613, 620-1, 625, 628, 633, 642, 659-60, 665-6, 671, 683-4, 689, 698-9, 728-9, 731, 734, 737, 739, 742, 744, 748, 750, 754-5, 760, 769, 775, 780, 784, 788, 793, 795, 799, 803, 805-6, 822, 827, 831, 840-1, 844, 849, 853, 859, 861, 876, 879, 883, 885, 887, 894, 926, 929-31, 933, 936-8, 941, 943, 945, 965, 970-3, 976, 984, 1004, 1007, 1012, 1018, 1025, 1031, 1033, 1036, 1055, 1078, 1128**
Seligman	Eugen Seligman, coin dealer in Frankfurt am Main **80**
Thieme	C. G. Th. Thieme, coin dealer in Leipzig **78, 187**
Timpe	C. T. Timpe, coin dealer in Berlin **83**
Vollard	Unidentified. This provenance is written on the tickets of the coins but it was not possible to explain it. **868, 870**
Webster	William Webster (1821-85), coin dealer in London **54, 57, 88, 93, 129, 152, 153, 155, 185, 890, 920**
Weyl	Adolph Weyl (1842-1901), coin dealer and auctioneer in Berlin **350**; auction 114 (1891): **52, 59, 95, 208, 377, 479, 573, 635, 824, 862, 863,**

866, 898; auction 127 (1893): **367, 439, 494, 527, 543, 560, 630, 752, 757, 779, 838, 939, 1034**

    Cf. also Poland, findspot unknown (no. 40) and Reval/Tallinn find (no. 47)

No provenance,
  other than year
  of acquisition   **1, 19, 27, 179, 300, 315, 708, 721, 958, 966–7, 982, 1081**

B. *Secondary sources: English collections and sales*

Boyne	W. Boyne, Sotheby, 21 January 1896
Cuff	J. D. Cuff, Sotheby, 8 June 1854
Dymock	T. F. Dymock, Sotheby, 1 June 1858
Marsham	R. Marsham, Sotheby, 19 November 1888
Montagu	H. Montagu, Sotheby, 18 November 1895; 11 May 1896; 16 November 1897
Murchison	R. M. Murchison, Sotheby, 28 May 1866
Nunn	J. J. Nunn, Sotheby, 27 November 1896
Richardson	A. B. Richardson, Sotheby, 22 May 1895
Sainthill	R. Sainthill, Sotheby, 27 April 1870
Shepherd	E. J. Shepherd, Sotheby, 22 July 1885

ABBREVIATIONS

The abbreviations of the rulers' names used in the summary of hoards above and in the indexes follow those in Smart 1981. Bibliographical abbreviations are set out in 'Bibliography' below.

Abp Cln   Ceolnoth, Archbishop of Canterbury (833–70).
Abp Enb   Eanbald, Archbishop of York (796–c.830?).
Abp Pl   Plegmund, Archbishop of Canterbury (890–923).
Abp Wfr   Wulfred, Archbishop of Canterbury (805–32).
Abp Wi   Wigmund, Archbishop of York (837–54?).
Æth II   Æthelred II (978–1016); types as BEH but A = *Last Small Cross* only, A1 = *First Small Cross*, Intermed A = *Intermediate Small Cross.*
Æth II Numbria   Æthelred II, king of Northumbria (841–4, 844–9?).
Æthbt   Æthelberht, king of Wessex (858–66); types as *BMC.*
Æthst   Æthelstan (924–39); types as *BMC.*
Æthst I   Æthelstan I, king of East Anglia (c.825–c.845).
Æthwd   Æthelweard, king of East Anglia (c.845–55).
Alfr   Ælfred, king of Wessex (871–99).
Bez   *Bezirk* (provinces of the GDR).
Bgr   Burgred, king of Mercia (852–74); types as *BMC.*
Bhtw   Berhtwulf, king of Mercia (840–52).
Bldr   Baldred, king of Kent (c.823–5).
Cn   Cnut (1016–35); types as BEH.
Cn I = HCn   BEH Cnut type I, now reattributed to Harthacnut.
Cnw   Coenwulf, king of Mercia (796–821).
Ean   Eanred, king of Northumbria (c.810–41).
Ecgb   Ecgberht, king of Wessex (802–39).
Ecgb Kent   Ecgberht, king of Kent (c.765–780?).
Edg   Eadgar (959–75); types as *BMC.*
Edm   Eadmund (939–46); types as *BMC.*

Edm EAng   Eadmund, king of East Anglia (855–69).
Edr   Eadred (946–55); types as *BMC.*
Edw I   Edward the Elder, king of Wessex (899–924); types as *BMC.*
Edw II   Edward the Martyr (975–8).
Edw III   Edward the Confessor (1042–66); types as BEH.
Edwg   Eadwig (955–9); types as *BMC.*
Har I   Harold I (1035–42); types as BEH.
Har II   Harold II (1066).
HCn   Harthacnut (1035–7, 1040–2); types as BEH.
HCn = Cn I   BEH Cnut type I, now reattributed to Harthacnut.
Hen I   Henry I (1100–35); types as *BMC.*
HibN   Hiberno-Norse; the coinage of the Norse kingdom of Dublin.
Kr   *Kreis* (districts in Germany).
MKB   Münzkabinett der Staatlichen Museen zu Berlin (Coin cabinet of the State Museum Berlin).
Osb   Osberht, king of Northumbria (849/50–867?).
pow   *powiat* (the older Polish districts as used in *PSW*).
Rb   *Regierungsbezirk* (Prussian provinces before 1918).
Rdw   Redwulf, king of Northumbria (844?).
Ste   Stephen (1135–54).
St Edm   St Edmund Memorial Coinage issued in East Anglia c.890–915.
tpq   *terminus post quem*
Wm I   William I (1066–87); types as *BMC.*
Wm II   William II (1087–1100); types as *BMC.*
woj   *wojewodstwo* (the new Polish provinces as used in *PSW* Atlas).
→   cross reference; see …
>   becoming, developing into.

BIBLIOGRAPHY

Anglo-Saxon Coins	*Anglo-Saxon Coins. Studies presented to F. M. Stenton on the occasion of his 80th birthday*, ed. R. H. M. Dolley (London 1961).
Archibald 1983	M. M. Archibald, 'Cash Credentials of King Beonna', *BM Soc. Bulletin* no. 42 (March 1983), p. 34.
Bahrfeldt 1888	E. Bahrfeldt, 'Nachträge zum Aufsatze von Dr Menadier Funde deutscher Münzen aus dem Mittelalter', *ZfN* 16 (1888), pp. 93-8.
Bahrfeldt 1896	E. Bahrfeldt, *Der Silberfund von Leissower Mühle* (Berlin 1896).
Bauer 1929	N. Bauer, 'Die russischen Funde abendländischer Münzen des 11. und 12. Jahrhunderts. I. Topographische Übersicht der Münzfunde des Ostbaltikums. II. Topographische Übersicht der in den Grenzen des heutigen Russlands (USSR) gefundenen Münzen', *ZfN* 39 (1929), pp. 1-187.
BBMSWK	*Berliner Blätter für Münz-, Siegel- und Wappenkunde*
BEH	B. E. Hildebrand, *Anglosachsiska mynt i Svenska Kongliga Myntkabinettet funna i Sveriges jord*, 2nd edn (Stockholm 1881).
Berghaus 1951	P. Berghaus, 'Die Münzen von Klein-Roscharden', *Oldenburger Jahrbuch* 51 (1951), pp. 196-206.
Berghaus 1954	P. Berghaus, 'Beiträge zur deutschen Münzkunde des 11. Jhs. 4. Polnische Funde des 11. Jhs. aus dem Nachlass Hermann Grotes', *HBN* 8 (1954), pp. 207-21.
Berghaus 1958	P. Berghaus, 'Die ostfriesischen Münzfunde', *Friesisches Jahrbuch* 1958, pp. 9-70.
Blackburn 1978	M. Blackburn, 'Anglo-Saxon Coins in Polish Museums', *NCirc* 86 (1978), pp. 518-20, 577-9.
Blackburn 1981a	M. Blackburn, 'An Imitative Workshop Active during Æthelred II's *Long Cross* Issue', *Studies in Northern Coinages*, pp. 29-88.
Blackburn 1981b	M. Blackburn, 'A Scandinavian Crux/Intermediate Small Cross Die-chain reappraised', *Viking-Age Coinage*, pp. 425-47.
Blackburn 1985	M. Blackburn, 'English Dies used in Scandinavian Imitative Coinages', *hikuin 11* (1985), pp. 101-24.
Blackburn (forthcoming)	M. Blackburn, 'Hiberno-Norse Coins of the *Helmet* type', *Numismatiska Meddelanden* (forthcoming).
Blackburn and Chown	M. Blackburn and J. Chown, 'A die-link between the Sigtuna coinage of Olof Skötkonung and some Long Cross imitations reading "OCLOD"', *NC* 144 (1984), pp. 166-72.
Blackburn and Dolley 1982	M. Blackburn and M. Dolley, 'The Anglo-Saxon and Anglo-Norman Coins at Dresden', *NCirc* 90 (1982), pp. 47-9, 85-6.
Blackburn and Jonsson	M. Blackburn and K. Jonsson, 'The Anglo-Saxon and Anglo-Norman Element of North European Coin Finds', *Viking-Age Coinage*, pp. 147-255.
Blunt 1961	C. E. Blunt, 'The Coinage of Offa', *Anglo-Saxon Coins*, pp. 39-62.

Blunt 1974   C. E. Blunt, 'The Coinage of Athelstan, King of England
                           924–939', *BNJ* 42 (special volume, 1974), pp. 35–158.

Blunt, Lyon, and Stewart   C. E. Blunt, C. S. S. Lyon, and B. H. I. H. Stewart, 'The coinage
                           of Southern England 796–840', *BNJ* 32 (1963), pp. 1–74.

BMC   *A Catalogue of English Coins in the British Museum. Anglo-Saxon
                           Series*, by H. A. Grueber and C. F. Keary, 2 vols. (London 1887–
                           93); *The Norman Kings*, by G. C. Brooke, 2 vols. (London 1916).

BNJ   *British Numismatic Journal*

Cappe 1857   H. Ph. Cappe, *Die Münzen der deutschen Kaiser und Könige des
                           Mittelalters*, vol. 3 (Dresden 1857).

CNS   *Corpus Nummorum saeculorum IX–XI qui in Suecia reperti sunt*
                           (Stockholm 1975–   ).

Cohn 1877   S. Cohn, 'Der Münzfund von Lübeck', *ZfN* 4 (1877), pp. 69–123
                           (Anglo-Saxon, Hiberno-Norse, Danish, Swedish coins, and
                           Scandinavian imitations).

Dannenberg 1857   H. Dannenberg, 'Zur Münzkunde des zehnten und elften Jahr-
                           hunderts', *Mitteilungen der Numismatischen Gesellschaft in
                           Berlin* 3 (1857), pp. 145–273 (Dannenberg *Studien*, pp. 48–177).

Dannenberg 1863   H. Dannenberg, 'Der Münzfund von Rummelsburg', *BBMSWK*
                           1 (1863), pp. 13–43 (Dannenberg *Studien*, pp. 179–209).

Dannenberg 1865   H. Dannenberg, 'Der Münzfund von Simoitzel', *BBMSWK* 2
                           (1865), pp. 150–65 (Dannenberg *Studien*, pp. 210–25).

Dannenberg 1871/3   H. Dannenberg, 'Der Münzfund von Plonsk', *BBMSWK* 6
                           (1871–3), pp. 150–9, 241–70 (Dannenberg *Studien*, pp. 226–66).

Dannenberg 1874   H. Dannenberg, 'Der Münzfund von Dobra', *ZfN* 1 (1874),
                           pp. 348–70 (Dannenberg *Studien*, pp. 268–90).

Dannenberg 1877   H. Dannenberg, 'Der Münzfund von Lübeck', *ZfN* 4 (1877),
                           pp. 50–68 (Dannenberg *Studien*, pp. 336–54) (German coins).

Dannenberg 1880   H. Dannenberg, 'Der Denarfund von Jarocin', *ZfN* 7 (1880),
                           pp. 146–56.

Dannenberg 1884   H. Dannenberg, 'Zwei Funde von Denaren des zehnten und
                           elften Jahrhunderts. B. Der Fund von Vossberg', *ZfN* 11 (1884),
                           pp. 264–330 (Dannenberg *Studien*, pp. 366–432).

Dannenberg 1887   H. Dannenberg, 'Der zweite Fund von Klein-Roscharden', *ZfN*
                           15 (1887), pp. 281–90.

Dannenberg 1897   H. Dannenberg, 'Unedirte Mittelaltermünzen meiner Samm-
                           lung', *ZfN* 20 (1897), pp. 1–27 (Dannenberg *Studien*, pp. 813–39).

Dannenberg 1897a   H. Dannenberg, 'Münzfunde aus Pommern und Mecklenburg.
                           A. Der Denarfund von Züssow', *ZfN* 20 (1897), pp. 122–6.

Dannenberg 1906   H. Dannenberg, 'Noch drei estnische Denarfunde. 2) Fund von
                           Odenpäh', *ZfN* 25 (1906), pp. 70–5.

Dannenberg 1906/9   H. Dannenberg, 'Der Hacksilberfund von Mgowo', *Berliner
                           Münzblätter* 27 (1906), pp. 335–40; 29 (1908), p. 165; 30 (1909),
                           pp. 322–7 (Dannenberg *Studien*, pp. 433–45).

Dannenberg *Studien*   H. Dannenberg, *Studien zur Münzkunde des Mittelalters (1848–
                           1905)*, ed. B. Kluge (Leipzig 1984).

Dbg   H. Dannenberg, *Die deutschen Münzen der sächsischen und
                           fränkischen Kaiserzeit*, 4 vols (Berlin 1876–1905).

DM   J. Menadier, *Deutsche Münzen. Gesammelte Aufsätze zur Geschichte des Deutschen Münzwesens*, 4 vols (Berlin 1891–1922).

Dolley 1957   R. H. M. Dolley, 'Two Anglo-Saxon Notes', *BNJ* 28 (1955–7), pp. 499–508.

Dolley 1967   M. Dolley, 'OE* Christthegn—An Unsuspected Instance of Early Middle Irish Influence on English Name-giving', *BNJ* 36 (1967), pp. 40–5.

Dolley 1981   M. Dolley, 'Imitation and Imitation of Imitation: Some Problems Posed by the non-English *Helmet* Pennies with the Name of Æthelræd II', *Studies in Northern Coinages*, pp. 89–111.

Dolley and Blunt 1961   R. H. M. Dolley and C. E. Blunt, 'The Chronology of the Coins of Ælfred the Great', *Anglo-Saxon Coins*, pp. 77–95.

Fiala 1916   E. Fiala, 'Der Nachmünzenfund von Lupow', in his *Münzen und Medaillen der Welfischen Lande. Part I. Prägungen der Zeit der Ludolfinger* (*Ottonen*), *Brunonen, Billunger, Supplingenburger etc.* (Prague 1916), pp. 98–126.

Flothow 1851   E. Flothow, 'Ein Schatzfund auf der Feldmark des Dorfes Ploetzig zwischen Cammin und Zempelburg', *Neue Preussische Provinzblätter* 11 (1851), pp. 318–20.

Friedlaender 1843   J. Friedlaender, 'Über einen Fund grösstentheils Deutscher Silbermünzen aus der ersten Hälfte des elften Jahrhunderts', *Zeitschrift für Münz-, Siegel- und Wappenkunde* 3 (1843), pp. 145–63.

Friedlaender 1877   J. Friedlaender, 'Der Fund von Althoefchen', *Münzstudien* 8 (1877), pp. 267–300.

Friedlaender 1879   J. Friedlaender, 'Der Fund von Witzmitz 991–1002', *ZfN* 6 (1879), pp. 242–51.

Friedlaender 1881   J. Friedlaender, 'Ein in der Provinz Posen gemachter Silberfund', *ZfN* 8 (1881), pp. 149–50.

Friedlaender and Müllenhoff 1850   J. Friedlaender and K. Müllenhoff, *Der Silberfund von Farve* (Kiel 1850).

Gariel   E. Gariel, *Les monnaies royales de France sous la race Carolingienne*, 2 vols (Strassburg 1883–4).

Hävernick   W. Hävernick, *Die Münzen von Köln vom Beginn der Prägung bis 1304* (Köln 1935).

Hahn   W. Hahn, *Moneta Radasponensis. Bayerns Münzprägung im 9., 10. und 11. Jahrhundert* (Braunschweig 1976).

Hauberg   P. Hauberg, *Myntforhold og Udmyntninger in Danmark indtil 1146* (Copenhagen 1900).

HBN   *Hamburger Beiträge zur Numismatik*

Hill 1977   D. Hill, 'The "Hanover" Hoard of Porcupine Sceattas', *NC* 137 (1977), pp. 173–4.

Jazdzewski 1879   W. Jazdzewski, *Wykopalisko jarocińskie a mianowicie monety Bolesławów czeskich* (Poznań 1879).

Kluge 1981   B. Kluge, 'Das angelsächsische Element in den slawischen Münzfunden des 10. bis 12. Jahrhunderts. Aspekte einer Analyse', *Viking-Age Coinage*, pp. 257–327.

Kluge 1985   B. Kluge, 'Der Hacksilberfund von Denzin/Dębczyno 1889', *Nummus et historia. Pieniądz Europy średniowiecznej* (Warszawa 1985), pp. 73–81.

Lagerquist 1970   L. O. Lagerquist, *Svenska mynt under Vikingatid och Medeltid (ca. 995–1521) samt Gotländska mynt (ca. 1140–1565)* (Stockholm 1970).

Lyon, van der Meer, and Dolley 1961   C. S. S. Lyon, G. van der Meer, and R. H. M. Dolley, 'Some Scandinavian Coins in the Names of Æthelred, Cnut and Harthacnut attributed by Hildebrand to English mints', *BNJ* 30 (1960–1), pp. 235–51.

Lyon and Stewart 1961   C. S. S. Lyon and B. H. I. H. Stewart, 'The Northumbrian Viking Coins in the Cuerdale Hoard', *Anglo-Saxon Coins*, pp. 96–121.

Lyon and Stewart 1964   C. S. S. Lyon and B. H. I. H. Stewart, 'The Classification of Northumbrian Viking Coins in the Cuerdale Hoard', *NC*[7] 4 (1964), pp. 281–2.

Malmer 1965   B. Malmer, *Olof Skötkonungs mynt och andra Ethelred-imitationer* (Antikvariskt arkiv 27, Lund 1965).

Malmer 1966   B. Malmer, *Nordiska mynt före år 1000* (Lund 1966).

van der Meer 1961   G. van der Meer, 'Some Corrections to and Comments on B. E. Hildebrand's Catalogue of the Anglo-Saxon Coins in Swedish Royal Coin Cabinet', *Anglo-Saxon Coins*, pp. 169–87.

van der Meer 1965   G. van der Meer, 'Some unpublished Anglo-Saxon Coins in the Berlin Coin Cabinet', *Dona Numismatica. Festschrift Walter Hävernick* (Hamburg 1965), pp. 67–71.

Menadier 1887   J. Menadier, 'Funde deutscher Münzen aus dem Mittelalter', *ZfN* 15 (1887), pp. 97–201.

Menadier 1888   J. Menadier, 'Gittelder Pfennige', *ZfN* 16 (1888), pp. 233–342.

Menadier 1898a   J. Menadier, 'Eine Nachlese zu dem Funde von der Leissower Mühle', *DM* 4 (1898), pp. 172–6.

Menadier 1898b   J. Menadier, 'Der Denarfund von Birglau bei Thorn', *ZfN* 21 (1898), pp. 288–304.

Menadier 1898c   J. Menadier, 'Ein russischer Fund deutscher Pfennige aus dem Ende des 11. Jahrhunderts', *DM* 4 (1898), pp. 195–234.

Menadier 1898d   J. Menadier, 'Der Fund von Ciechanow', *DM* 4 (1898), pp. 163–71.

Menadier 1902   J. Menadier, 'Der Fund von Kinno', *ZfN* 23 (1902), pp. 95–106.

Menadier 1924   J. Menadier, 'Fund von Seemark bei Schneidemühl', *ZfN* 34 (1924), pp. 107–12.

Metcalf 1966a   D. M. Metcalf, 'A Stylistic Analysis of the "Porcupine" Sceattas', *NC*[7] 4 (1966), pp. 179–205.

Metcalf 1966b   D. M. Metcalf, 'Artistic borrowing, Imitation and Forgery in the eighth century', *HBN* 20 (1966), pp. 379–92.

Metcalf 1969   D. M. Metcalf, 'A Hoard of "Porcupine" Sceattas', *American Numismatic Society Museum Notes* 15 (1969), pp. 108–18.

Morrison and Grunthal   K. F. Morrison and H. Grunthal, *Carolingian Coinage* (Numismatic Notes and Monographs 158, New York 1967).

Mossop	H. R. Mossop and others, *The Lincoln Mint c.890–1279* (Newcastle 1970).
NC	*Numismatic Chronicle*
NCirc	*Numismatic Circular* (Spink)
North	J. J. North, *English Hammered Coinage. Vol. I: Early Anglo-Saxon to Henry III, c.600–1272*, 2nd edn (London 1980).
Pagan 1969	H. E. Pagan, 'Northumbrian Numismatic Chronology in the Ninth Century', *BNJ* 38 (1969), pp. 1–15.
Pagan 1971	H. E. Pagan, 'Mr. Emery's Mint', *BNJ* 40 (1971), pp. 139–70.
Pagan 1982	H. E. Pagan, 'The Coinage of the East Anglian Kingdom from 825 to 870', *BNJ* 52 (1982), pp. 41–81.
Pagan and Rhodes	H. E. Pagan and N. G. Rhodes, 'Anglo-Saxon Coins in the Westminster School Collection', *BNJ* 31(1962), pp. 11–26.
Połabia	R. Kiersnowski, *Wczesnośredniowieczne skarby srebrne z Połabia* (Wrocław/Warszawa/Kraków 1964).
Potin 1967	V. M. Potin, 'Topografija nachodok zapadnoevropejskich monet 10–13 vv. na territorii drevnej Rusi', *Trudy Gosudarstvennogo Ermitaža* 9 (1967), pp. 106–88.
PSW	*Polskie skarby wczesnośredniowieczne. Inwentarze* (Polskie Badania Archeologiczne, vols 1, 4, 10, 12; Wrocław/Warszawa/Kraków 1959–66): I. J. Ślaski and St. Tabaczyński, *Wczesnośredniowieczne skarby srebrne Wielkopolski* (1959). II. T. and R. Kiersnowscy, *Wczesnośredniowieczne skarby srebrne z Pomorza* (1959). III. A. Gupieniec, T. and R. Kiersnowscy, *Wczesnośredniowieczne skarby srebrne z Polski środkowej, Mazowsza i Podlasia* (1965). IV. M. Haisig, R. Kiersnowski, J. Reyman, *Wczesnośredniowieczne skarby srebrne z Małopolski, Śląska, Warmii i Mazur* (1966).
PSW Atlas	L. Gajewski, J. Gorska, L. Paderewska, J. Pyrgala and W. Szymański, *Skarby wczesnośredniowieczne z obszaru Polski. Atlas* (Early Mediaeval Hoards in Poland. Atlas) (Wrocław/Warszawa/Kraków/Gdańsk/Łódź 1982).
Pyl 1897	Th. Pyl, *Die Greifswalder Sammlungen vaterländischer Alterthümer*, fasc. 2 (Greifswald 1897), pp. 60–84.
Rigold 1960	S. E. Rigold, 'The Two Primary Series of Sceattas', *BNJ* 30 (1960–1), pp. 6–53.
Rigold 1966	S. E. Rigold, 'The Two Primary Series of Sceattas. Addenda and Corrigenda', *BNJ* 35 (1966), pp. 1–6.
Rigold 1977	S. E. Rigold, 'The Principal Series of English Sceattas', *BNJ* 47 (1977), pp. 21–30.
SCBI	*Sylloge of Coins of the British Isles.*
SCBI Belfast	*Ulster Museum Belfast.* Part II. *Hiberno-Norse Coins*, by W. Seaby (London 1984) (*SCBI* 32).
SCBI BM HibN	*The Hiberno-Norse Coins in the British Museum*, by R. H. M. Dolley (London 1966) (*SCBI* 8).

SCBI Cambridge   *The Fitzwilliam Museum*. Part I. *Ancient British and Anglo-Saxon Coins*, by P. Grierson (London 1958) (*SCBI* 1).

SCBI Copenhagen   *The Royal Danish Collection Copenhagen.*
Part I. *Ancient British and Anglo-Saxon Coins before Æthelred II*, by G. Galster, (London 1964).
Part II. *Anglo-Saxon Coins. Æthelred II*, by G. Galster (London 1966).
Part III. A, B and C. *Anglo-Saxon Coins. Cnut*, by G. Galster (London 1970).
Part IV. *Anglo-Saxon Coins from Harold I and Anglo-Norman Coins.* by G. Galster (London 1972).
Part V. *Hiberno-Norse and Anglo-Irish Coins*, by G. Galster with M. Dolley and J. S. Jensen (London 1975).
(*SCBI* 4, 7, 13–15, 18, 22).

SCBI East Anglia   *Museums in East Anglia. The Morley St Peter Hoard and Anglo-Saxon, Norman, and Angevin coins, and later Coins of the Norwich Mint*, by T. H. McK. Clough (London 1980) (*SCBI* 26).

SCBI Glasgow   *Hunterian and Coats Collections, University of Glasgow.* Part I. *Anglo-Saxon Coins* by A. S. Robertson (London 1961) (*SCBI* 2).

SCBI Helsinki   *The National Museum, Helsinki. Anglo-Saxon, Anglo-Norman, and Hiberno-Norse Coins*, by T. Talvio (London 1978) (*SCBI* 25).

SCBI Mack   *Ancient British, Anglo-Saxon, and Norman Coins in the collection formed by Commander R. P. Mack*, by R. P. Mack (London 1973) (*SCBI* 20).

SCBI Merseyside   *Merseyside County Museums. Ancient British Issues and later Coins from English, Irish and Scottish Mints to 1279 and associated Foreign Coins*, by M. Warhurst (London 1982) (*SCBI* 29).

SCBI Midlands   *Ancient British, Anglo-Saxon and Norman Coins in Midlands Museums*, by A. J. H. Gunstone (London 1971) (*SCBI* 17).

SCBI Oxford   *Ashmolean Museum, Oxford.* Part I. *Anglo-Saxon Pennies*, by J. D. A. Thompson (London 1967) (*SCBI* 9).

SCBI Reading   *Reading University. Anglo-Saxon and Norman Coins*, by C. E. Blunt and M. Dolley (London 1969) (*SCBI* 11a).

SCBI Stockholm   *Royal Coin Cabinet Stockholm. Anglo-Norman Pennies*, by M. Dolley (London 1969) (*SCBI* 11b).

SCBI Yorkshire   *Coins in Yorkshire Collections.* Part I. *Coins from Northumbrian Mints, c.895–1279.* Part II. *Ancient British Issues and later Coins from other English, Irish, and Scottish Mints to 1279*, by E. J. E. Pirie (London 1975) (*SCBI* 21).

Seger 1928   H. Seger, 'Die schlesischen Silberfunde der spät-slawischen Zeit', *Altschlesien* 2 (1928), pp. 129–62.

Skaare 1976   K. Skaare, *Coins and Coinage in Viking-Age Norway* (Oslo 1976).

Smart 1965   V. J. Smart, 'A Subsidiary Issue of Æthelred II's *Long Cross*', *BNJ* 34 (1965), pp. 37–41.

Smart 1968   V. J. Smart, 'Moneyers of the late Anglo-Saxon Coinage 973–1016', *Commentationes de nummis saec. IX-XI in Suecia repertis*, II (Stockholm 1968), pp. 194–276.

Lastly the provenances of the coins are given. The Museum's acquisitions number, consisting of a serial number and the year of acquisition (eg. 588/1894), is given for coins acquired after 1868, unless they were part of one of the major collections for which individual coin numbers were not assigned. References should be made to the section 'Collections, Dealers, and Donors', as well as for the major collections to the introductory chapter above, and for the find provenances to 'Finds represented in the Berlin coin cabinet'. In view of the great importance of the hoard evidence, a careful check has been made of the Acquisitions Journal and of the archives of the MKB.

The indexes follow the example now given by Smart 1981 and should help to make the material easy to use and to compare with other *SCBI* volumes especially with regard to moneyers' names.

PLATES

ANGLO-SAXON SERIES

GOLD AND ELECTRUM ('THRYMSAS')

	Weight		Die	
	gm	gr	axis	
1	1.23	19.0	0	*Pada* (in runic characters). Rigold 1960, class P IIa. Same *rev.* die as *SCBI* Cambridge 219. Normally in silver (North 154). Provenance uncertain, acquired between *c*.1870 and 1890.

EARLY SILVER PENNIES ('SCEATTAS')

The series classification is that of Rigold 1977. See also Rigold 1960 and 1966, and for series E ('porcupines') Metcalf 1966a and 1969.

Series A

2	1.29	19.9	180	*BMC* 2a, North 40. Grote coll. 1879.

Series D ('Continental Runic')

3	1.21	18.7		*BMC* 2c, North 168. 943/1953, ex Reichsbank coll.
4	1.12	17.3		*BMC* 2c, North 168. Broken. Ruehle coll. 1842.
5	0.77	11.9		*BMC* 2c, North 168. Ruehle coll. 1842.

Series E ('Porcupine')

Nos. 6–25 are derivatives of Metcalf's classes A, C, E, F and are probably Frisian (Metcalf 1966a and 1969). The attribution of no. 26, an early 'porcupine' type, is uncertain. Nos. 27–8 are probably English.

6	1.30	20.1		Grote coll. 1879, ex Barthe find 1835.
7	1.29	19.9		Grote coll. 1879, ex Barthe find 1835.
8	1.29	19.9		Grote coll. 1879, ex Barthe find 1835.
9	1.28	19.8		Grote coll. 1879, ex Barthe find 1835.
10	1.28	19.8		Grote coll. 1879, ex Barthe find 1835.
11	1.27	19.6		Gansauge coll. 1873.
12	1.25	19.3		Grote coll. 1879, ex Barthe find 1835.
13	1.25	19.3		Ex coll. Landesmuseum Kassel 1925.
14	1.24	19.1		Grote coll. 1879, ex Barthe find 1835.
15	1.24	19.1		Grote coll. 1879, ex Barthe find 1835.
16	1.22	18.8		Old collection.
17	1.20	18.5		940/1953, ex Reichsbank coll.
18	1.17	18.1		Grote coll. 1879, ex Barthe find 1835.
19	1.17	18.1		7559/1953, bt. from a private collector.
20	1.09	16.8		941/1953, ex Reichsbank coll.
21	0.99	15.3		Old collection.
22	0.99	15.3		Ruehle coll. 1842.
23	0.98	15.2		Ruehle coll. 1842.
24	0.92	14.2		Old collection.
25	0.79	12.2		Ruehle coll. 1842.
26	1.22	18.8		'Plumed bird' variety. *BMC* 6, Metcalf 1966, class J. Ex coll. Landesmuseum Kassel 1925.
27	1.25	19.3		*Æthilirǣd* (in runic characters). *BMC* Mercia Æthelred 4, North 155. Provenance uncertain, acquired after 1900.
28	1.11	17.1		*Æthilrǣd* (in runic characters). *BMC* Mercia Æthelred 4, North 155. Gansauge coll. 1873.

Series F

29	1.18	18.2		*BMC* 24b, North 62. 942/1953, ex Reichsbank coll.

Series X ('Woden/Monster')

30	1.25	19.3	0	*BMC* 31, North 117. Gansauge coll. 1873.
31	0.91	14.1	90	*BMC* 31, North 117. Grote coll. 1879.
32	0.54	8.4	0	*BMC* 31, North 117. This coin is of copper. Ruehle coll. 1842.

PLATE 1

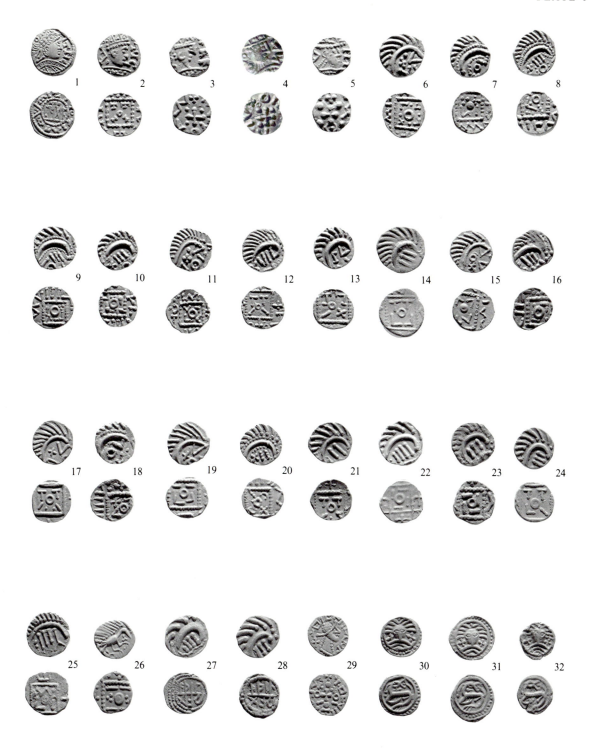

8TH-CENTURY SILVER 'SCEATTAS'

EADBERHT, 737-58

	Weight		Die	
	gm	gr	axis	
33	1.08	16.6		+EOTBEREHTVΓ. North 178, *BMC* 4. 399/1884, bt. Hirsch.

9TH-CENTURY COPPER 'STYCAS'

The traditional dates are given, followed in parentheses by an alternative dating proposed by Pagan 1969.

EANRED, *c.*810-41 (*c.*825-*c.*854)

The *obv.* reads +EANRED REX unless otherwise indicated (North 186).

(a) Early phase, in base silver.

34	1.20	18.5	180	*Vilheah* (Wilheah). Gansauge coll. 1873.

(b) Late phase, in copper alloy.

35	1.52	23.4	180	*Brodr* (Brother). *Obv.* +EAHRED R. Gansauge coll. 1873.
36	1.03	15.9	0	*Eordred* (Fordræd), retrograde. Dannenberg coll. 1870.
37	0.95	14.6	180	*Fordred* (Fordræd). Gansauge coll. 1873.
38	1.28	19.7	270	*Monne* (Man/Manna/Monna). *Obv.* initial E reversed. Grote coll. 1879.
39	0.97	14.9	180	*Monne* (Man/Manna/Monna). *Obv.* initial E reversed. Ruehle coll. 1842.

ÆTHELRED II, first reign 841-4 (*c.*854-8)

The *obv.* reads +EDILRED REX (L often inverted) unless otherwise indicated (North 188).

40	0.78 (chipped)	12.1	130	*Aldhere* (Ealhhere). *Obv.* AEDILRE RX (RX ligatured). Gansauge coll. 1873.
41	1.13	17.4	180	*Brother*. Ruehle coll. 1842.
42	1.19	18.4	270	*Eanred* (Eanræd). Gansauge coll. 1873.
43	1.15	17.7	90	*Eanred* (Eanræd). Grote coll. 1879.
44	1.08	16.7	340	*Eanred* (Eanræd). *Obv.* AEILRED R. Gansauge coll. 1873.
45	1.27	19.6	0	*Fordred* (Fordræd). Grote coll. 1879.
46	1.12	17.3	90	*Fordred* (Fordræd). *Obv.* EDFLRED RE. Dannenberg coll. 1892.
47	1.07	16.5	270	*Vendelberht* (Wendelbeorht), letters N and L inverted. Gansauge coll. 1873.
48	1.21	18.7	180	*Vulfred* (Wulfræd). *Obv.* EDILRED RE. Grote coll. 1879.

REDWULF, 844 (*c.*858)

North 189

49	1.06	16.4	0	*Brother*. *Obv.* +REDVL RE. Gansauge coll. 1873.
50	1.29	19.9	90	*Eordred* (Fordræd). *Obv.* +REDVLF RE. 470/1872, bt. Meinardus, ex Ehrentraut coll. Miss Pirie comments that this coin belongs to a die-chain which includes coins in the name of Æthelred II of the moneyers Fordræd, Brother, Monne, Odilo, and Wulfræd. Some of which are clearly irregular.

ÆTHELRED II, second reign 844-9 (*c.*858-62)

The *obv.* reads +EDILRED REX (North 190).

51	1.25	19.3	0	*Eardvulf* (Eardwulf). Grote coll. 1879.
52	1.22	18.8	90	*Eardvulf* (Eardwulf). Slightly double-struck. 291/1892, ex Weyl auction 114 (1891), 1442.
53	1.14	17.6	50	*Eardvulf* (Eardwulf). *Obv.* legend retrograde. Gansauge coll. 1873.

OSBERHT, 849/50-867 (862-7)

North 191

54	1.19	18.4	180	*Eannle* (Eanwulf?), letters A and L reversed. *Obv.* OSBERCHT EX, letters S and T inverted. 671/1872, bt. Webster.
55	1.00	15.4	270	*Monne* (Man/Manna/Monna), retrograde. *Obv.* OSBERHT RCX, partly inverted. 167/1928, ex L. Hamburger auction Feb. 1928, 1373 (Prince Philipp of Saxe-Coburg coll.).

[*continued overleaf*]

PLATE 2

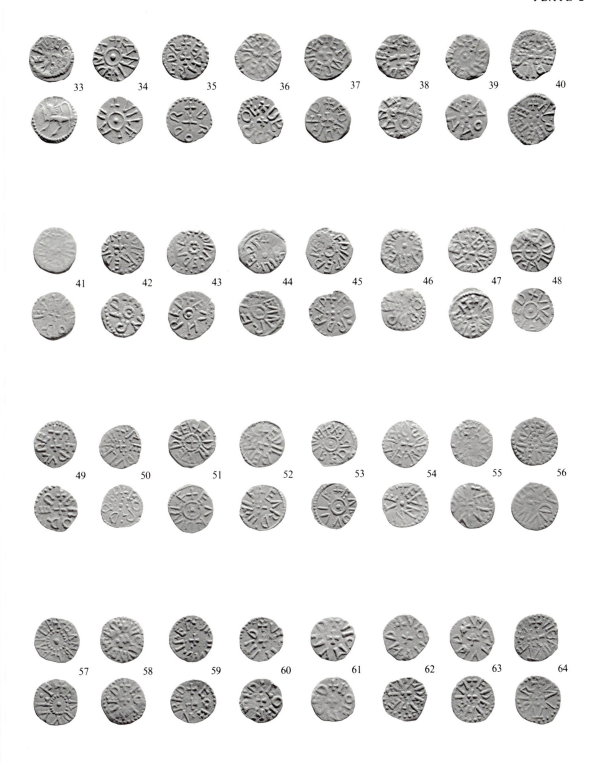

Plate 3 (*cont.*)

KINGS OF KENT

ECGBERHT, *c*.765–*c*.780 or later

	Weight		Die	
	gm	*gr*	*axis*	
84	1.17	18.1	0	*Udd. Obv.* **EGCBERHT**. Canterbury. Blunt 1961, 118, North 200. Same *rev.* die as *BMC* 1 and *SCBI* Cambridge 428. 487/1875, bt. Hirsch.

BALDRED, *c*.823–5

85	1.23	19.0	0	*Werheard* (Wærheard). Canterbury. *Obv.* **BELDRED REX**. *BMC* 19, North 213, Blunt, Lyon, and Stewart, 16(b). 919/1905, ex Murdoch 37, 'found in East Coker churchyard, near Yeovil, Dorset, between 1860 and 1870'.

ARCHBISHOPS OF CANTERBURY

WULFRED, 805–32

86	1.27	19.6	0	*Swefherd* (Swefheard). Regular monogram type (pre 823). *Obv.* no pellets by face. North 240/1, Blunt, Lyon, and Stewart, group iii (specimen not mentioned). 923/1905, ex Murdoch 39, 'from a find in Ireland', probably Delgany 1874 hoard (Pagan and Rhodes 1962, p. 15, this coin discussed).
87	1.28	19.8	270	Unspecified moneyer. **DOROBERNIA CIVITAS**. *Obv.* **VVLFRED**, letters **V** and **D** later corrected by the die-cutter, two pellets on each side of the face. North 237/1, Blunt, Lyon, and Stewart, p. 71, no. 16. 923/1905, ex Murdoch 40, ex Montagu (1897), 4, ex Montagu (1895), 310, ex Marsham 112, ex Sainthill 155, who obtained it in France. Blunt, Lyon, and Stewart regard this as a mule between the 'Baldred' type and the Anonymous Archiepiscopal coinage, *c*.823.

CEOLNOTH, 833–70

88	1.34	20.7	0	*Liabincg* (Leofing/Lifing). Open Cross type. *Obv.* **+CEOLNOÐ ARCHIEP**, three pellets on each side of the bust. North 245. 673/1872, bt. Webster.

PLEGMUND, 890–923

Earlier group (*temp.* Ælfred)

89	1.47	22.7	210	*Elfstan* (Ælfstan). *Obv.* **+PLEGMVND EPIZC**. North 253. 921/1905, ex Murdoch 46, ex Montagu 330, ex Shepherd 55, ex Murchison 217, ex Cuff 405, ex Cuerdale hoard.
90	1.51	23.3	270	*Hunfreth* (Hunfrith). *Obv.* legend begins at 3 o'clock **+PLEGMVND ARCHIEP**. North 254. 920/1905, ex Murdoch 45.

Later group (*temp.* Edward the Elder)

91	0.88	13.6	90	*—ulf* (moneyer uncertain, probably Æthelwulf). *Obv.* **(+P)LEGMVND A——**. North 256. 544/1897,
	(fragment)			ex Gesellschaft für pommersche Geschichte und Altertumskunde Stettin, probably from a Pomeranian hoard. This appears to be one of the earliest known coins of the archbishop in Edward the Elder's reign; see C. E. Blunt, I. H. Stewart, and C. S. S. Lyon, *Coinage in Tenth-Century England* (forthcoming).

PENCE *(cont.)* GROUP II *(cont.)*

	Weight		Die	
	gm	gr	axis	

II(d) *Obv.* Pellet in two angles of cross. *Rev.* **CNVT REX**. Plain cross, no pellets in angles. C-1b/CR-F (North 499)

120	1.44	22.2	30	Grote coll. 1879.
121	1.27	19.6	40	Gariel–Ferrari coll. 1911.

II(e) *Obv.* as (d). *Rev.* as (b). C-1b/CR-G (North 501).

122	1.44	22.2	0	Gariel–Ferrari coll. 1911.
123	1.44	22.2	60	Gariel–Ferrari coll. 1911.
124	1.41	21.8	0	Gariel–Ferrari coll. 1911.
125	1.39	21.5	220	Grote coll. 1879
126	1.31	20.2	140	Gariel–Ferrari coll. 1911.
127	1.27	19.6	140	Two peck-marks on *obv.*, one on *rev.* Grote coll. 1879.

GROUP III. *Obv.* **SIEFREDVS**. Small cross pattée.

III(a) *Obv.* Two pellets in each angle of cross. *Rev.* **REX+**. Cross crosslet with groups of pellets between each letter. S-1a/REX—E (North 502).

128	1.26	19.4	60	Same *obv.* die as *SCBI* Copenhagen i 555-6. Gariel–Ferrari coll. 1911.

III(c) *Obv.* Pellet in two angles of cross. *Rev.* **REX+**. Plain cross, no pellets. S-1b/REX—F (North 503)

129	1.32	20.4	180	Same dies as 130 and *SCBI* Copenhagen i 554. 672/1872, bt. Webster.
130	1.16	17.9	180	Same dies as 129 and *SCBI* Copenhagen i 554. Gariel–Ferrari coll. 1911.

III(d) *Obv.* as (c). *Rev.* **CNVT REX**. Patriarchal cross, groups of pellets between letters S-1b/CR-G (North 504).

131	1.48	22.8	50	Same dies as *SCBI* Oxford 191. Gariel–Ferrari coll. 1911.
132	1.29	19.9	0	Same dies as *SCBI* Oxford 193. Gariel–Ferrari coll. 1911.

GROUP V. *Obv.* **DNS DS REX**. Small cross pattée with pellet in two angles.

V(a) *Rev.* **SIEVERT REX**. Patriarchal cross. DDR-1/SR-G (North 506)

133	1.39	21.5	130	Same dies as *SCBI* Copenhagen i 561, same *rev.* die as *SCBI* Oxford 195. Dannenberg coll. 1892.
134	1.38	21.3	220	Gariel–Ferrari coll. 1911.

GROUP VI. *Obv.* **MIRABILIA FECIT**. Small cross pattée with pellet in two angles.

VI(a) *Rev.* **DNS DS O REX** in two lines. MF-1/DDOR-Aii (North 509).

135	1.32	20.4	0	Same dies as *SCBI* Copenhagen i 577-8 and *SCBI* Oxford 201. Dannenberg coll. 1870.

VI(c) *Rev.* **EBRAICE**. Patriarchal cross. MF-1/EC-G (North 512).

136	1.40	21.6	120	**MIRABILIA FC**. Same *obv.* die as *SCBI* Copenhagen i 567-70. Gariel–Ferrari coll. 1911.
137	1.39	21.5	180	Gansauge coll. 1873.
138	1.37	21.1	20	Same *obv.* die as *SCBI* Oxford 216. Gariel–Ferrari coll. 1911.
139	1.28	19.8	260	Same *rev.* die as 140. Gariel–Ferrari coll. 1911.
140	1.13	17.4	220	**MIRABIIAN FCT**. Two peck-marks on *rev.* Same dies as *SCBI* Oxford 215, same *obv.* die as **139**. Gansauge coll. 1873.

VI(d) *Rev.* **CNVT REX**. Patriarchal cross. MF-1/CR-G (North 511)

141	1.27	19.6	90	**MIRABILIA FEC**. Gariel–Ferrari coll. 1911.
142	1.19	18.4	240	**MIRABILIA FC**. Dannenberg coll. 1892.

GROUP VII. *Obv.* **QVENTOVICI**. Small cross pattée. *Rev.* **CNVT REX** (blundered). Plain cross, pellet in each angle. 1-CR-C (North 524).

143	1.39	21.5	0	*Rev.* **CIRTENV**. Gariel–Ferrari coll. 1911.

[continued overleaf]

PLATE 5

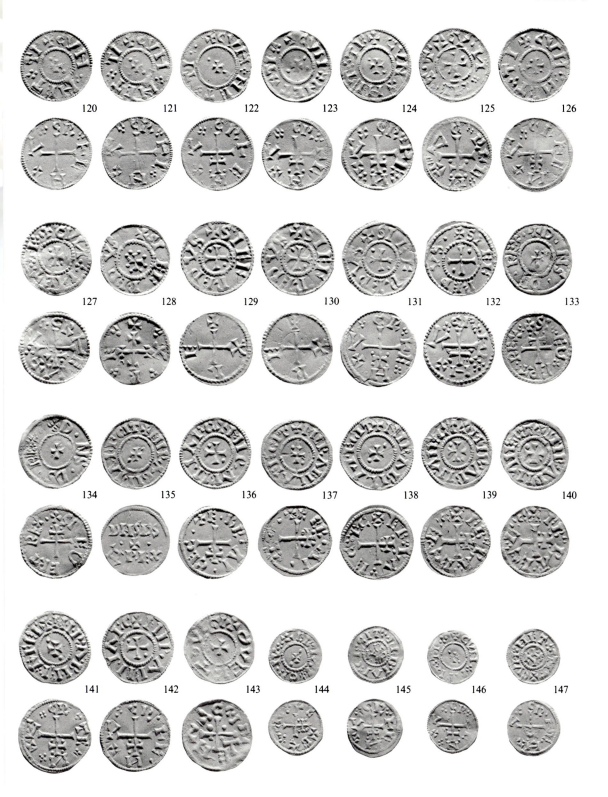

120   121   122   123   124   125   126

127   128   129   130   131   132   133

134   135   136   137   138   139   140

141   142   143   144   145   146   147

Plate 6 (*cont.*)

KINGS OF ALL ENGLAND

ÆTHELSTAN, 924–39

Two-line (*BMC* i, North 668).
The *obv.* reads **ÆÐELSTAN REX**. References are to Blunt 1974.

	Weight		Die		
	gm	gr	axis		
162	1.45	22.4	0	*Abba.* Blunt 7. North Western style. Gansauge coll. 1873.
163	1.53	23.6	0	*Abonel* (Abenel), Blunt 8 (Anglian style but now regarded by Blunt as North Eastern I style). Ruehle coll. 1842.
164	1.51	23.3	270	*Nother.* Blunt 396. North Eastern I style. Ruehle coll. 1842.
165	1.54	23.8	0	*Stefanus.* Blunt 404. North Eastern I style. Ruehle coll. 1842.

Cross. With mint name (*BMC* v, North 672)

166	1.26	19.4	90	*York* (**EFORPIC**), *Regnald* (Ragnaldr or Reinald). *Obv.* **EÐELSTAN REX TO BRIT**. Four pellets around the cross. Blunt 230. Gansauge coll. 1873.

Crowned bust. With mint name (*BMC* viii, North 675). The *obv.* reads **+ÆÐELSTAN REX**

167	1.27	19.6	90	*Canterbury* (**DOR CI**), *Torhtelm* (Torhthelm). Blunt 264. Ruehle coll. 1842.
168	1.39	21.5	270	*Hertford* (**HIORT**), *Abonel* (Abenel). Blunt 265. Ruehle coll. 1842.
169	1.59	24.5	40	*London* (**LONDEI**), *Beahred* (Beagræd). Blunt 270. Ruehle coll. 1842.
170	1.58	24.4	90	*London* (**LONDCI**), *Biorneard* (Beornheard or possibly Berenhard). Blunt 271. Ruehle coll. 1842.
171	1.62	25.0	180	*London* (**LONDCI**), *Grimwald.* Blunt 273. Ruehle coll. 1842.
172	1.64	25.3	0	*London* (**LONDCIVI**), *Igere* (Ighar). Irregular lettering. Blunt 275. Ruehle coll. 1842.

ÆTHELSTAN *(cont.)*

Crowned bust (cont.)

	Weight		Die	Pecks	
	gm	gr	axis	o./r.	
173	1.10	17.0	0	0/0	*Norwich* (N——), *Manticen*. Blunt 286. 544/1897, ex Gesellschaft für pommersche Geschichte und Altertumskunde Stettin, probably from a Pomeranian hoard.
	(fragment)				

Bust-in-relief (North East) (*BMC* x, North 676)

| 174 | 1.50 | 23.1 | 130 | 0/0 | ISNELOCNDE, *Isnel* (Snell). *Obv.* bust left in high relief, +AEDELZTAN RE, letter T inverted. Blunt 433. Ruehle coll. 1842. |

Cross/Rosette (West Mercia) (*BMC* vc, North 681)

| 175 | 1.54 | 23.8 | 0 | 0/0 | *Chester* (LEGC), *Wlfstan* (Wulfstan). Gansauge coll. 1873. |

EADMUND, 939–46

Two-line (*BMC* i)

| 176 | 1.40 | 21.6 | 270 | 0/0 | *Are* (Ari). *Obv.* +EADMVND RE. North 688. Adler coll. 1821. |
| 177 | 1.51 | 23.3 | 140 | 0/0 | *Frard* (Eoforheard). *Obv.* EADMVND REX. North 691. 36/1892, bt. Hamburger. |

Crowned bust. Without mint name (*BMC* vi, North 697)

| 178 | 1.36 | 21.0 | 0 | 0/0 | PPINIPE (Winide?). *Obv.* +EADMVND EX. Same dies as *SCBI* Reading 52. 1228/1878, bt. Hirsch. |

EADRED, 946–55

Two-line (*BMC* i)

The *obv.* reads +EADRED REX unless otherwise indicated.

179	1.64	25.3	270	0/0	*Heremod.* Above and below a trefoil. North 706. Provenance uncertain, acquired between *c.*1870 and 1900.
180	1.45	22.4	180	0/0	*Hunred* (Hunræd). *Obv.* +EADRED REX S. North 706. 471/1872, bt. Meinardus, ex Ehrentraut coll.
181	1.23	19.0	230	0/0	*Hunred* (Hunræd). North 706. Grote coll. 1879.
	(damaged)				
182	1.52	23.5	0	0/0	*Regther(es)* (Hreitharr). North 708. *Obv.* EADRED RE. Gansauge coll. 1873.
183	1.42	21.9	130	0/0	*Theodmaer.* North 706. *Obv.* EADRED REXⲄ. 1095/1905, bt. Morchio and Mayer.
184	0.77	11.9	0	0/0	*Warin.* North 706. Gansauge coll. 1873.

EADWIG, 955–9

Three-line (*BMC* ii)

| 185 | 1.21 | 18.7 | 90 | 0/0 | *Bedford* (BEDA), *Baldwine* (Baldwin). North 728. *Obv.* EADVVIG RE: 677/1872, bt. Webster. |

EADGAR, 959–75

Two-line (before *c.*973) (*BMC* i)

Obv. BEH A, North 741

186	1.21	18.7	0	0/0	*Copman* (Kaupman). *Obv.* +EADGAR REX. Gansauge coll. 1873.
187	1.41	21.8	160	0/0	*Durand.* *Obv.* +EADGAR RE:C. 168/1892, bt. Thieme.
188	1.21	18.7	250	0/0	*Eanulf* (Eanwulf). *Obv.* +EADGAR RE⋰ Gansauge coll. 1873

Reform Small Cross (*c.*973–5) (BEH C2, *BMC* vi, North 752)

The *obv.* reads +EADGAR REX ANGLORX

189	1.75	27.0	180	0/0	*Leicester* (LIGAR), *Man.* (Man/Manna/Monna) 377–4/1846, ex Stolp/Słupsk find 1846. Dannenberg 1848, p. 108.
190	1.64	25.3	0	11/15	*Oxford* (OXNA), *Æthelwine.* Same *rev.* die as *SCBI* Oxford 418. Ruehle coll. 1842.
191	1.25	19.3	90	2/0	*Stamford* (STANFORD), *Oge* (Oio). Ruehle coll. 1842 (or Dannenberg coll. 1870).

[*continued overleaf*]

PLATE 7

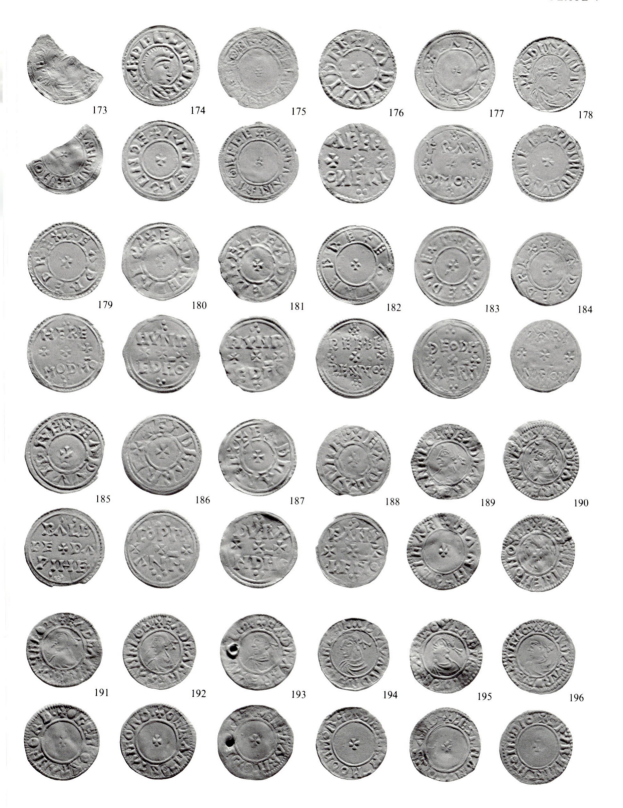

173   174   175   176   177   178

179   180   181   182   183   184

185   186   187   188   189   190

191   192   193   194   195   196

ÆTHELRÆD II (*cont.*)

Second Hand (*cont.*)

	Weight		Die	Pecks	
	gm	gr	axis	o./r.	
225	1.54	23.8	90	0/0	London (**LVND**), *Eadwine*. Ruehle coll. 1842.
226	1.44	22.2	90	15/10	London (**LVND**), *Leofstan*. Ruehle coll. 1842.
227	1.54	23.8	270	2/5	London (**LVNDO**), *Leofwine*. Ruehle coll. 1842.
228	1.40	21.6	90	0/3	London (**LVND**), *Osferth* (Asferthr). Same dies as *SCBI* Copenhagen ii 913. 556/1872, ex Althoefchen/Starydworek find 1872. Friedlaender 1877, no. 170.
229	0.99	15.3	270	0/1	Lymne (**LIMNA**), *L——*. The moneyer is Leofric, cf. *SCBI* Glasgow 822 and BEH 1613.
	(fragment)				992/1878, ex Witzmitz/Wicimice find 1878. Friedlaender 1879, p. 249.
230	1.43	22.1	270	11/3	Thetford (**ÐEOT**), *Swyrling* (Sperling). Same dies as *SCBI* East Anglia 1154. 1270/1896, ex Leissow/Lisówek find 1894. Menadier 1898a, p. 176, no. 50.
231	1.16	17.9	90	5/2	Totnes (**TOTAN**), *Dodda*. 588/1894, ex Mgowo find 1893.

Benediction Hand (BEH B3, *BMC* iif, North 769)

232	1.59	24.5	180	3/3	Canterbury (**CÆNT**), *Duda* (Dud/Duda). *Obv.* **ANG**. Grote coll. 1879.
233	1.50	23.1	270	2/2	Lymne (**LIM—**), *Lefric* (Leofric). *Obv.* **Æ-ÐELRÆD RE ANGLORX**, letters **O, R, X** ligatured. Remains of suspension loop. Cf. BEH 1611 (reads **LIMÆ**). 308/1890, bt. Weyl, ex Reval/Tallinn find.
234	1.47	22.7	270	1/2	Wilton (**PILTV**), *S——ne*. The moneyer is Sæwine, cf. BEH 4009. Gansauge coll. 1873.
	(chipped)				

Second Hand/Crux mule (BEH Cc, North 772)

235	1.65	25.5	0	3/0	London (**LVND**), *Edwine* (Eadwine). Same dies as *CNS* 1.2.4: 1004–5, same *obv.* die as ibid. 1006. Dannenberg coll. 1870.

Crux (BEH C, *BMC* iiia, North 770)

Contraction of king's title is **ANGLORX** (**NG** and **OR** ligatured), unless otherwise indicated.

236	1.76	27.2	270	1/3	Bath (**BA-Ð**), *Æthelric*. 996/1878, ex Witzmitz/Wicimice find 1878. Friedlaender 1879, p. 249.
237	1.65	25.5	270	2/3	Bedford (**BEDA**), *Leofnoth*. Ruehle coll. 1842.
238	1.18	18.2	180	7/7	Cambridge (**GRANT**), *Ælfric*. 385/1903, bt. Friedensburg, ex Zottwitz/Sobocisko find 1902.
239	1.16	17.9	270	11/9	Cambridge (**GRANT**), *Ælfwine*. 556/1872, ex Althoefchen/Starydworek find 1872. Friedlaender 1877, no. 145.
240	1.50	23.1	180	0/0	Cambridge (**GRANT**), *Edric* (Eadric). Dannenberg coll. 1870.
241	1.29	19.9	270	3/9	Cambridge (**GRANT**), *Edwine* (Eadwine). *Obv.* **ÆDELRD**. Same dies as **242** and *SCBI* Copenhagen ii 375. Grote coll. 1879.
242	1.14	17.6	180	11/1	Cambridge (**GRANT**), *Edwine* (Eadwine). Same dies as **241**. 931/1953, ex Reichsbank coll.
243	1.14	17.6	0	5/3	Cambridge (**GRANT**), *Edwine* (Eadwine). Dannenberg coll. 1870, ex Dobra find 1869.
	(chipped)				Dannenberg 1874, p. 367, no. 103.
244	1.62	25.0	180	2/4	Canterbury (**CÆNT**), *Duda* (Dud/Duda). Dannenberg coll. 1892, ex Lübeck find 1875. Cohn 1877, p. 69, no. 2.
245	1.69	26.1	180	7/1	Canterbury (**CÆNT**), *Godwine*. 1270/1896, ex Leissow/Lisówek find 1894. Menadier 1898a, p. 176, no. 45.
246	1.65	25.5	0	0/2	Canterbury (**CÆNT**), *Lifinc* (Leofing/Lifing). 556/1872, ex Althoefchen/Starydworek find 1872. Friedlaender 1877, no. 134.
247	1.54	23.8	0	1/2	Canterbury (**CÆNT**), *Lifinc* (Leofing/Lifing). 556/1872, ex Althoefchen/Starydworek find 1872. Friedlaender 1877, no. 134.
248	1.57	24.2	270	2/3	Canterbury (**CÆNT**), *Wulfwi* (Wulfwig). Same *obv.* die as *SCBI* Copenhagen ii 96. Adler coll. 1821.
249	1.43	22.1	90	0/6	Colchester (**COLE**), *Godwine*. Ruehle coll. 1842.
250	1.14	17.6	270	8/2	Colchester (**CEOL**), *Toca* (Toki). Adler coll. 1821.
251	1.45	22.4	180	0/3	Dorchester (**DOR**), *Wulfnoth*. Dannenberg coll. 1870.
252	1.37	21.1	90	11/3	Exeter (**EAXE**), *Ælfstan*. 556/1872, ex Althoefchen/Starydworek find 1872. Friedlaender 1877, no. 139.

PLATE 9

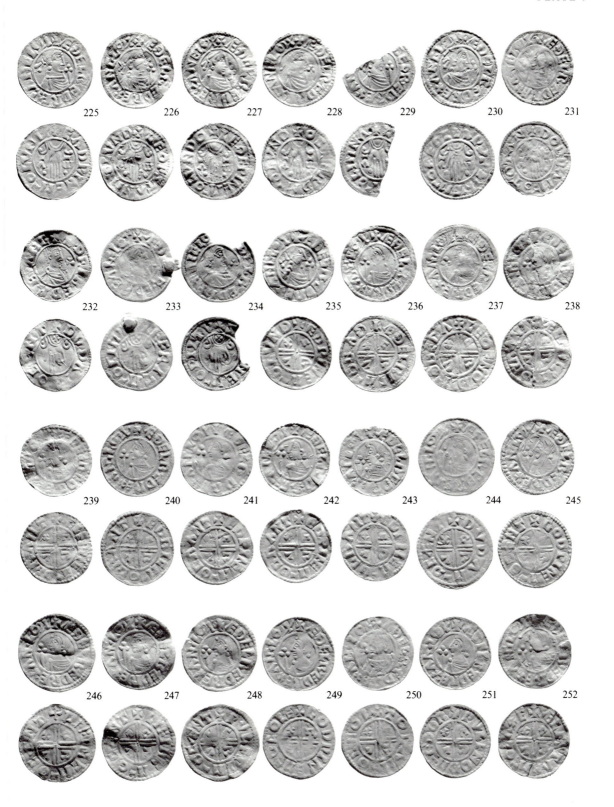

225   226   227   228   229   230   231

232   233   234   235   236   237   238

239   240   241   242   243   244   245

246   247   248   249   250   251   252

Crux (*cont.*)

	Weight		Die	Pecks	
	gm	gr	axis	o./r.	
309	1.56	24.1	0	3/2	*Thetford* (**ÐEOD**), *Osber* (Osbern). Same *rev.* die as *SCBI* Helsinki 118. Gansauge coll. 1873.
310	1.62	25.0	90	1/0	*Totnes* (**TOTAN**), *Doda* (Doda/Dodda). Same dies as *SCBI* Copenhagen ii 1257. Grote coll. 1879, ex Ciechanow find 1868. Cf. Berghaus 1954, p. 218.
311	1.66	25.6	90	1/2	*Wallingford* (**ÞELIA**), *Eoda*. Same dies as *SCBI* Copenhagen ii 1286. Ruehle coll. 1842.
312	1.68	25.9	0	3/3	*Wallingford* (**ÞELIA**), *Sigeulf* (Sigewulf). Friedlaender coll. 1861, ex 'Frankfurt' find 1840. Friedlaender 1843, p. 159, no. 68.
313	1.70	26.2	270	0/0	*Wilton* (**ÞILTV**), *Sæwine*. Gansauge coll. 1873.
314	1.67	25.8	90	0/0	*Wilton* (**ÞILTV**), *Sæwine*. 556/1872, ex Althoefchen/Starydworek find 1872. Friedlaender 1877, no. 188.
315	1.41 (chipped)	21.8	180	3/3	*Winchester* (**ÞINT**), *Ælfsi* (Ælfsige). Same *obv.* die as *SCBI* Copenhagen ii 1329. 834/1921. Acquired in 1921, details unknown.
316	1.68	25.9	90	10/2	*Winchester* (**ÞIN**), *Æthelgar*. 556/1872, ex Althoefchen/Starydworek find 1872. Friedlaender 1877, no. 189.
317	1.64	25.3	0	4/0	*Winchester* (**ÞINT**), *Byrhsige* (Beorhtsige). 1170/1898, ex Birglau/Bierzgłowo find 1898. Menadier 1898b, p. 302, no. 122.
318	1.59	24.5	90	0/0	*Winchester* (**ÞINT**), *Edsige* (Eadsige). Grote coll. 1879.
319	1.66	25.6	90	8/1	*Winchester* (**ÞINT**), *Leofwold* (Leofweald). Gansauge coll. 1873.
320	1.66	25.6	90	7/0	*Worcester* (**ÞIHR**), *Durant* (Durand). Adler coll. 1821.
321	1.37	21.1	90	8/0	*York* (**EOFRI**), *Leofwine*. *Obv.* **Æ-ÐERED**. Ruehle coll. 1842.
322	1.28	19.8	100	8/1	*York* (**EOF**), *Swertinc* (Svertingr). *Obv.* **Æ-ÐERED**. Pellet in fourth quarter of *rev.* Same dies as *SCBI* Merseyside 546, cf. *SCBI* Reading 78 and *SCBI* Helsinki 142 from different dies. Old collection.
323	1.54	23.8	90	5/1	*York* (**EOF**), *Thurstan* (Thorsteinn). Grote coll. 1879.

Small Crux variety (BEH Ca)

Contraction of king's title is **ANGLOR** (**OR** ligatured), unless otherwise indicated.

324	1.25	19.3	180	4/4	*Canterbury* (**CÆNT**), *Eadwold* (Eadweald). Adler coll. 1821.
325	1.40	21.6	0	7/6	*Canterbury* (**CÆNTÞ**), *Godwine*. 934/1953, ex Reichsbank coll.
326	1.40	21.6	90	7/2	*Canterbury* (**CÆNTI**), *Leofric*. Anomalous **R-V-X-C**. Old collection (?).
327	1.30	20.1	0	6/1	*Colchester* (**COLNIO**), *Edwi*[1] (Eadwig). *Obv.* **ANGLOX**. Pellet in first and second quarter of *rev.* Adler coll. 1821.
328	1.35	20.8	90	8/8	*Dover* (**DOVER**), *Wulfstan*. 556/1872, ex Althoefchen/Starydworek find 1872. Friedlaender 1877, no. 137.
329	1.12	17.3	180	5/5	*Exeter* (**EAXEC**). *Goda* (God/Goda). *Obv.* **Æ-ÐELRCD RCX ANGLORX**. 932/1953, ex Reichsbank coll.
330	1.29	19.9	180	3/11	*London* (**LVN**), *Ælfstan*. *Obv.* **ANGLO**. Pellet in first and second quarter of *rev.* 556/1872, ex Althoefchen/Starydworek find 1872. Friedlaender 1877, no. 153.
331	1.36	21.0	270	1/5	*London* (**LVN**), *Ælfwine*. *Obv.* **ANGLOX**. Pellet in first and second quarter of *rev.* Ruehle coll. 1842.
332	1.47	22.7	270	12/4	*London* (**LVND**), *Godric*. Pellet in first and second quarter of *rev.* 556/1872, ex Althoefchen/Starydworek find 1872. Friedlaender 1877, no. 163.
333	1.32	20.4	180	5/1	*Rochester* (**ROFEC**). *Sidwine* (Siduwine). Same dies as *SCBI* Copenhagen ii 1070. Ruehle coll. 1842.

Intermediate Small Cross/Crux mule (BEH Cb, *BMC* iii, North 773/770)

334	1.70	26.2	90	2/2	*Winchester* (**ÞIN**), *Æthelgar*. *Obv.* **ANGLORX**. Same *obv.* die as *SCBI* Copenhagen ii 1337. Grote coll. 1879, ex Ciechanow find 1868. Cf. Berghaus 1954, p. 218.

Intermediate Small Cross (BEH A, *BMC* i, North 773)

335	1.73	26.7	0	2/6	*Wilton* (**ÞILTVN**), *Sæwine*. *Obv.* **ANGLORX**. Same *obv.* die as *SCBI* Copenhagen ii 1315 and *CNS* 1.2.4: 1284. Ruehle coll. 1842.

[1] Moneyer not recorded in BEH, *BMC*, or Smart 1981 for type for mint.

PLATE 12

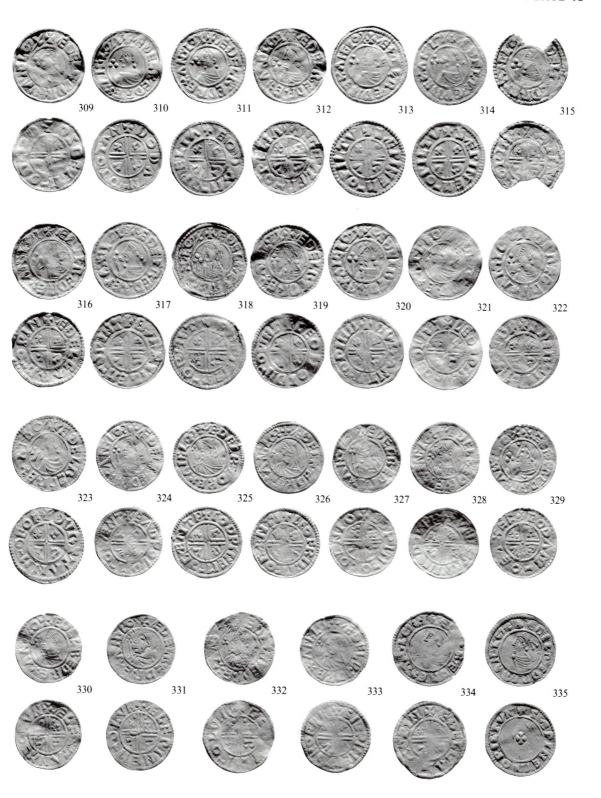

309 310 311 312 313 314 315

316 317 318 319 320 321 322

323 324 325 326 327 328 329

330 331 332 333 334 335

Long Cross (BEH D, *BMC* iva, North 774)

Contraction of king's title is **ANGLO**, **ANGLOR**, or **ANGLORX** (**OR** often ligatured) unless otherwise indicated. For 'subsidiary' style, see Smart 1965.

	Weight		Die	Pecks	
	gm	gr	axis	o./r.	
336	1.75	27.0	0	0/1	*Bath* (**BA-Ð**), *Ælfric. Obv.* **ANGLORI**. 677/1901, ex Kinno find 1900. Menadier 1902, p. 105, no. 38.
337	1.62	25.0	180	1/8	*Bath* (**BA-Ð**), *Edstan* (Eadstan). Same dies as *SCBI* Copenhagen ii 23 and *SCBI* Helsinki 164. Ruehle coll. 1842.
338	1.65	25.5	0	0/5	*Bath* (**BA-Ð**), *Wynstan*. 1186/1878, Roemer gift, ex Visby, Gotland, find.
339	1.55	23.9	180	2/6	*Cambridge* (**GRANT**), *Edwine* (Eadwine). Same dies a *SCBI* Helsinki 169–70, same *rev.* dies as *SCBI* Cambridge 679. 69/1893, bt. Loewenstimm, ex unknown Russian hoard.
340	1.66	25.6	0	4/7	*Canterbury* (**CÆNT**), *Ælfryd* (Ælfræd). Ruehle coll. 1842.
341	1.65	25.5	180	1/0	*Canterbury* (**CÆNT**), *Leofstan*. Ruehle coll. 1842.
342	1.61	24.8	0	0/0	*Canterbury* (**CÆNT**), *Leofstan*. Same *rev.* die as *SCBI* Helsinki 180–1. Grote coll. 1879, ex
	(pierced)				Ciechanow find 1868. Cf. Berghaus 1954, p. 218.
343	1.75	27.0	90	0/5	*Chester* (**LEIG**), *Ælfstan*. Same dies as *SCBI* Copenhagen ii 478, same *obv.* die as **344** below. Ruehle coll. 1842.
344	1.74	26.9	0	0/3	*Chester* (**LEGC**), *Ælfstan*. Same *obv.* as **343** above and *SCBI* Copenhagen ii 478. 517/1883, ex Borzecice find 1883. Menadier 1887, p. 175.
345	1.70	26.2	90	0/4	*Chester* (**LEIG**), *Swegen* (Sveinn). Ruehle coll. 1842.
346	1.74	26.9	180	1/2	*Chichester* (**CISE**), *Æthelm* (Æthelhelm). Ruehle col. 1842.
347	1.52	23.5	180	0/7	*Chichester* (**CISE**), *Cynna*. Same dies as *SCBI* Copenhagen ii 102. Ruehle coll. 1842.
348	1.37	21.1	90	0/6	*Colchester* (**COL**), *Leofwold* (Leofweald). 677/1901, ex Kinno find 1900. Menadier 1902, p. 105, no. 103.
349	1.65	25.5	270	4/8	*Cricklade* (**GROC**), *Leofgod*. Adler coll. 1821.
350	1.70	26.2	0	0/4	*Dover* (**DOFE**), *Godwine*. Same dies a *SCBI* Helsinki 186–7. 387/1892, bt. Weyl.
351	1.64	25.3	180	5/1	*Dover* (**DOF**), *Wulfstan*. Same dies as *SCBI* Copenhagen ii 134. Gansauge coll. 1873.
352	1.76	27.2	270	0/0	*Exeter* (**EAXE**), *Dunstan*. Ruehle coll. 1842.
353	1.62	25.0	0	3/4	*Exeter* (**EAXE**), *Dunstan*. Same dies as *SCBI* Copenhagen ii 169, same *obv.* die as ibid. 168.
	(pierced)				Dannenberg coll. 1870.
354	1.79	27.6	90	5/23	*Exeter* (**EAXEC**), *God* (God/Goda). Same dies as *SCBI* Copenhagen ii 181. Old collection.
355	1.40	21.6	0	5/2	*Exeter* (**EAXE**), *Manna* (Man/Manna/Monna). *Obv.* **ANGL**. Friedlaender coll. 1861, ex 'Frankfurt' find 1840. Friedlaender 1843, p. 158, no. 63.
356	1.77	27.3	0	1/1	*Exeter* (**EAXE**), *Wynsige. Obv.* **ANGL**. Same *obv.* die as *SCBI* Helsinki 204. 556/1872, ex Althoefchen/Starydworek find 1872. Friedlaender 1877, no. 142.
357	1.47	22.7	90	6/11	*Exeter* (**EAXE**), *Wynsige. Obv.* **AN**. Same dies as *SCBI* Copenhagen ii 218, *SCBI* Helsinki 202–3. Grote coll. 1879, ex Ciechanow find 1868. Cf. Berghaus 1954, p. 218.
358	1.56	24.1	0	1/1	*Hereford* (**HERE**), *Ælfget* (Ælfgeat). 556/1872, ex Althoefchen/Starydworek find 1872. Friedlaender 1877, no. 149.
359	1.45	22.4	180	0/4	*Ipswich* (**GIPS**), *Leofsige. Obv.* **E-ÐELRED**. 117/1896, bt. Kirsch.
360	1.47	22.7	0	1/0	*Leicester* (**LIHER**), *Wuleget* (Wulfgeat). Old collection.
361	1.57	24.2	270	0/0	*Lewes* (**LÆÞE**), *Ælfgar*. Probably same dies as *SCBI* Copenhagen ii 448. Ruehle coll. 1842.
362	1.73	26.7	90	3/1	*Lewes* (**LÆÞ**), *Herebyrht* (Herebeorht). Probably same *rev.* die as *SCBI* Copenhagen ii 456. Ruehle coll. 1842.
363	1.62	25.0	0	0/1	*Lincoln* (**LNIC**), *Ælfsi* (Ælfsige). *Obv.* **Æ-ÐELRED ERX ANGLO**. Mossop VIII:11. Adler coll. 1821.

PLATE 13

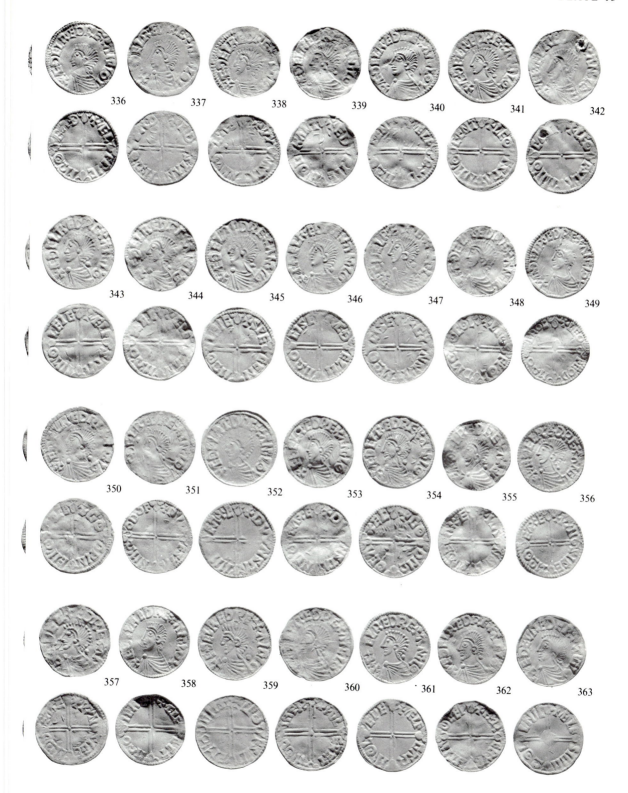

336   337   338   339   340   341   342

343   344   345   346   347   348   349

350   351   352   353   354   355   356

357   358   359   360   361   362   363

ÆTHELRÆD II (*cont.*)

Long Cross (*cont.*)

	Weight		Die	Pecks	
	gm	gr	axis	o./r.	
448	1.61	24.8	180	3/8	*Warwick* (**ÞÆRNG**), *Æthestan* (Æthelstan). 192/1899, ex Birglau/Bierzgłowo find 1898. Menadier 1898b, p. 302, no. 120.
449	1.54	23.8	0	3/1	*Warwick* (**ÞÆRI**), *Æthestan* (Æthelstan). Same dies as *SCBI* Copenhagen ii 1268. 556/1872, ex Althoefchen/Starydworek find 1872. Friedlaender 1877, no. 186.
450	1.73	26.7	90	3/3	*Warwick or Wareham* (**ÞÆRI**), *Byrhsige* (Beorhtsige). Same dies as *SCBI* Copenhagen ii 1269 (as Warwick), *SCBI* Midlands 257-9 (as Warwick) and *SCBI* Mack 960 (as Wareham). For the attribution to Warwick/Wareham, see Smart 1981, p. 108. Ruehle coll. 1842.
451	1.78	27.5	90	2/4	*Wilton* (**ÞILT**), *Sæwine*. Same *obv.* die as **452** and *SCBI* Copenhagen ii 1318. 1170/1898, ex Birglau/Bierzgłowo find 1898. Menadier 1898b, p. 302, no. 121.
452	1.72	26.5	0	0/4	*Wilton* (**ÞILT**), *Sæwine*. Same dies as *SCBI* Copenhagen ii 1318, same *obv.* die as **457**. Old collection.
453	1.75	27.0	0	0/2	*Wilton* (**ÞILTVN**), *Sæwine*. Same dies as *SCBI* Copenhagen ii 1319. Ruehle coll. 1842.
454	1.76	27.2	270	1/1	*Winchester* (**ÞINT**), *Byrhsige* (Beorhtsige). Friedlaender coll. 1861, ex 'Frankfurt' find 1840. Friedlaender 1843, p. 158, no. 64.
455	1.75	27.0	0	0/10	*Winchester* (**ÞINT**), *Byrhsige* (Beorhtsige). Probably same dies as *SCBI* Copenhagen ii 1365 and same *obv.* die as *SCBI* Helsinki 348. 936/1953, ex Reichsbank coll.
456	1.71	26.4	270	0/6	*Winchester* (**ÞIN**), *Byrhtnod* (Beorhtnoth). Same dies as *SCBI* Copenhagen ii 1372. 556/1872, ex Althoefchen/Starydworek find 1872. Friedlaender 1877, no. 190.
457	1.72	26.5	180	0/1	*Winchester* (**ÞINT**), *Godeman* (Godman). Probably same dies as *SCBI* Copenhagen ii 1391. Ruehle coll. 1842.
458	1.57	24.2	0	1/0	*York* (**EOFR**), *Eadric*. Blackburn 1981a, p. 64, no. 19A. 677/1901, ex Kinno find 1900. Menadier 1902, p. 105, no. 101.
459	1.38	21.3	0	1/2	*York* (**EOFR**), *Ira* (Iri). *Obv.* **ANGL**. Same dies as BEH 741. Blackburn 1981a, p. 62, no. 2c. Grote coll. 1879, ex Ciechanow find 1868. Cf. Berghaus 1954, p. 218.
460	1.44	22.2	180	2/4	*York* (**EOFR**), *Oban*. Same dies as BEH 776. Blackburn 1981a, p. 64, no. 25b. Ruehle coll. 1842.
461	1.84	28.4	90	2/0	*York* (**EOFR**), *Steorcer* (Styrkarr). Same dies as *SCBI* Copenhagen ii 296, same *rev.* die as *SCBI* Helsinki 359, *SCBI* Merseyside 560. 556/1872, ex Althoefchen/Starydworek find 1872. Friedlaender 1877, no. 143.
462	1.61	24.8	270	1/4	*York* (**EOFR**), *Sunulf* (Sunnulfr). Same dies as *SCBI* Merseyside 563, same *obv.* die as *SCBI* Copenhagen ii 304. Old collection.
463	1.68	25.9	250	0/12	*York* (**EOFR**), *Thurulf* (Thorulfr). Same *rev.* die as *SCBI* Copenhagen ii 313 and *SCBI* Merseyside 567. 69/1893, bt. Loewenstimm, ex unknown Russian hoard.
464	1.29	19.9	180	1/0	*York* (**EOFI**), *Wulfsige*. Pellet in first quarter of *rev.* Friedlaender coll. 1861, ex 'Frankfurt' find 1840. Friedlaender 1843, p. 158, no. 65.

Helmet (BEH E, *BMC* viii, North 775)

Contraction of king's title is **ANGLO**, unless otherwise indicated.

465	1.52	23.5	180	0/0	*Bath* (**BA-Ð**), *Æthestan* (Æthelstan). *Obv.* **ANGL**. Same dies as *SCBI* Copenhagen ii 19. Dannenberg coll. 1892.
466	1.49	23.0	180	1/0	*Chester* (**LEIG**), *Ælfstan*. Same *obv.* die as *SCBI* Copenhagen ii 479. 588/1894, ex Mgowo find 1893.
467	1.47	22.7	270	0/0	*Chester* (**LEIG**), *Ælfstan*. 69/1893, bt. Loewenstimm, ex unknown Russian hoard.
468	1.16	17.9	0	3/10	*Exeter* (**EAXE**), *Ælfmær*. 556/1872, ex Althoefchen/Starydworek find 1872. Friedlaender 1877, no. 138.
469	1.46	22.5	270	3/2	*Exeter* (**EAXE**), *Ælfnoth*. Ruehle coll. 1842.
470	1.12	17.3	180	2/2	*Exeter* (**EAXE**), *Carla*. *Obv.* **ANGL**. 69/1893, bt. Loewenstimm, ex unknown Russian hoard.
471	1.16	17.9	180	0/1	*Hertford* (**HEOR**), *Wulfric*. Annulet in second and third quarter of *rev.* Same dies as *SCBI* Copenhagen ii 424. Old collection.
472	1.17	18.1	180	1/0	*Ipswich* (**GI**), *Æthelbyrht*[1] (Æthelbeorht). 556/1872, ex Althoefchen/Starydworek find 1872. Friedlaender 1877, no. 146 (as **GR** for *Cambridge*).

[1] Moneyer not in BEH, *BMC*, and Smart 1981 for Æthelræd II.

[*continued overleaf*]

PLATE 17

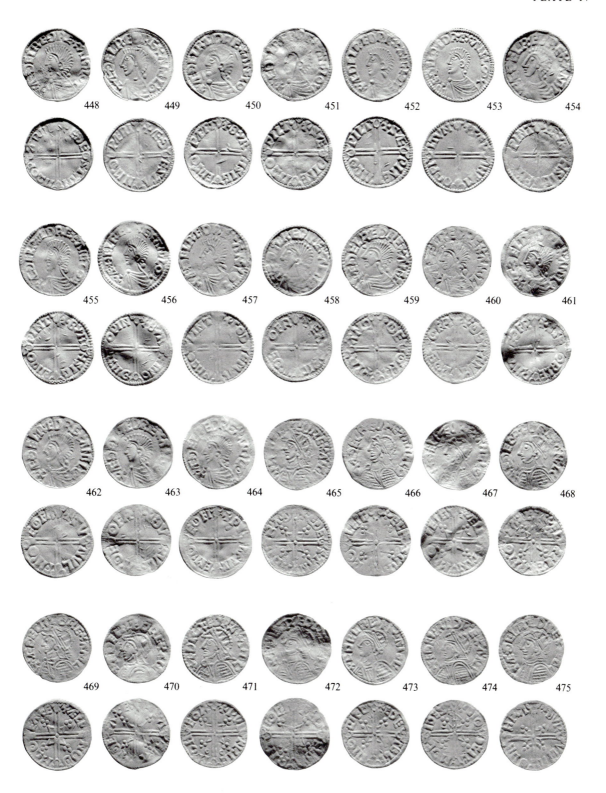

448   449   450   451   452   453   454

455   456   457   458   459   460   461

462   463   464   465   466   467   468

469   470   471   472   473   474   475

Plate 17 (*cont.*)

	Weight		Die	Pecks
	gm	*gr*	*axis*	*o./r.*
473	1.09	16.8	0	2/2
474	1.06	16.4	270	6/12
475	1.30	20.1	0	0/2

473 *Ipswich* (**GIPE**), *Edælbrct* (Æthelbeorht?). *Obv.* **CDELRED**. Some letters inverted in first, second, and fourth quarter of *rev.* Ruehle coll. 1842.

474 *Ipswich* (**GIDES**), *Giodcic* (Godric?). *Obv.* **ANG**. Cf. *SCBI* Copenhagen ii 338 from different dies. Grote collection 1879. Michael Dolley gave coins with this *rev.* legend to Dublin, but see Blackburn (forthcoming) for arguments that they are English.

475 *Leicester* (**LEHR A**), *Thurulf* (Thorulfr). *Obv.* **ANGL**. Same *rev.* die as *SCBI* Copenhagen ii 513. Friedlaender coll. 1861, ex 'Frankfurt' find 1840. Friedlaender 1843, p. 160, no. 73.

Helmet (*cont.*)

	Weight		Die	Pecks	
	gm	gr	axis	o./r.	
476	1.44	22.2	270	8/11	*Lewes* (**LÆE**), *Lofwne* (Leofwine). Same dies as *SCBI* Copenhagen ii 464. Ruehle coll. 1842.
477	1.46	22.5	270	3/4	*Lincoln* (**LINT**), *Osferth* (Asferthr). Mossop XVII : 27. 7/1897, ex Juura/Odenpäh find 1888.
	(pierced)				Menadier 1898c, p. 232, no. 135 (reads ÞINT, *Winchester*).
478	1.45	22.4	270	2/2	*Lincoln* (**LINC**), *Osgut* (Asgautr). Mossop XVIII : 1. Adler coll. 1821.
479	1.47	22.7	90	1/2	*Lincoln* (**LINC**), *Osmund*. Obv. **ANGL**. Mossop XVIII : 9. 293/1892, ex Weyl auction 114 (1892), lot 1446.
480	1.32	20.4	180	3/6	*Lincoln* (**LII**), *Ræienold* (Ragnaldr or Reinald). Obv. **EÐELRED REX AN**. Mossop XVIII : 27. Old collection.
481	1.45	22.4	90	0/0	*London* (**LVND**), *Æthelwerd* (Æthelweard). 677/1901, ex Kinno find 1900. Menadier 1902, p. 105, no. 106.
482	1.27	19.6	0	2/1	*London* (**LVNDENE**), *Edwi* (Eadwig). Obv. **ANGL**. 556/1872, ex Althoefchen/Starydworek find 1872. Friedlaender 1877, no. 162.
483	1.41	21.8	180	0/2	*London* (**LVND**), *Godric*. Adler coll. 1821.
484	1.37	21.1	0	0/4	*London* (**LVND**), *Godwne* (Godwine). Pellet behind bust on *obv.* 556/1872, ex Althoefchen/ Starydworek find 1872. Friedlaender 1877, no. 165.
485	1.48	22.8	270	0/0	*London* (**LVND**), *Leofric*. Adler coll. 1821.
486	1.26	19.4	270	3/4	*London* (**LVNDE**), *Leofric*. Obv. **AN**. Gansauge coll. 1873.
487	1.46	22.5	270	0/2	*London* (**LVND**), *Leofwne* (Leofwine). Same *obv.* die as *SCBI* Helsinki 409. Old collection.
488	1.16	17.9	180	1/0	*London* (**LVNDEN**), *Liofryd* (Leofræd?). Moneyer in this form not in BEH or Smart 1981. Old collection.
489	1.47	22.7	0	0/2	*London* (**LVNDN**), *Osulf* (Asulfr or Oswulf). Same dies as *SCBI* Helsinki 411. 556/1872, ex Althoefchen/Starydworek find 1872. Friedlaender 1877, no. 171.
490	1.60	24.7	180	5/10	*London* (**LVNDENE**), *Toca* (Toki). Same dies as *SCBI* Copenhagen ii 950, *SCBI* Helsinki 413, 414. Adler coll. 1821.
491	1.45	22.4	180	0/3	*London* (**LVND**), *Wulfwine*. Same dies as *SCBI* Copenhagen ii 975. Old collection.
492	1.46	22.5	270	2/1	*Lydford* (**LYDA**), *Bruna* (Brun/Bruna). 137/1895, bt. Lau.
493	1.52	23.5	90	1/2	*Norwich* (**NORÐ**), *Hwateman* (Hwætman). Dannenberg coll. 1870.
494	1.48	22.8	180	0/4	*Oxford* (**OXNA**), *Æthelric*. Obv. **ANGL**. 369/1895, ex Weyl auction 127 (1893), lot 1300.
495	1.50	23.1	90	1/6	*Oxford* (**OXNA**), *Brihtwine* (Beorhtwine). Same dies as *SCBI* Oxford 602. 69/1893, bt. Loewenstimm, ex unknown Russian hoard.
496	1.20	18.5	90	0/1	*Southampton* (**HEAM**), *Æthelsige*. Same dies as *SCBI* Copenhagen ii 997. Ruehle coll. 1842.
497	1.42	21.9	270	0/0	*Stamford* (**SAN**), *Swartgar* (Svartgeirr). Same dies as *SCBI* Copenhagen ii 1142. Ruehle coll. 1842.
498	1.44	22.2	180	4/4	*Tamworth* (**TAM**), *Ælfgar*. Obv. **ANGL**. Grote coll. 1879, ex Richnau/Rychnowo find. Cf. Berghaus 1954, p. 220 (as *Long Cross* type).
499	1.34	20.7	0	3/7	*York* (**EOFI**), *Colgrim* (Kolgrimr). Obv. **ANG**. Small cross behind bust and at the beginning of the legend on *obv.* Gansauge coll. 1873. The *obv.* die is probably of Hiberno-Norse manufacture, though the coins struck from it are thought to be official York products, see Blackburn (forthcoming).
500	1.32	20.4	90	6/11	*York* (**EOFI**), *Hildulf* (Hildulfr). Obv. **EDELRED**. Same *rev.* die as *SCBI* Merseyside 575. Grote coll. 1879.

Last Small Cross (BEH A, *BMC* i, North 777)

Contraction of king's title is **ANGL** or **ANGLO**, unless otherwise indicated.

501	1.27	19.6	270	0/2	*Cadbury* (**CADEBY**), *Ælfwine*. Pellet in front of bust on *obv.* and two pellets on *rev.* Same dies as *SCBI* Copenhagen ii 38. Adler coll. 1821.
502	1.49	23.0	180	0/9	*Canterbury* (**CENTÞ:**), *Ælered* (Ælfræd). Obv. **EDELRED NX AHNLO**. Old collection.
	(pierced)				
503	0.92	14.2	90	1/1	*Canterbury* (**CENTÞ**), *Ælfred* (Ælfræd). Same dies as *SCBI* Copenhagen ii 43 and probably same dies as *SCBI* Helsinki 444. 556/1872, ex Althoefchen/Starydworek find 1872. Friedlaender 1877, no. 133.
	(cracked)				

PLATE 18

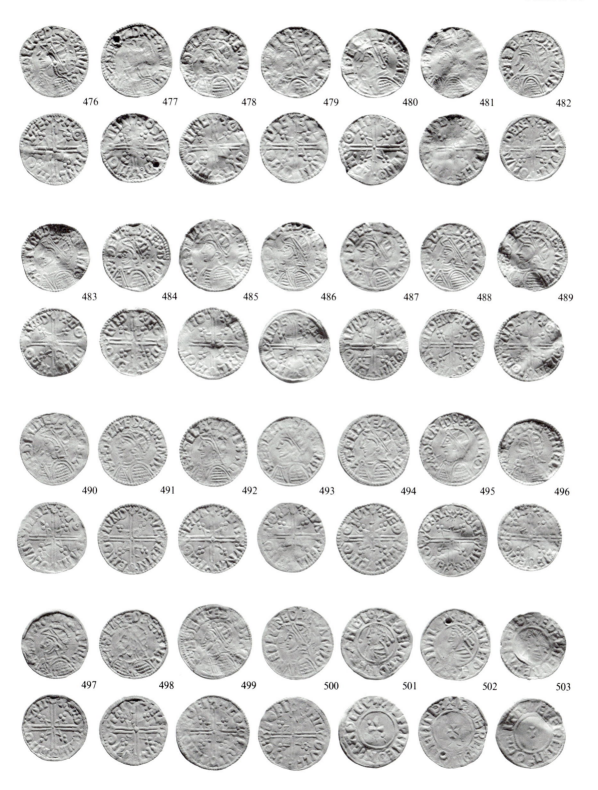

476 477 478 479 480 481 482

483 484 485 486 487 488 489

490 491 492 493 494 495 496

497 498 499 500 501 502 503

Last Small Cross (*cont.*)

	Weight		Die	Pecks	
	gm	gr	axis	o./r.	
504	1.44	22.2	180	0/0	Canterbury (**CANTƿ**), *Eadwold* (Eadweald). Friedlaender coll. 1861, ex 'Frankfurt' find 1840. Friedlaender 1843, p. 159, no. 69.
505	1.68	25.9	90	5/1	Chester (**LEIG**), *Ælewnie* (Æthelwine). Obv. **ANG**. Ruehle coll. 1842.
506	1.72	26.5	90	1/5	Chester (**LEGEGE:**), *Elcsige* (Ælfsige or Ealhsige). Obv. **E-ÐELRED**, legend starts at 2 o'clock. Same dies as *SCBI* Copenhagen ii 488. Adler coll. 1821.
507	1.03	15.9	90	0/0	Chester (**LECCI**), *Elenod* (Ælfnoth). Obv. **ÆÐELRÆD EX ANGLO**. Same dies as *SCBI* Helsinki 450. Ruehle coll. 1842.
508	1.63	25.2	180	1/9	Chester (**LEIG**), *Leofnoth*. Obv. **ANG**. Same dies as *SCBI* Copenhagen ii 493. Ruehle coll. 1842.
509	1.26	19.4	0	0/2	Chester (**LECEST**), *Swartinc* (Svertingr). Obv. **ANG**. Same dies as *SCBI* Copenhagen ii 502. Dannenberg coll. 1892.
510	1.46	22.5	0	4/0	Cricklade (**GROC**), *Ælwine* (Æthelwine). Obv. **ANG**. 556/1872, ex Althoefchen/Starydworek find 1872. Friedlaender 1877, no. 135.
511	1.22	18.8	0	1/3	Dover (**DOFER**), *Manninc* (Manning). Same dies as *SCBI* Copenhagen ii 133. Ruehle coll. 1842.
512	1.71	26.4	90	1/7	Gloucester (**GLEA**), *Sigered* (Sigeræd). Obv. **ANG**. Ruehle coll. 1842.
513	1.46	22.5	270	1/3	Leicester (**LIHPA**), *Æthelwig*. Same dies as *SCBI* Copenhagen ii 509. Ruehle coll. 1842.
514	1.11	17.1	0	0/2	Lincoln (**LIN**), *Æthelmær*. E in field of *rev.* Mossop XX:8. Grote coll. 1879, ex Ciechanow find 1868. Cf. Berghaus 1954, p. 217.
515	1.14	17.6	180	2/1	Lincoln (**LIIC**), *Æthelnoth*. Obv. **E-ÐELRED REX ANGL**. Mossop XXI:3. Ruehle coll. 1842.
516	1.38	21.3	180	0/2	Lincoln (**LINCO**), *Colsweign*[1] (Kolsveinn). Obv. **ANGLOR**. Mossop XXII:25. Ruehle coll. 1842.
517	1.42	21.9	0	0/7	Lincoln (**LINC**), *Cytlern* (Ketilbjorn?). Mossop XXII:31. 7/1897, ex Juura/Odenpäh find 1888. Menadier 1898c, p. 231, no. 128.
518	1.37	21.1	180	0/0	Lincoln (**LINCOLN**), *Dreng* (Drengr). Mossop XXIII:7. 518/1920, bt. Grunthal/Ball.
519	0.97	14.9	0	2/0	Lincoln (**LINCO:**), *Iustan* (Iosteinn). E in field of *rev.* Mossop XXIV:8. 100/1880, ex Rawicz find. Menadier 1887, p. 107.
520	1.45	22.4	0	0/2	Lincoln (**LINCOL**), *Osferth* (Asferthr). Obv. **ANG**. Mossop XXV:22. 534/1897, bt. Weyl, ex unknown Polish find.
521	1.00 (pierced)	15.4	180	1/4	Lincoln (**LINC:**), *Othbern* (Authbjorn). E in field of rev. Remains of suspension loop. Mossop XXVI:17. Ruehle coll. 1842.
522	1.12	17.3	180	2/3	Lincoln (**LINCOL**), *Othgrim* (Authgrimr). Obv. **ANG**. Mossop XXVI:22 Ruehle coll. 1842.
523	1.15	17.7	270	0/2	Lincoln (**LINC**), *Sumerlæth* (Sumarlithr). Cross behind bust on *obv.*, **V** in field of *rev.* Mossop XXVIII:8. Friedlaender coll. 1861, ex 'Frankfurt' find 1840. Friedlaender 1843, p. 159, no. 70.
524	1.07	16.5	90	0/0	Lincoln (**LIIC**), *Sumerleth* (Sumarlithr). Cross behind bust on *obv.*, **V** in field of *rev.* Mossop XXVIII:21. Grote coll. 1879, ex Ciechanow find 1868. Cf. Berghaus 1954, p. 217.
525	1.39	21.5	0	1/5	Lincoln (**LINCOL**), *Thorcetel* (Thorketill). Mossop XXIX:7. Adler coll. 1821.
526	1.59	24.5	270	1/5	Lincoln (**LINC**), *Ulfcetel* (Ulfketill). Pellet in field of *rev.* Mossop XXIX:13. Ruehle coll. 1842.
527	1.30	20.1	270	1/2	Lincoln (**LIN**), *Ulfcetel* (Ulfketill). Trefoil in field of *rev.* Mossop XXIX:11. 369/1895, ex Weyl auction 127 (1893), lot 1300.
528	1.22	18.8	180	4/1	Lincoln (**LINCO**), *Wulfgrim* (Ulfgrimr). Mossop XXX:18. Ruehle coll. 1842.
529	1.51	23.3	90	1/1	Lincoln (**LINCOLNE**), *Wulfric*. Obv. **ANGLRO**. Mossop XXXI:5. Ruehle coll. 1842.
530	1.33	20.5	0	1/0	London (**LVNDENE**), *Ælfnoth*. Obv. **EDELRÆD**. Old collection.
531	1.73	26.7	90	2/6	London (**LVNDENE**), *Ælfric*. Obv. **AN**. Same dies as *SCBI* Copenhagen ii 653. 937/1953, ex Reichsbank coll.

[1] Moneyer not in BEH, *BMC*, or Smart 1981 for Æthelræd II. Normalized form by V. Smart (pers. comm.).

PLATE 19

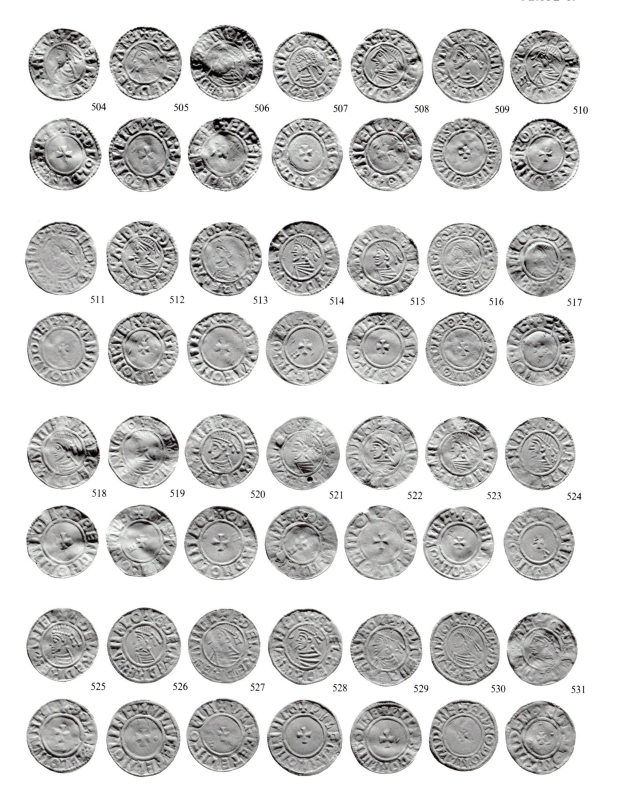

504   505   506   507   508   509   510

511   512   513   514   515   516   517

518   519   520   521   522   523   524

525   526   527   528   529   530   531

Last Small Cross (*cont.*)

	Weight		Die	Pecks	
	gm	gr	axis	o./r.	
532	1.33	20.5	270	0/3	*London* (**LVNDENE**), *Ælfwi* (Ælfwig). Remains of suspension loop. Old collection.
533	1.10	17.0	290	0/8	*London* (**LVNDE**), *Ælfwi* (Ælfwig). Obv. **ANG**. Same *obv.* die as *SCBI* Copenhagen ii 666. Gansauge coll. 1873.
534	0.96	14.8	180	8/16	*London* (**LVND**), *Ælfwine*. Obv. **ANG**. 556/1872, ex Althoefchen/Starydworek find 1872. Friedlaender 1877, no. 154.
535	1.16	17.9	90	0/10	*London* (**LVND**), *Æthelwi* (Æthelwig). Obv. **E-ÐELRD RE+ ANGLO**. 7/1897, ex Juura/Odenpäh find 1888. Menadier 1898c, p. 231, no. 130.
	(pierced)				
536	1.32	20.4	0	0/0	*London* (**LVN**), *Æthelwine*. Obv. **ANGLOR**. Old collection.
537	1.19	18.4	0	8/10	*London* (**LVN**), *Eadwerd* (Eadweard). 556/1872, ex Althoefchen/Starydworek find 1872. Friedlaender 1877, no. 158.
538	1.33	20.5	0	1/6	*London* (**LVND**), *Eadwine*. Obv. **ANGLOR**. Adler coll. 1821.
539	1.16	17.9	0	1/5	*London* (**LVND**), *Edsige* (Eadsige). Obv. **ANG**. Friedlaender coll. 1861.
540	1.10	17.0	90	0/6	*London* (**LVND:**), *Edsige* (Eadsige). Obv. **AN**. 534/1897, bt. Weyl, ex unknown Polish find.
541	1.23	19.0	0	10/7	*London* (**LVND**), *Goderæ* (Godhere). Obv. **Æ-ÐELRÆD RÆX ANG**. Same dies as *SCBI* Copenhagen ii 819. Ruehle coll. 1842.
542	1.08	16.7	270	0/0	*London* (**LVND**), *Goderæ* (Godhere). Obv. **Æ-ÐELRDE RÆX ANG**. 7/1897, ex Juura/Odenpäh find 1888. Menadier 1898c, p. 232, no. 131.
543	1.28	19.8	0	0/2	*London* (**LVNDE**), *Godric*. Obv. **Æ-ÐELRDE REX ANGL**. 369/1895, ex Weyl auction 127 (1893), lot 1300.
544	1.15	17.7	0	0/0	*London* (**LVNDEN**), *Godwine*. Obv. **EDELRÆD REX ANGL**. Grote coll. 1879, ex Ciechanow find 1868. Cf. Berghaus 1954, p. 217.
545	1.33	20.5	180	0/2	*London* (**LVN**), *Goldwine*. Grote coll. 1879.
546	1.17	18.1	90	0/0	*London* (**LV⸞**), *Leofsta* (Leofstan). Obv. **ANGLOX**. Same dies as **547**. Ruehle coll. 1842.
547	1.01	15.6	90	1/14	*London* (**LV⸞**), *Leofsta* (Leofstan). Obv. **ANGLOX**. Same dies as **546**. Grote coll. 1879.
548	0.86	13.2	0	0/0	*London* (**LVID**), *Leofwine*. Obv. **E-ÐELRED**. York style *obv.* die (inf. M. Blackburn). Grote coll. 1879, ex Ciechanow find 1868. Cf. Berghaus 1954, p. 218.
549	1.22	18.8	180	3/15	*London* (**LVN·D:E**), *Lioewi* (Leofwig). Obv. **E-ÐELRÆD REX ANGLORV:**. 556/1872, ex Althoefchen/Starydworek find 1872. Friedlaender 1877, no. 168.
550	1.20	18.5	90	0/3	*London* (**LVN**), *Liofheh*[1] (Leofheah). Obv. **ANG**. 588/1894, ex Mgowo find 1893.
551	1.17	18.1	270	1/1	*London* (**LVNDENE**), *Lyofwine* (Leofwine). Obv. **ÆDELRÆD REX ANGO**. 588/1894, ex Mgowo find 1893.
552	1.66	25.6	90	3/1	*London* (**LVNDE**), *Osulf* (Asulfr or Oswulf). Obv. **ANGLOR**. Old collection.
553	1.31	20.2	0	1/1	*Lydford* (**LYDAFOR**), *Bruna*. Pellet behind bust. Probably same dies as *SCBI* Copenhagen ii 978, *SCBI* Helsinki 536. 556/1872, ex Althoefchen/Starydworek find 1872. Friedlaender 1877, no. 176.
554	1.26	19.4	270	1/3	*Lydford* (**LYDA:FOR:**), *Goda*. Same dies as *SCBI* Copenhagen ii 980 and same *obv.* die as ibid. 981. Dannenberg coll. 1892.
555	1.27	19.6	90	4/17	*Norwich* (**NOR-ÐÞI**), *Edwecær* (Eadwacer). Obv. **EDELRED RE ANG**. Same dies as *SCBI* Copenhagen ii 1011, *SCBI* East Anglia 1207. Old collection.
556	1.45	22.4	180	0/8	*Rochester* (**ROFEC**), *Eadwerd* (Eadweard). Obv. **ANG**. Same dies as *SCBI* Copenhagen ii 1058. Ruehle coll. 1842.
557	1.43	22.1	90	2/3	*Salisbury* (**SEABRI**), *Sæman* (Sæmann). Obv. **ANGLO**. Ruehle coll. 1842.
558	1.43	22.1	270	1/12	*Shaftesbury* (**SCEFTES:**), *Ælfwine*. Same dies as *SCBI* Copenhagen ii 1075. 385/1903, bt. Friedensburg, ex Zottwitz/Sobocisko find 1902.
559	0.87	13.4	90	2/2	*Shrewsbury* (**CROBE**), *Æ——th* (Æthelnoth?). Obv. **ANG**. York style *obv.* die (inf. M. Blackburn). 7/1897, ex Juura/Odenpäh find 1888. Menadier 1898c, p. 231, no. 127.
	(chipped)				

[1] Moneyer not in BEH, *BMC*, and Smart 1981 for Æthelræd II.

PLATE 20

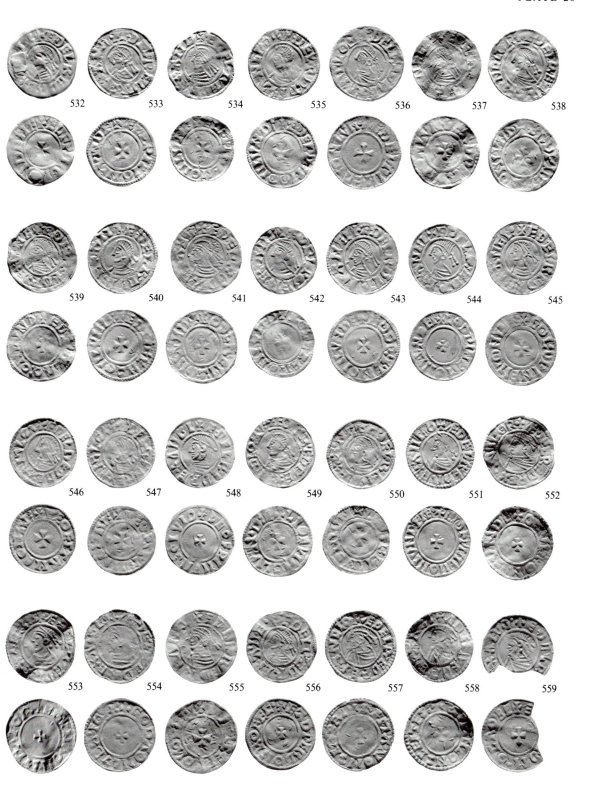

532 533 534 535 536 537 538

539 540 541 542 543 544 545

546 547 548 549 550 551 552

553 554 555 556 557 558 559

Last Small Cross (*cont.*)

	Weight		Die	Pecks	
	gm	gr	axis	o./r.	
560	1.48	22.8	270	2/0	*Stamford* (**STANFORD**), *Æscwig*. Probably same dies as *SCBI* Copenhagen ii 1112. 369/1895, ex Weyl auction 127 (1893), lot 1300.
561	1.43	22.1	90	2/4	*Stamford* (**STANFO**), *Æswig* (Æscwig). Same *rev.* die as *SCBI* Copenhagen ii 1115. 78/1890, ex Denzin/Dębczyno find 1889. Kluge 1985, no. 32.
562	1.35	20.8	90	0/4	*Stamford* (**STI**), *Æthelwine*. *Obv.* **ANG**. **S** in field of *rev.* 556/1872, ex Althoefchen/Starydworek find 1872. Friedlaender 1877, no. 183.
563	1.24	19.1	90	4/12	*Stamford* (**STANF**), *Godeleof* (Godleof). *Obv.* **ÆDELREDRÆD REX ANG**. Same dies as *SCBI* Helsinki 550. Adler coll. 1821.
564	1.32	20.4	0	3/10	*Stamford* (**STAN**), *Leofwine*. *Obv.* **ANG**. Small cross in field of *rev.* Adler coll. 1821.
565	1.10 (pierced twice)	17.0	0	0/1	*Stamford* (**STAN**), *Swertgar* (Svartgeirr). Pellet in field of *rev.* Same *obv.* die as *SCBI* Copenhagen ii 1146. 588/1894, ex Mgowo find 1893.
566	1.55	23.9	270	2/3	*Thetford* (**ÐEOTF**), *Edwine* (Eadwine). Ruehle coll. 1842.
567	1.27	19.6	270	2/12	*Thetford* (**ÐEOTF**), *Edwine* (Eadwine). *Obv.* **EDELRED**. Small cross behind bust. Same dies as *SCBI* Helsinki 556. Dannenberg coll. 1870, ex 'Berlin I' find 1856. Dannenberg 1857, p. 211, no. 140.
568	1.24 (pierced twice)	19.1	0	0/2	*Thetford* (**ÐEOTF**), *Mana* (Man). *Obv.* **ANG**. 69/1893, bt. Loewenstimm, ex unknown Russian hoard.
569	0.99	15.3	0	1/1	*Thetford* (**ÐEOD**), *Walgizt* (Wælgist). *Obv.* **EDELRED**. Same dies as *SCBI* Copenhagen ii 1248. 7/1897, ex Juura/Odenpäh find 1888. Menadier 1898c, p. 232, no. 133.
570	1.19	18.4	0	0/7	*Thetford* (**ETFO**), *Wulfnoth*. *Obv.* **E·ÐELRED REX ANGLORV**. Ruehle coll. 1842.
571	1.64	25.3	180	1/7	*Wallingford* (**ÞELIHGA**), *Winn* (Wine). *Obv.* **ANGLORX**. Ruehle coll. 1842.
572	1.49	23.0	180	0/6	*Winchester* (**ÞINTESTR**), *Cyna* (Cynna). 677/1901, ex Kinno find 1900. Menadier 1902, p. 106, no. 115.
573	1.25	19.3	0	0/1	*Winchester* (**ÞINCSTER**), *Cynna*. 293/1892, ex Weyl auction 114 (1891), lot 1450.
574	1.24	19.1	270	8/7	*Winchester* (**ÞINCSTR**), *Cynna*. Grote coll. 1879.
575	1.22	18.8	90	1/2	*Winchester* (**ÞINCST:**), *Cynna*. Grote coll. 1879, ex Ciechanow find 1868. Cf. Berghaus 1954, p. 218.
576	1.73	26.7	270	0/2	*Winchester* (**ÞINTCEST**), *Leofwne* (Leofwine). Same *obv.* die as *SCBI* Copenhagen ii 1408. Old collection.
577	1.23	19.0	0	0/8	*Winchester* (**ÞINCST**), *Leofwine*. Same *obv.* die as *SCBI* Copenhagen ii 1407. 588/1894, ex Mgowo find 1893.
578	1.46	22.5	90	2/2	*Winchester* (**ÞINSCESRE**), *Oda*. Grote coll. 1879.
579	1.38	21.3	0	2/10	*Winchester* (**ÞINCESTRE**), *Oda*. Ruehle coll. 1842.
580	1.25	19.3	0	0/4	*Winchester* (**ÞINCS**), *Ordbriht* (Ordbeorht). Same dies as *SCBI* Helsinki 579, same *obv.* die as **581**. Ruehle coll. 1842.
581	1.22	18.8	0	0/2	*Winchester* (**ÞINCS**), *Ordbriht* (Ordbeorht). Same *obv.* die as **580** and *SCBI* Helsinki 579. Ruehle coll. 1842.
582	1.11	17.1	180	3/7	*Winchester* (**ÞINCST**), *Seolca*. 165/1895, ex Thurow-Züssow find 1893.
583	1.46	22.5	0	1/22	*Winchester* (**ÞINTCSR**), *Spileman*. *Obv.* **ANGLOV**, legend starts at 8 o'clock. **A** in field of *rev.* Same *obv.* die as *SCBI* Copenhagen ii 1431. Ruehle coll. 1842.
584	1.69	26.1	180	5/10	*Worcester* (**ÞIHRACS**), *Leofgod*. *Obv.* legend starts at 9 o'clock. Same dies as *SCBI* Copenhagen ii 1306. 385/1903, bt. Friedensburg, ex Zottwitz/Sobocisko find 1902.
585	1.52 (chipped)	23.5	90	0/4	*York* (**EORÞI**), *Hildolf* (Hildulfr). *Obv.* **E·ÐELRED REX ANGLOR**. Old collection.
586	1.58	24.4	110	0/1	*York* (**EOFRÞIC**), *Osgot* (Asgautr). *Obv.* **E·ÐELRED REX ANGLORV**. Same *obv.* die as *SCBI* Copenhagen ii 287 and probably same *rev.* die as ibid. 286. Adler coll. 1821.
587	1.17	18.1	90	6/11	*York* (**EOFRÞI**), *Osgot* (Asgautr). Old collection.

PLATE 21

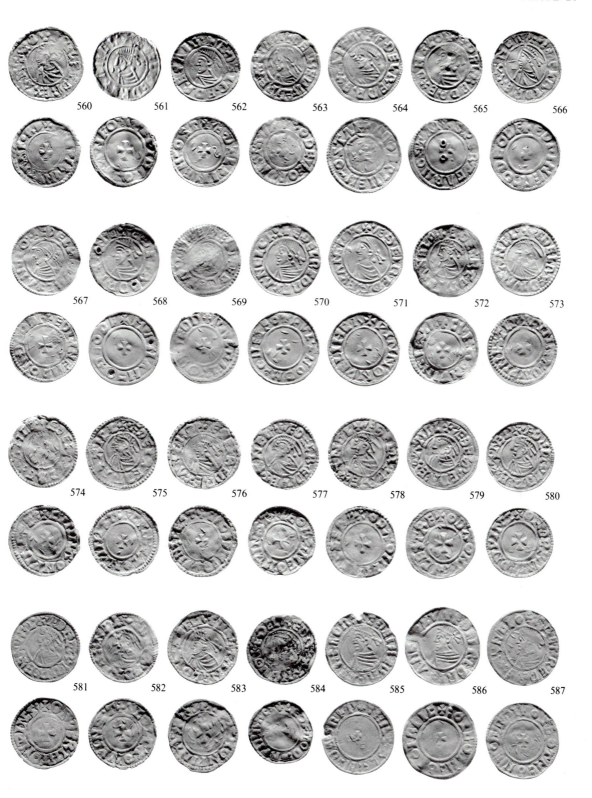

560 561 562 563 564 565 566

567 568 569 570 571 572 573

574 575 576 577 578 579 580

581 582 583 584 585 586 587

Last Small Cross (*cont.*)

	Weight		Die	Pecks	
	gm	gr	axis	o./r.	
588	1.23	19.0	310	0/0	*York* (**EOFRI**), *Stircol* (Styrkollr). *Obv.* E-ÐELRED REX ANGLOR. Grote coll. 1879, ex Ciechanow find 1868. Cf. Berghaus 1954, p. 218.
589	1.44	22.2	180	1/3	*York* (**EOF**), *Sumerlethi* (Sumarlithr). *Obv.* E-ÐELRED. Same dies as *SCBI* Copenhagen ii 239. Friedlaender coll. 1861, ex 'Frankfurt' find 1840. Friedlaender 1843, p. 153, no. 72.
590	1.39	21.5	110	1/15	*York* (**EOFR**), *Sumerlethi* (Sumarlithr). *Obv.* E-ÐELRED REX ANGLOR. Same dies as *SCBI* Merseyside 592. 69/1893, bt. Loewenstimm, ex unknown Russian hoard.
591	1.20	18.5	270	0/4	*York* (**EOFR**), *Sumrlethi* (Sumarlithr). *Obv.* E-ÐELRED REX ANGLOR. Grote coll. 1879, ex Ciechanow find 1868. Cf. Berghaus 1954, p. 218.
592	1.62	25.0	180	1/13	*York* (**EOFRÞC**), *Thorolf* (Thorulfr). *Obv.* E-ÐELRED REX ANGLORV:. Same *obv.* die as *SCBI* Helsinki 592. Friedlaender coll. 1861, ex 'Frankfurt' find 1840. Friedlaender 1843, no. 72.

Last Small Cross: Right facing variety (BEH Aa, North 780)

| 593 | 1.33 | 20.5 | 180 | 2/11 | *Dover* (**DOFR**), *Godman*. *Obv.* ANGLOR. Same dies as *SCBI* Copenhagen ii 130. 556/1872, ex Althoefchen/Starydworek find 1872. Friedlaender 1877, no. 136 (as Lodman). |

CNUT, 1016–35

Quatrefoil (BEH E, *BMC* viii, North 781)

The obverse legend reads +CNVT REX ANGLORVM. Contractions of ANGLORVM are indicated, followed by the starting point of the obverse legend according to the hours of the clock.

594	0.96	14.8	0	0/2	*Barnstaple* (**BARDA**), *Byrhsie* (Beorhtsige). *Obv.* ANGLOI (12 o'clock). Same *rev.* die as *SCBI* Copenhagen iiia 12. 261/1856, ex Wielowies find 1856. Cf. Menadier 1887, p. 176.
595	1.16	17.9	180	5/11	*Bath* (**BA-Ð**), *Alfwald* (Ælfweald). (12 o'clock). Ruehle coll. 1842.
596	1.12	17.3	90	1/1	*Bath* (**BA-Ð**), *Æthestan* (Æthelstan). (9 o'clock). Ruehle coll. 1842.
597	0.75	11.5	180	1/2	*Bristol* (**BRIC**), *Ælfwine*. *Obv.* ANGLORV (12 o'clock). Diademed bust variety (BEH Ed, North 785). Ruehle coll. 1842.
598	0.95	14.6	0	4/2	*Bristol* (**BRIC**), *Godaman* (Godman). *Obv.* ANGLOR (12 o'clock). Diademed bust variety (BEH Ed, North 785). Same dies as *SCBI* Copenhagen iiia 89. 386/1903, bt. Friedensburg, ex Zottwitz/Sobocisko find 1902.
599	0.91	14.1	270	0/6	*Cambridge* (**GRANT**), *Orst* (Orest/Ornost). *Obv.* ANGLOR (8 o'clock). 1534/1951, bt. Grabow.
600	1.11	17.1	0	0/0	*Canterbury* (**CÆ**), *Godric*. *Obv.* ANI (4 o'clock). Grote coll. 1879.
601	0.97	14.9	270	1/1	*Canterbury* (**CÆNT**), *Wulfstan*. *Obv.* ANGLOR (8 o'clock). Old collection.
602	1.01	15.7	270	6/3	*Chester* (**LEI**), *Godwine*. (10 o'clock). Adler coll. 1821.
603	1.07	16.5	90	1/1	*Chester* (**LEG**), *Leonoth* (Leofnoth). *Obv.* ANGLOR (9 o'clock). Probably same *rev.* die as *SCBI* Copenhagen iiia 1446. 677/1901, ex Kinno find 1900. Menadier 1902, p. 106, no. 118.
604	0.91	14.1	180	0/2	*Colchester* (**COL**), *Godric*. *Obv.* ANGLOX (12 o'clock). Same dies as *SCBI* Copenhagen iiia 259, same *obv.* die as ibid. 258. Ruehle coll. 1842.
605	1.11	17.1	0	2/1	*Exeter* (**EAXCES**), *God* (Goda). *Obv.* ANGLORV (12 o'clock). Same dies as *SCBI* Copenhagen iiia 450, 452, *rev.* die uncertain. 14/1851, ex Ploetzig/Plocko find 1850.
606	1.10	17.0	90	0/0	*Exeter* (**EAX**), *Isegod* (Isengod). *Obv.* ANGLO (12 o'clock). Ruehle coll. 1842.
607	1.16	17.9	0	3/0	*Gloucester* (**GLE**), *Godwine*. *Obv.* ANGLOR (12 o'clock). Same dies as *SCBI* Copenhagen iiia 1027–8. Friedlaender coll. 1861.
608	0.85	13.1	0	0/1	*Hastings* (**HÆSTII**), *Ælsig* (Æthelsige). *Obv.* ANGLO: (8 o'clock). Probably same dies as *SCBI* Copenhagen iiia 1153. 533/1897, bt. Weyl, ex unknown Polish find.
609	0.97	14.9	90	2/0	*Hastings* (**HESTIN**), *Elsi* (Æthelsige). *Obv.* ANGLORVMM (9 o'clock). Dannenberg coll. 1870.
610	1.03 (cracked)	15.9	180	1/1	*Huntingdon* (**HVN**), *Eadnoth*. (6 o'clock). 589/1894, ex Mgowo find 1893.
611	0.81	12.5	0	4/5	*Huntingdon* (**HVNTI**), *Wulfric*.[1] *Obv.* ANGLO: (8 o'clock). Pellet behind bust. Dannenberg coll. 1870.
612	0.89	13.7	270	1/0	*Ilchester* (**GIIL**), *Ælfwine*. *Obv.* ANGLORV (12 o'clock). Same *obv.* die as *SCBI* Helsinki 622. 533/1897, bt. Weyl, ex unknown Polish find.
613	1.07	16.5	270	1/0	*Ipswich* (**GIP**), *Edric* (Eadric). (8 o'clock). Ruehle coll. 1842.
614	0.94	14.5	0	3/0	*Lewes* (**LÆÐ**), *Ælfwerd* (Ælfweard). *Obv.* ANGL (8 o'clock). 589/1894, ex Mgowo find 1893.
615	1.33	20.5	90	3/0	*Lewes* (**LÆÐ**), *Leofnoth*. *Obv.* ANGLOVI. Old collection.

[1] Moneyer not in BEH, *BMC*, or Smart 1981 for mint.

PLATE 22

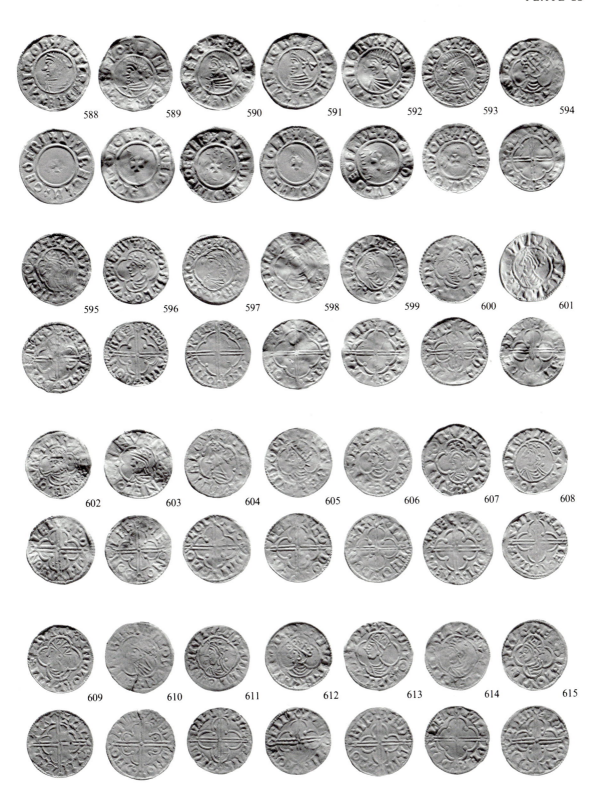

588 589 590 591 592 593 594

595 596 597 598 599 600 601

602 603 604 605 606 607 608

609 610 611 612 613 614 615

Quatrefoil (*cont.*)

	Weight		Die	Pecks	
	gm	gr	axis	o./r.	
616	0.87	13.4	270	0/0	*Lincoln* (**LIN**), *Bruntat.* *Obv.* ANGLORVMI (6 o'clock). Small cross in first quarter of *rev.* Mossop XXXIII: 7. 589/1894, ex Mgowo find 1893.
617	1.09	16.8	90	0/1	*Lincoln* (**LINC**), *Godric.* *Obv.* ANGLORV. (5 o'clock). York style *obv.* die. Small cross in first quarter of *rev.* Mossop XXXIV: 3. Old collection.
618	0.88	13.6	90	1/2	*Lincoln* (**LINC**), *Iustan* (Iosteinn). *Obv.* ANGLORV. (6 o'clock). Small cross in first quarter of *rev.* Mossop XXXIV: 29. Grote coll. 1879.
619	0.94	14.5	270	2/3	*Lincoln* (**LINC:**), *Leofing.* *Obv.* ANGLORV: (6 o'clock). Mossop XXXV: 9. 70/1893, bt. Loewenstimm, ex unknown Russian hoard.
620	1.40	21.6	90	0/1	*Lincoln* (**LINC**), *Osferth* (Asferthr). *Obv.* ANGLORVI (6 o'clock). Mossop XXXVIII: 9. Ruehle coll. 1842.
621	1.03	15.9	0	5/6	*Lincoln* (**LIN**), *Sumerlth* (Sumarlithr). *Obv.* ANGLORV: (6 o'clock). Small cross behind bust. Mossop XXXIX: 23. Ruehle coll. 1842.
622	1.02	15.7	90	2/0	*Lincoln* (**LIN**), *Sumerlth* (Sumarlithr). *Obv.* ANGLORV (6 o'clock). Small cross behind bust. Mossop XXXIX: 26. 556/1872, ex Althoefchen/Starydworek find 1872. Friedlaender 1877, no. 193.
623	1.30	20.1	270	1/0	*Lincoln* (**LINC:**), *Sunegod.* *Obv.* ANGLORVI (7 o'clock). Mossop XL: 5. 521/1883, ex Borzecice find 1883. Cf. Menadier 1887, p. 175.
624	1.11	17.1	270	0/4	*Lincoln* (**LIN**), *Wulfgat* (Wulfgeat). *Obv.* ANGLORV (6 o'clock). Mossop XLI: 13. 589/1894, ex Mgowo find 1893.
625	1.08	16.7	180	1/15	*London* (**LVND**), *Dunstan.* *Obv.* ANGLOT (8 o'clock). Probably same dies as *SCBI* Helsinki 651. Ruehle coll. 1842.
626	1.05 (cracked)	16.2	90	2/7	*London* (**LVNDEI**), *Eadnod* (Eadnoth). *Obv.* ANGLORV (8 o'clock). 589/1894, ex Mgowo find 1893.
627	1.02	15.7	90	4/2	*London* (**LVNDENE**), *Eadsi* (Eadsige). *Obv.* ANGLO (8 o'clock). Gansauge coll. 1873.
628	0.98	15.1	270	0/0	*London* (**LVNDI**), *Eadwn* (Eadwine). *Obv.* ANGLO (8 o'clock). Ruehle coll. 1842.
629	1.01	15.6	90	0/1	*London* (**LVND**), *Edwold* (Eadweald). *Obv.* ANGL (7 o'clock). Grote coll. 1879, ex Richnau/Rychnowo find 1854. Cf. Berghaus 1954, p. 220.
630	1.03	15.9	270	1/5	*London* (**LVIDEN**), *Elefwi* (Ælfwig or Ælfwine). *Obv.* ANGLO (8 o'clock). 370/1895, ex Weyl auction 127 (1893), lot 1302.
631	0.98	15.1	0	0/0	*London* (**LVND**), *Erdnoth* (Eardnoth). *Obv.* ANGLOR (8 o'clock). Same *obv.* die as *SCBI* Copenhagen iiib 2505. Adler coll. 1821.
632	0.94	14.5	0	1/8	*London* (**LVND**), *Frethewine* (Freothuwine). *Obv.* ANGLOX (7 o'clock). Cf. *SCBI* Copenhagen iiib 2521, possibly same *obv.* die. 1334/1951, bt. Grabow
633	1.07	16.5	270	0/0	*London* (**LVNDEN**), *Frethi.* *Obv.* ANGLOR (8 o'clock). Ruehle coll. 1842.
634	0.96	14.8	90	1/2	*London* (**LVND**), *Frethi.* *Obv.* ANGLO (8 o'clock). 939/1953, ex Reichsbank coll.
635	1.49	23.0	90	0/0	*London* (**LVND**), *Godere* (Godhere). *Obv.* ANGLORV: (6 o'clock). Same dies as *SCBI* Copenhagen iiib 2548-9, *SCBI* Helsinki 658. 294/1892, ex Weyl auction 114 (1891), lot 1452.
636	1.03 (cracked)	15.9	0	1/1	*London* (**LVN**), *Leofwine.* *Obv.* ANGLOR (8 o'clock). 519/1883, ex Borzecice find 1883. Cf. Menadier 1887, p. 175.
637	0.85	13.1	180	5/4	*London* (**LVND**), *Liofwine* (Leofwine). *Obv.* ANGLO: (8 o'clock). Same dies as *SCBI* Copenhagen iiib 2880, *obv.* die uncertain. 7/1897, ex Juura/Odenpäh find 1888. Menadier 1898c, no. 149.
638	1.04	16.0	180	0/2	*London* (**LVNE**), *Osulf* (Asulfr or Oswulf). *Obv.* ANGLORV (12 o'clock). Same *obv.* die as *SCBI* Copenhagen iiib 2892-3, 2896. 556/1872, ex Althoefchen/Starydworek find 1872. Friedlaender 1877, no. 194.
639	1.05	16.2	0	0/2	*London* (**LVND**), *Wulfgar.* *Obv.* ANGLO (8 o'clock). Probably same *rev.* die as *SCBI* Copenhagen iiib 2965. 7/1897, ex Juura/Odenpäh find 1888. Menadier 1898c, no. 144.
640	1.01	15.6	90	0/0	*London* (**LVND**), *Wulfgar.* *Obv.* ANGLOR (7 o'clock). Probably same dies as *SCBI* Copenhagen iiib 2962. Gansauge coll. 1873.
641	0.99	15.3	180	0/0	*London* (**LVND**), *Wulfgar.* *Obv.* ANGL (8 o'clock). Same *obv.* die as *SCBI* Copenhagen iiib 2961, 2964. Grote coll. 1879, ex Baranow/Baranowo find. Berghaus 1954, p. 219.
642	1.37	21.1	180	0/0	*London* (**LVN**), *Wulfnooth* (Wulfnoth). *Obv.* ANGLOR (8 o'clock). Same *rev.* die as *SCBI* Copenhagen iiib 2967. Ruehle coll. 1842.
643	1.06	16.4	180	0/0	*London* (**LVND**), *Wulfred* (Wulfræd). *Obv.* ANGLO (8 o'clock). 261/1856, ex Wielowies find 1856. Cf. Menadier 1887, p. 176.

PLATE 23

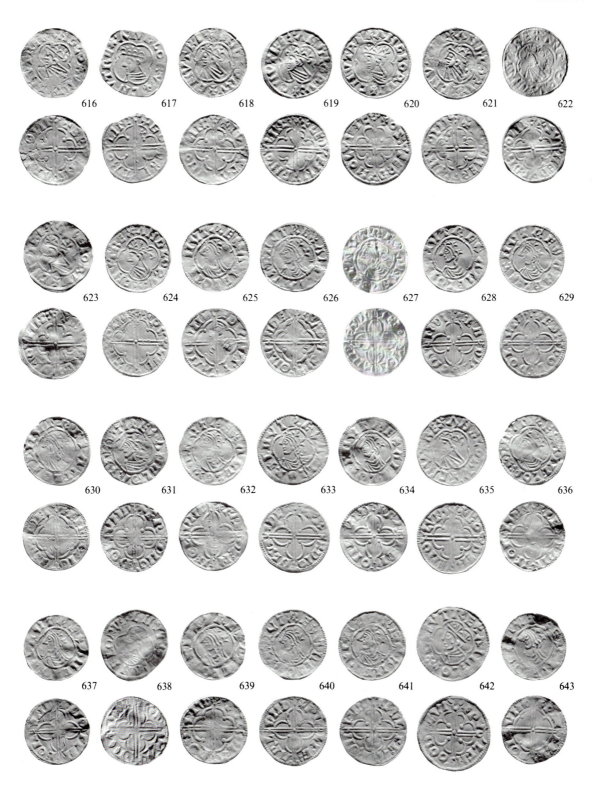

616 617 618 619 620 621 622

623 624 625 626 627 628 629

630 631 632 633 634 635 636

637 638 639 640 641 642 643

Quatrefoil (*cont.*)

	Weight		Die	Pecks	
	gm	gr	axis	o./r.	
644	1.22	18.8	180	0/0	*Lymne* (**LIMEN**), *Iounus* (Johannes). *Obv.* **ANGLO** (8 o'clock). Cf. BEH 1462. Dannenberg coll. 1892.
645	0.90	13.9	180	0/0	*Norwich* (**NOR-Ð**), *Edmund* (Eadmund). *Obv.* **ANGLO** (9 o'clock). 677/1901, ex Kinno find 1900. Menadier 1902, p. 106, no. 121.
646	0.91 (cracked)	14.1	270	1/1	*Norwich* (**NOR**), *Godwine*. *Obv.* **ANGLORVI** (6 o'clock). Probably same dies as *SCBI* Copenhagen iiic 3162. 261/1856, ex Wielowies find 1856. Cf. Menadier 1887, p. 176.
647	1.03	15.9	0	3/2	*Norwich* (**NOR**), *Oswold* (Osweald). *Obv.* **ANGLORV** (7 o'clock). Probably same *rev.* die as *SCBI* Copenhagen iiic 3214–15. Old collection.
648	1.20	18.5	0	1/2	*Norwich* (**NOR**), *Thurferd* (Thorfrithr). *Obv.* **ANGLORX** (12 o'clock). Grote coll. 1879.
649	1.48	22.8	180	0/0	*Oxford* (**OXE**), *Brihtwine* (Beorhtwine). (12 o'clock). Dannenberg coll. 1892.
650	0.91	14.1	90	0/0	*Peterborough* (**ME-Ð**[1]), *Leofdæi* (Leofdæg). *Obv.* **ANGLORV:** (6 o'clock). Van der Meer 1965, p. 70, pl. VII, 2. 677/1901, ex Kinno find 1900. Menadier 1902, p. 106, no. 120.
651	0.98 (pierced)	15.1	180	0/7	*Salisbury* (**SER**), *Godwne* (Godwine). (6 o'clock). 167/1926, Ball gift.
652	0.97	14.9	0	0/0	*Southampton* (**HAMT**), *Ælfwerd* (Ælfweard). (12 o'clock). Grote coll. 1879.
653	1.00	15.5	270	0/0	*Southwark* (**SVG:**), *Ælfwerd* (Ælfweard). *Obv.* **ANGLORVI** (8 o'clock). Grote coll. 1879.
654	0.88 (cracked)	13.6	0	0/0	*Stamford* (**ST**), *Godeleof* (Godleof). *Obv.* **ANGLORV** (6 o'clock). Same dies as *SCBI* Copenhagen iiic 3537. 556/1872, ex Althoefchen/Starydworek find 1872. Friedlaender 1877, no. 195.
655	0.94 (cracked)	14.5	180	1/0	*Stamford* (**STA**), *Godwine*. *Obv.* **ANGLOI** (6 o'clock). Adler coll. 1821.
656	0.96	14.8	180	7/13	*Sudbury* (**SVB**), *Swrlync* (Sperling). *Obv.* **ANGLORX** (12 o'clock). Grote coll. 1879.
657	0.94	14.5	0	0/0	*Taunton* (**TANTV**), *Edric* (Eadric). (12 o'clock). Probably same *rev.* die as *SCBI* Helsinki 710. Grote coll. 1879.
658	1.40	21.6	90	1/0	*Thetford* (**-ÐETF**), *Mana* (Man). (6 o'clock). Same *rev.* die as *SCBI* Copenhagen iiic 3842. 7/1897, ex Juura/Odenpäh find 1888. Menadier 1898c, no. 153.
659	0.80 (cracked)	12.3	180	9/4	*Thetford* (**ÐEO**), *Wlgist* (Wælgist). *Obv.* **ANGLORVI** (6 o'clock). Same dies as *SCBI* Copenhagen iiic 3875. Ruehle coll. 1842.
660	1.30	20.1	270	1/3	*Winchester* (**ÞINCST**), *Ælfsige*. (12 o'clock). Same dies as *SCBI* Copenhagen iiic 4018. Ruehle coll. 1842.
661	1.23	19.0	0	4/2	*Winchester* (**ÞINCST**), *Ælfstan*. (12 o'clock). 294/1892, ex Weyl auction 114 (1891), lot 1453, probably ex 'Berlin II' find. Dannenberg 1857, p. 257, no. 99.
662	1.11	17.1	270	1/7	*Winchester* (**ÞINCS**), *Leifinc*[2] (Leofwine or Leofinc). *Obv.* **ANGLORV:** (12 o'clock). Old collection.
663	1.02 (cracked)	15.7	0	0/0	*Winchester* (**ÞINCST**), *Leofstan*. (12 o'clock). Grote coll. 1879.
664	1.13	17.4	0	0/0	*Winchester* (**ÞINCST**), *Leofwold* (Leofweald). *Obv.* **ANGLORV:** (12 o'clock). Grote coll. 1879.
665	1.06	16.4	270	3/2	*Winchester* (**ÞINCSTR**), *Ode* (Oda/Odda). *Obv.* **ANGLORV** (12 o'clock). Ruehle coll. 1842.
666	1.22	18.8	0	0/0	*Winchester* (**ÞINCS**), *Ordbriht* (Ordbeorht). (12 o'clock). Same dies as *SCBI* Copenhagen iiic 4151, same *obv.* die as ibid. 4153. Ruehle coll. 1842.
667	1.12	17.3	90	0/1	*Winchester* (**ÞINCST**), *Sibdoa* (Sigeboda). *Obv.* **ANGLORV** (12 o'clock). 556/1872, ex Althoefchen/Starydworek find 1872. Friedlaender 1877, no. 196.
668	1.56	24.1	90	0/0	*Worcester* (**ÞIH**), *Garulf* (Garwulf). *Obv.* **ANGLORV** (7 o'clock). Same dies BEH 3741 and *SCBI* Helsinki 730. 70/1893, bt. Loewenstimm, ex unknown Russian hoard.
669	1.17	18.1	60	0/0	*York* (**EOI**), *Arncetel* (Arnketill). *Obv.* **ANGLORV:** (7 o'clock). Grote coll. 1879.
670	1.09	16.8	0	0/0	*York* (**EO:**), *Bretecol* (Bretakollr). (5 o'clock). Same dies as *SCBI* Copenhagen iiia 560–1. 532/1897, bt. Weyl, ex unknown Polish find.
671	1.05	16.2	160	2/7	*York* (**EO**), *Fargrim* (Fargrimr). *Obv.* **ANGLOI** (5 o'clock). Probably same dies as *SCBI* Copenhagen iiia 621. Ruehle coll. 1842.

[1] Mint not in BEH, *BMC*, or Smart 1981; unique coin. For mint signature Medeshamstede (Peterborough), see Dolley, *BNJ* 27 (1954), pp. 263–5. Leofdæg is known as a Stamford moneyer for *Short Cross* type, cf. BEH 3289–98, *SCBI* Copenhagen iiic 3574–84, *BMC* 520–1.

[2] Moneyer in this form not in BEH, *BMC*, or Smart 1981. It is probably Leofwine who is known as Winchester moneyer of *Quatrefoil*, cf. BEH 3787–9, *SCBI* Copenhagen iiic 4125–7, 4129, 4135, *SCBI* Helsinki 725.

PLATE 24

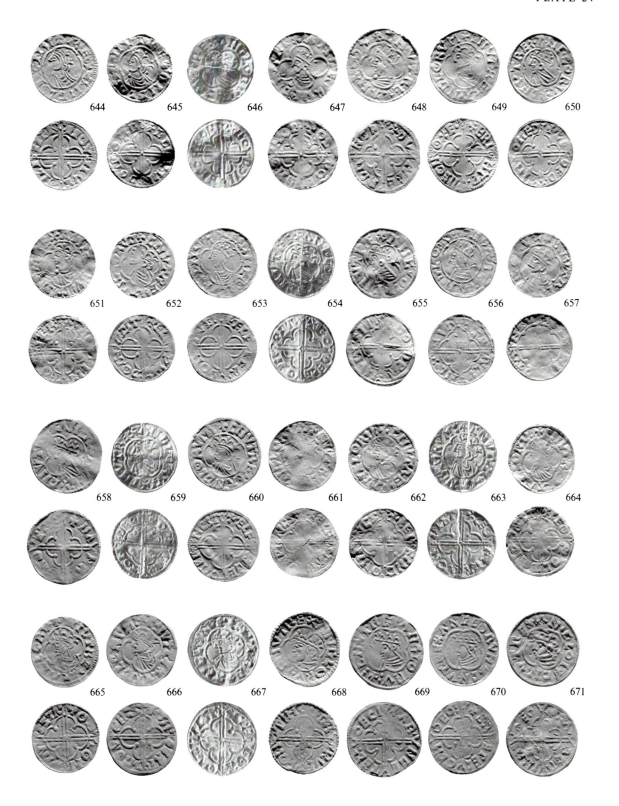

644 645 646 647 648 649 650

651 652 653 654 655 656 657

658 659 660 661 662 663 664

665 666 667 668 669 670 671

CNUT (*cont.*)

Quatrefoil (*cont.*)

	Weight		Die	Pecks	
	gm	gr	axis	o./r.	
672	1.03	15.9	90	1/2	*York* (**EO**), *Hildolf* (Hildulfr). *Obv.* **ANGLORVI** (5 o'clock). Same *obv.* die as *SCBI* Copenhagen iiia 714. Adler coll. 1821.
673	1.04	16.0	90	0/0	*York* (**EO**), *Selecol* (Selakollr). *Obv.* **ANGLOR** (5 o'clock). Same *obv.* die as *SCBI* Copenhagen iiia 808. Grote coll. 1879.
674	1.09	16.8	180	3/0	*York* (**EO**), *Stircer* (Styrkarr). *Obv.* **ANGLOR** (5 o'clock). Probably same dies as *SCBI* Copenhagen iiia 812, same *obv.* die as ibid. 813. 518/1883, ex Borzecice find 1883. Cf. Menadier 1887, p. 175.
675	0.91	14.1	180	5/5	*York* (**EO**), *Stircol* (Styrkollr). *Obv.* **ANGLORV** (5 o'clock). 556/1872, ex Althoefchen/ Starydworek find 1872. Friedlaender 1877, no. 192.
	(cracked)				
676	0.95	14.6	180	0/0	*York* (**EO**), *Sunolf* (Sunnulfr). *Obv.* **ANGLORV**. (5 o'clock). Probably same *rev.* die as *SCBI* Helsinki 745. 589/1894, ex Mgowo find 1893.

Pointed Helmet (BEH G, *BMC* xiv, North 787)

The obverse legend reads **CNVT RE[C]X [ANG]**; REX or RECX and contractions of **ANGLORVM** are indicated. The legend normally starts at 12 or 1 o'clock, exceptions are indicated.

677	1.04	16.0	90	1/0	*Cambridge* (**GRANTEB**), *Ada. Obv.* **RECX:** Dannenberg coll. 1892.
678	1.05	16.2	270	0/1	*Cambridge* (**GRAN**), *Wulsige* (Wulfsige). *Obv.* **ECX ANG**. Same dies as *SCBI* Copenhagen iiia 1122, same *obv.* die as ibid. 1121, 1124. 589/1894, ex Mgowo find 1893.
679	0.91	14.0	0	0/0	*Canterbury* (**CÆNT**), *Godman. Obv.* **ECX ANG**. 533/1897, bt. Weyl, ex unknown Polish find.
680	0.91	14.1	0	2/1	*Canterbury* (**CÆNT**), *Leofnoth. Obv.* **REX ANGL** (8 o'clock). Same dies as *SCBI* Copenhagen iiia 150. Gansauge coll. 1873.
681	1.05	16.2	270	0/1	*Chester* (**LEIGIC**), *Gunleof* (Gunnleifr). *Obv.* **RECX**. 7/1897, ex Juura/Odenpäh find 1888. Menadier 1898c, no. 141 (as Leicester).
682	0.88	13.6	180	0/2	*Chester* (**LCICST**), *Wulnoth* (Wulfnoth). *Obv.* **RCX AI**. Old collection.
	(cracked)				
683	1.01	15.6	270	0/0	*Dover* (**DOFRA**), *Lufwine* (Leofwine). *Obv.* **RECX A**. Same dies as *SCBI* Copenhagen iiia 401, same *obv.* die as ibid. 395–6. Ruehle coll. 1842.
684	1.13	17.4	180	2/4	*Huntingdon* (**HVNT**), *Godeleof* (Godleof). *Obv.* **REXX ANG**. Ruehle coll. 1842.
685	1.06	16.3	90	0/0	*Huntingdon* (**HVN**), *Godeleof* (Godleof). *Obv.* **RECX A**. Same dies as *SCBI* Copenhagen iiia 1276–7. Dannenberg coll. 1870.
686	0.98	15.1	180	0/1	*Ilchester* (**GIFE**), *Ægelwig* (Æthelwig). *Obv.* **RECX**. Same dies as *SCBI* Copenhagen iiia 929–30. Dannenberg coll. 1892.
687	1.13	17.4	270	0/5	*Ipswich* (**GIPESPI**), *Liifinc* (Leofing/Lifing). *Obv.* **RECX A**. Same dies as *SCBI* Copenhagen iiia 1007–8. 7/1897, ex Juura/Odenpäh find 1888. Menadier 1898c, no. 138.
688	1.06	16.4	0	0/2	*Langport* (**LANCFOR**), *Edric* (Eadric). *Obv.* **RECX AN**. Same dies as *BMC* 266, *SCBI* Copenhagen iiia 1295–6. Adler coll. 1821.
689	1.12	17.3	270	7/8	*Lincoln* (**LINC**), *Ægelmær* (Æthelmær). *Obv.* **REX ANG**. Mossop XLII:8. Ruehle coll. 1842.
	(cracked)				
690	1.03	15.9	270	1/0	*Lincoln* (**LINCOLN**), *Aslac* (Asleikr). *Obv.* **EX ANGL**. Mossop XLII:17. Dannenberg coll. 1892.
691	0.94	14.5	270	0/0	*Lincoln* (**LINCO:**), *Godwine. Obv.* **REX AN**. Mossop XLIII:14. 343/1874, ex Parlin find 1874. Cf. Menadier 1887, pp. 176–7.
692	0.92	14.2	180	2/1	*Lincoln* (**LIN**), *Godwine. Obv.* **REX A**. Mossop XLIII:25. 1137/1892, bt. Hahlo.
693	0.83	12.8	270	1/0	*Lincoln* (**LINCO**), *Goinie* (Godwine?). *Obv.* **RCEX A**. Mossop XLIII:26. 121/1933, bt. Drachenfels.
694	1.00	15.4	90	3/6	*Lincoln* (**LIN**), *Grimcetel* (Grimkell). *Obv.* **REX AI**. Mossop XLIII:28 (*rev.*). 294/1892, ex Weyl auction 114 (1891), lot 1451, ex 'Berlin I' find 1856. Dannenberg 1857, p. 212, no. 145.
695	1.04	16.0	90	0/0	*Lincoln* (**LIN**), *Grimcytel* (Grimkell). *Obv.* **EX ANG**. Mossop XLIV:2. Adler coll. 1821.
696	0.96	14.8	90	1/1	*Lincoln* (**LINCO**), *Gustan* (Iosteinn). *Obv.* **REX AN**. Mossop XLIV:18. Friedlaender coll. 1861, ex 'Frankfurt' find 1840. Friedlaender 1843, p. 160, no. 74.
697	0.85	13.1	180	10/6	*Lincoln* (**LINCOL**), *Gustan* (Iosteinn). *Obv.* **REX AI**. Mossop XLIV:16. 7/1897, ex Juura/ Odenpäh find 1888. Menadier 1898c, no. 142.
	(pierced and cracked)				
698	1.13	17.4	90	5/3	*Lincoln* (**LINCOL**), *Oslac* (Asleikr). *Obv.* **REX AN**. Mossop XLII:22. Ruehle coll. 1842.
699	0.95	14.7	270	3/4	*Lincoln* (**L**), *Swartbrand* (Svartbrandr). *Obv.* **REX ANG**. Small cross behind bust. Mossop XLVII:28. Ruehle coll. 1842.

PLATE 25

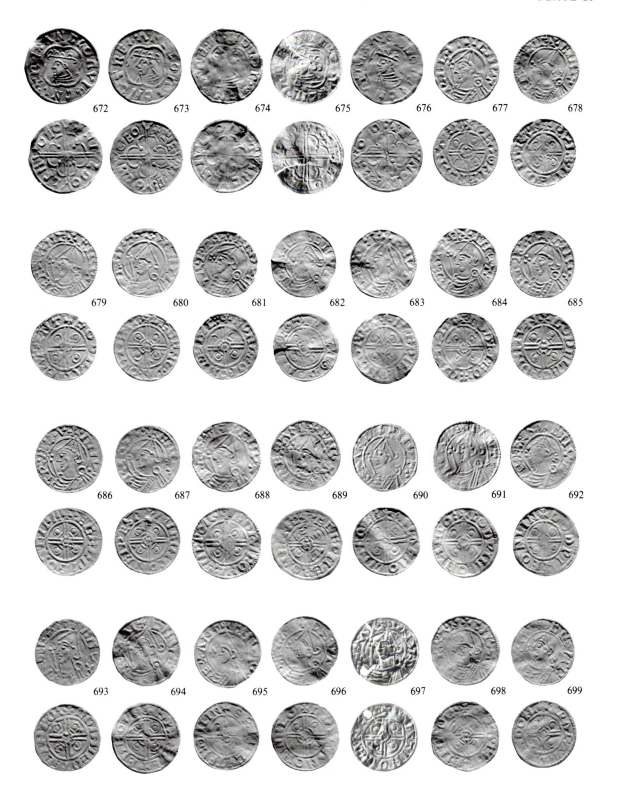

672   673   674   675   676   677   678

679   680   681   682   683   684   685

686   687   688   689   690   691   692

693   694   695   696   697   698   699

Pointed Helmet (*cont.*)

	Weight		Die	Pecks	
	gm	gr	axis	o./r.	
700	1.16	17.9	90	4/2	*Lincoln* (**LI**), *Swweartabrad* (Svartbrandr). *Obv.* **RECX A⋮**. Mossop XLVII : 29. 261/1856, ex Wielowies find 1856. Cf. Menadier 1887, p. 176.
701	0.97	14.9	180	2/6	*London* (**LVN⋮**), *Ægelwine* (Æthelwine). *Obv.* **RECX A**. Same *rev.* die as *SCBI* Copenhagen iiib 1957–9. 589/1894, ex Mgowo find 1893.
702	1.02 (cracked)	15.7	0	9/6	*London* (**LVDEN**), *Ælfwerd* (Ælfweard). *Obv.* **REX ANGL**. Same dies as *SCBI* Copenhagen iiib 2029, same *obv.* die as ibid. 2026–8, 2030–1. Old collection.
703	1.03	15.9	90	0/3	*London* (**LVNND**), *Ælfwig*. *Obv.* **RECX AN**. Same dies as *SCBI* Copenhagen iiib 2080, *SCBI* Helsinki 779. Same *obv.* die as *SCBI* Copenhagen iiib 2076–8. Adler coll. 1821.
704	1.05	16.2	0	0/0	*London* (**LVNDEN**), *Ælric* (Æthelric). *Obv.* **REX AN**. Same dies as SCBI Copenhagen iiib 2120–2. Friedlaender coll. 1861, ex 'Frankfurt' find 1840. Friedlaender 1843, p. 160, no. 75.
705	1.03	15.9	0	3/2	*London* (**LVND**), *Ælwerd* (Æthelweard). *Obv.* **RECX A**. Same *rev.* die as *SCBI* Copenhagen iiib 2127–8. 589/1894, ex Mgowo find 1893.
706	0.97	14.9	270	0/1	*London* (**LVN⋮**), *Brungar*. *Obv.* **RECX A**. Same dies as *SCBI* Copenhagen iiib 2243. Adler coll. 1821.
707	1.02	15.7	0	0/1	*London* (**LVNDE⋮**), *Edricc* (Eadric). *Obv.* **RECX A**. Same *obv.* die as *SCBI* Copenhagen iiib 2436–8. Grote coll. 1879.
708	0.94	14.5	270	0/1	*London* (**LVNDEN**), *Edwig* (Eadwig). *Obv.* **RECX A⋮**. 1278/1905.
709	0.85	13.1	0	2/0	*London* (**LVND**), *Elewine* (Æthelwine). *Obv.* **REX AN**. Same dies as *SCBI* Copenhagen iiib 2499, 2500. 7/1897, ex Juura/Odenpäh find 1888. Menadier 1898c, no. 145.
710	1.08	16.7	0	3/1	*London* (**LVDENE⋮**), *Etsige* (Eadsige). *Obv.* **REX AN⋮**. Same dies as *SCBI* Copenhagen iiib 2507, same *rev.* die as ibid. 2506. 14/1851, ex Ploetzig/Plocko find 1850.
711	1.02	15.7	180	0/0	*London* (**LVNDE**), *Godere* (Godhere). *Obv.* **REX AN⋮**. Same *obv.* die as *SCBI* Copenhagen iiib 2552–3. Same *rev.* die as ibid. 2558–61. Gansauge coll. 1873.
712	1.07	16.5	270	0/1	*London* (**LVNDEN⋮**), *Godric*. *Obv.* **RECX A**. Same dies as *SCBI* Copenhagen iiib 2630. 1538/1951, bt. Grabow.
713	1.06	16.4	90	0/0	*London* (**LVDDEN**), *Godric*. *Obv.* **EX ANGL**. Same dies as *SCBI* Copenhagen iiib 2620. Old collection.
714	1.04	16.0	90	3/7	*London* (**LVNN**), *Godwine*. *Obv.* **RECX ANG**. Probably same dies as *SCBI* Helsinki 797. Old collection.
715	1.05	16.2	90	1/0	*London* (**LVDDEN⋮**), *Lifinc* (Leofing/Lifing). *Obv.* **REX ANG**. Same dies as *SCBI* Copenhagen iiib 2839, same *obv.* die as ibid. 2840–3, same *rev.* die as **716** and *SCBI* Copenhagen iiib 2837–8. Gansauge coll. 1873.
716	1.02	15.7	270	3/3	*London* (**LVDDEN⋮**), *Lifinc* (Leofing/Lifing). *Obv.* **RECX A**. Same dies as *SCBI* Copenhagen iiib 2837–8. Same *rev.* die as **715** and *SCBI* Copenhagen iiib 2839. 264/1892, ex Hornikau/Horniki find 1890.
717	1.03 (pierced)	15.9	0	0/0	*London* (**LVND⋮**), *Leofstan*. *Obv.* **RECX⋮**. Same *obv.* die as **718-19**. 589/1894, ex Mgowo find 1893.
718	1.01	15.6	270	0/0	*London* (**LVND⋮**), *Leofstan*. *Obv.* **RECX⋮**. Same *obv.* die as **717, 719**. Friedlaender coll. 1861, ex 'Frankfurt' find 1840. Friedlaender 1843, p. 160, no. 76.
719	0.98	15.1	0	5/3	*London* (**LVN⋮**), *Leofstan*. *Obv.* **RECX**. Same *obv.* die as **717-18**. Same *rev.* die as *SCBI* Copenhagen iiib 2744, 2747. 7/1897, ex Juura/Odenpäh find 1888. Menadier 1898c, no. 148.
720	0.87 (cracked)	13.5	0	2/1	*London* (**LVNDEN**), *Sired* (Sigeræd). *Obv.* **RECX A**. Same *rev.* die as *SCBI* Copenhagen iiib 2902–3. Grote coll. 1879.
721	1.05	16.2	90	1/4	*London* (**LVND⋮**), *Wynsige*. *Obv.* **RCCX A⋮**. Same dies as *SCBI* Copenhagen iiib 3045–6. No provenance, acquired after 1950.
722	1.12	17.3	0	0/0	*London* (**LVND⋮**), *Wynstan*. *Obv.* **EX ANG**. Same dies as *SCBI* Copenhagen iiib 3073–4. 533/1897, bt. Weyl, ex unknown Polish find.
723	1.09	16.8	90	3/4	*London* (**LVN⋮**), *Wynstan*. *Obv.* **REX ANG**. Same dies as *SCBI* Copenhagen iiib 3067, *SCBI* Helsinki 810. Old collection.
724	0.98	15.1	90	4/2	*London* (**LVN⋮**), *Wynstan*. *Obv.* **RECX⋮**. Same dies as *SCBI* Copenhagen iiib 3068–9. Adler coll. 1821.
725	1.04	16.0	180	1/1	*Milborne Port* (**MYLE**), *Godwine*. *Obv.* **REEX**. Adler coll. 1821.
726	1.05	16.2	180	0/0	*Norwich* (**NOR-ÐVICS**), *Mana* (Man/Manna/Monna). *Obv.* **REX ANG**. Dannenberg coll. 1892.
727	0.99	15.3	90	0/0	*Norwich* (**NOR-ÐVI**), *Mana* (Man/Manna/Monna). *Obv.* **RECX A⋮**. Same *obv.* die as *SCBI* Copenhagen iiic 3199. Adler coll. 1821.

PLATE 26

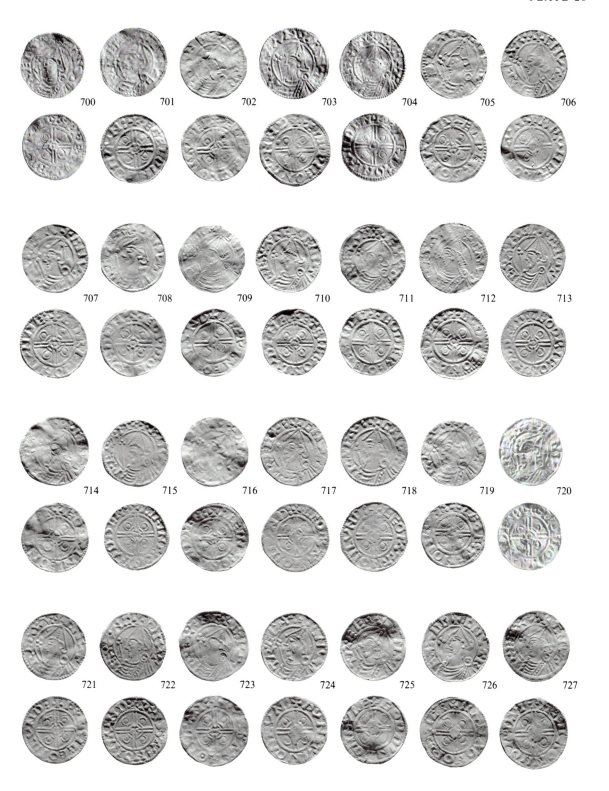

Pointed Helmet (*cont.*)

	Weight		Die	Pecks	
	gm	gr	axis	o./r.	
728	1.09	16.8	180	5/3	*Norwich* (**NOR·ÐƿP**), *Ricnulf* (Hringwulf). *Obv.* **REX ANGL:**. Same dies as *SCBI* Copenhagen iiic 3216. Ruehle coll. 1842.
729	1.05	16.2	180	2/5	*Oxford* (**ORXEN**), *Ælfwine. Obv.* **REX ANGL**. Same dies as *SCBI* Copenhagen iiic 3239–40. Ruehle coll. 1842.
730	1.18	18.2	0	0/1	*Oxford* (**OCXENE**), *Lifincc* (Leofing/Lifing). *Obv.* **REX ANG**. Same dies as *SCBI* Oxford 698, *SCBI* Copenhagen iiic 3285–6, same *obv.* die as ibid. 3278. Adler coll. 1821.
731	1.04	16.0	90	0/4	*Salisbury* (**SERE**), *Winstan* (Wynstan). *Obv.* **REX A**. Same dies as *SCBI* Copenhagen iiic 3463. Ruehle coll. 1842.
732	0.87	13.5	180	0/0	*Southwark* (**SV·Ð**), *Ælfgar. Obv.* **RECX A**. Same dies as *SCBI* Copenhagen iiic 3687. Dannenberg coll. 1892.
733	0.90	13.9	0	0/0	*Southwark* (**SV·Ð**), *Leofinc* (Leofing/Lifing). *Obv.* **REX A**. Same dies as *SCBI* Helsinki 818. 589/1894, ex Mgowo find 1893.
734	1.03	15.9	90	0/0	*Thetford* (**ÐEOTF:**), *Edwine* (Eadwine). *Obv.* **CNVT EX ANGLOR**. Ruehle coll. 1842.
	(cracked)				
735	1.16	17.9	0	0/0	*Wallingford* (**ƿPELIN**), *Edwerd* (Eadweard). *Obv.* **REX ANGL**. Same dies as *SCBI* Copenhagen iiic 3937. 589/1894, ex Mgowo find 1893.
736	1.15	17.7	270	1/3	*Warwick* (**ƿPÆRI**), *Godwine. Obv.* **REX ANG**. Adler coll. 1821.
737	1.11	17.1	270	3/4	*Winchcombe* (**ƿPINCEL**), *Dropa. Obv.* **REX ANG**. Same dies as *SCBI* Copenhagen iiic 3993, same *obv.* die as ibid. 3994. Ruehle coll. 1842.
738	1.14	17.6	180	0/0	*Winchester* (**ƿPINC:**), *Burwold* (Burhweald). *Obv.* **REX AN**. Same dies as *SCBI* Copenhagen iiic 4067, same *obv.* die as ibid. 4065–6. 7/1897, ex Juura/Odenpäh find 1888. Menadier 1898c, no. 152.
739	1.13	17.4	270	4/4	*Worcester* (**ƿPIHRACE**), *God* (God/Goda). *Obv.* **REX AN:**. Ruehle coll. 1842.
740	1.07	16.5	90	2/1	*Worcester* (**ƿPINRACE**), *God* (God/Goda). *Obv.* **+CN:+ — REC A:**. 533/1897, bt. Weyl, ex unknown Polish find.
741	1.05	16.2	0	3/0	*York* (**EOFR**), *Asgod* (Asgautr). *Obv.* **REX AN**. Same dies as *SCBI* Copenhagen iiia 531, same *obv.* die as **742**. 14/1851, ex Ploetzig/Plocko find 1850.
742	0.96	14.8	240	3/0	*York* (**EOFRƿPIC**), *Asgout* (Asgautr). *Obv.* **REX AN**. Same *obv.* die as **741**. Ruehle coll. 1842.
743	1.13	17.4	270	0/0	*York* (**EOFRƿPIC**), *Cetel* (Ketill). *Obv.* **REX ANG**. Same dies as *SCBI* Copenhagen iiia 573, 575, same *rev.* die as ibid. 574. 7/1897, ex Juura/Odenpäh find 1888. Menadier 1898c, no. 139.
744	1.03	15.9	270	0/0	*York* (**EOFR**), *Grimolf* (Grimulfr). *Obv.* **REX A**. Same *obv.* die as *SCBI* Copenhagen iiia 686, *SCBI* Merseyside 633. Ruehle coll. 1842.
745	0.95	14.7	40	0/0	*York* (**EOFR**), *Hildolf* (Hildulfr). *Obv.* **REX ANG**. Same dies as *SCBI* Copenhagen iiia 724. Old collection.
746	0.93	14.4	250	0/0	*York* (**EOFRƿPIC**), *Ire* (Iri). *Obv.* **REX AI**. 70/1893, bt. Loewenstimm, ex Russian hoard.
747	0.94	14.5	180	3/0	*York* (**EOFRƿP**), *Withrin* (Witherwine). *Obv.* **REX AN:**. Adler coll. 1821.
748	1.06	16.3	20	1/1	*York* (**EOFRI**), *Wulfnoth. Obv.* **REX ANGLO**. Same dies as *SCBI* Copenhagen iiia 906 (*rev.* die uncertain). Ruehle coll. 1842.

Short Cross (BEH H, *BMC* xvi, North 790)

The obverse legend reads **+CNVT RE[C]X**; **REX** or **RECX** and the contraction of **ANGLORVM**, if present, are indicated.

749	0.99	15.3	90	0/0	*Bristol* (**BRⱵC**), *Leofwine. Obv.* **RECX**. 7/1879, ex Juura/Odenpäh find 1888. Menadier 1898c, no. 137.
750	1.14	17.6	0	0/0	*Cambridge* (**GRA:**), *Ælfwig. Obv.* **CREC**. Ruehle coll. 1842.
751	1.16	17.9	180	4/4	*Canterbury* (**CENT**), *Ælfred* (Ælfræd). *Obv.* **CNV RECX A**. Same *obv.* die as *SCBI* Copenhagen iiia 125. 70/1893, bt. Loewenstimm, ex unknown Russian hoard.
752	1.16	17.9	270	0/0	*Canterbury* (**CENT**), *Leofwine. Obv.* **RECX**. 370/1895, ex Weyl auction 127 (1893), lot 1302.
753	1.15	17.7	90	2/1	*Chichester* (**CICC**), *Leofric. Obv.* **RECX**. Probably same dies as *SCBI* Copenhagen iiia 233. Grote coll. 1879.
754	1.02	15.7	90	0/2	*Colchester* (**COL**), *Wulfwine. Obv.* **RECX**. Same dies as *SCBI* Copenhagen iiia 275. Ruehle coll. 1842.
755	1.12	17.3	0	0/2	*Crewkerne* (**CRVC**), *Brihtwig* (Beorthwig). *Obv.* **RECX**. Pellet in fourth quarter of *rev.* Ruehle coll. 1842.

PLATE 27

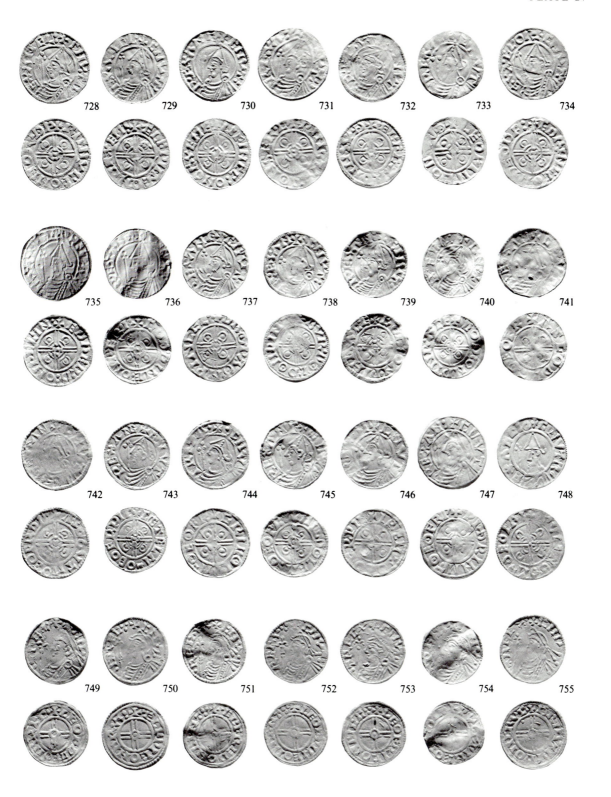

728 729 730 731 732 733 734

735 736 737 738 739 740 741

742 743 744 745 746 747 748

749 750 751 752 753 754 755

Short Cross (*cont.*)

	Weight		Die	Pecks	
	gm	*gr*	*axis*	*o./r.*	
756	0.82	12.6	270	1/1	*Dover* (**DOFF**), *Ælfwine*.[1] *Obv.* **REX**. Provenance uncertain, possibly ex Altranft find 1901.
757	1.12	17.3	0	1/3	*Dover* (**DOFER**), *Leofwine*. *Obv.* **RECX**. Same dies as *SCBI* Copenhagen iiia 388. 370/1895, ex Weyl auction 127 (1893), lot 1302.
758	1.04 (cracked)	16.0	90	3/4	*Lincoln* (**LINC**), *Ælfnoth*. *Obv.* **RE+**. Mossop XLIX:27. 264/1892, ex Hornikau/Horniki find 1890.
759	1.15	17.7	180	0/6	*Lincoln* (**LINC**), *Brihtric* (Beorhtric). *Obv.* **RECX**. Mossop L:6. Grote coll. 1879.
760	0.99	15.3	0	0/0	*Lincoln* (**LINCO**), *Colgrim* (Kolgrimr). *Obv.* **RE+**. Mossop LI:8. Ruehle coll. 1842.
761	0.87	13.4	0	0/0	*Lincoln* (**LI**), *Herthecnut* (Harthacnut). *Obv.* **RE+**. Mossop LI:24 (*rev.*). 7/1897, ex Juura/Odenpäh find 1888. Menadier 1898c, no. 140 (as Hertford, moneyer Cnut).
762	1.17	18.1	180	0/0	*Lincoln* (**LINCO**), *Wulfric*. *Obv.* **RECX**. Mossop LVI:26. 121/1933, bt. Drachenfels.
763	0.96 (pierced twice)	14.8	180	0/0	*London* (**LVND:**), *Ælfwine*. *Obv.* **RE+**. Same dies as *SCBI* Copenhagen iiib 2111. 520/1883, ex Borzecice find 1883; not recorded in Menadier 1887, p. 175.
764	1.13	17.4	270	0/0	*London* (**LVN**), *Brungar*. *Obv.* **RECX**. Adler coll. 1821.
765	1.12 (cracked)	17.3	90	0/0	*London* (**LV:**), *Brungar*. *Obv.* **RECX**. Grote coll. 1879.
766	1.10	17.0	270	0/0	*London* (**LV:**), *Brungar*. *Obv.* **REIX**. 1335/1951, bt. Grabow.
767	1.07	16.5	180	0/1	*London* (**LV**), *Eadmund*. *Obv.* **RECX**. Old collection.
768	1.17	17.9	270	5/11	*London* (**LVND**), *Eadwold?* (Eadweald). *Obv.* **RECX:**. 1536/1951, bt. Grabow.
769	1.00	15.4	270	0/3	*London* (**LVHD:**), *Godgod* (God/Goda). *Obv.* **REX**. Same dies as *SCBI* Copenhagen iiib 2571. Ruehle coll. 1842.
770	1.15	17.7	180	0/0	*London* (**LVND**), *Godric*. *Obv.* **RCCX**. 70/1893, bt. Loewenstimm, ex unknown Russian hoard.
771	1.03	15.9	0	1/0	*London* (**LVND**), *Leofred* (Leofræd). *Obv.* **RCX**. 7/1897, ex Juura/Odenpäh find 1888. Menadier 1898c, no. 146.
772	1.07	16.5	270	0/3	*London* (**LVND**), *Leofric*. *Obv.* **REX**. 386/1903, bt. Friedensburg, ex Zottwitz/Sobocisko find 1902.
773	1.08	16.7	180	2/0	*London* (**LVN**), *Leofstan*. *Obv.* **CNV RECX A**. Adler coll. 1821.
774	1.02	15.7	0	4/2	*London* (**LVND**), *Leofwerd*[2] (Leofweard). *Obv.* **REX**. 7/1897, ex Juura/Odenpäh find 1888. Menadier 1898c, no. 147.
775	1.12	17.3	0	0/1	*London* (**LVND**), *Swan* (Sveinn). *Obv.* **RECX**. Same dies as *SCBI* Copenhagen iiib 2919. Ruehle coll. 1842.
776	1.11	17.1	180	6/5	*Salisbury* (**SE:**), *Ælfred* (Ælfræd). *Obv.* **RECX**. Probably same dies as *SCBI* Copenhagen iiic 3418. 264/1892, ex Hornikau/Horniki find 1890.
777	0.81	12.5	0	0/0	*Stamford* (**STA**), *Thurstan* (Thorsteinn). *Obv.* **RCX**. Dannenberg coll. 1870.
778	1.08	16.7	0	4/6	*Steyning* (**STEI**), *Frthiwine* (Freothuwine). *Obv.* **REX A**. Dannenberg coll. 1892.
779	1.07	16.5	270	0/0	*Thetford* (**ÐE**), *Brunstan*. *Obv.* **RCCX:**. Same dies as *SCBI* Copenhagen iiic 3793. 370/1895, ex Weyl auction 127 (1893), lot 1302.
780	1.16	17.9	0	3/2	*Winchester* (**ÞINCE**), *Ælfeh* (Ælfheah). *Obv.* **CNV: RECX**. Same *obv.* die as *SCBI* Copenhagen iiic 4002. Ruehle coll. 1842.
781	1.18	18.2	180	1/0	*Winchester* (**ÞINC**), *Æthestan* (Æthelstan). *Obv.* **RECX**. Same *obv.* die as *SCBI* Copenhagen iiic 4053, 4056–7. Old collection.
782	0.95	14.6	180	0/0	*York* (**EOFFR**), *Beorn*. *Obv.* **RCX:**. 70/1893, bt. Loewenstimm, ex unknown Russian hoard.
783	1.06	16.4	0	0/0	*York* (**EOF**), *Earngrim* (Arngrimr). *Obv.* **REEC+:**. Same dies as *SCBI* Copenhagen iiia 609, same *obv.* die as ibid. 607–8. 532/1897, bt. Weyl, ex unknown Polish find.

[1] Moneyer not in BEH, *BMC*, or Smart 1981 for mint.
[2] Moneyer not in BEH, *BMC*, or Smart 1981 for type. Cf. BEH 2521 Leofrerd.

PLATE 28

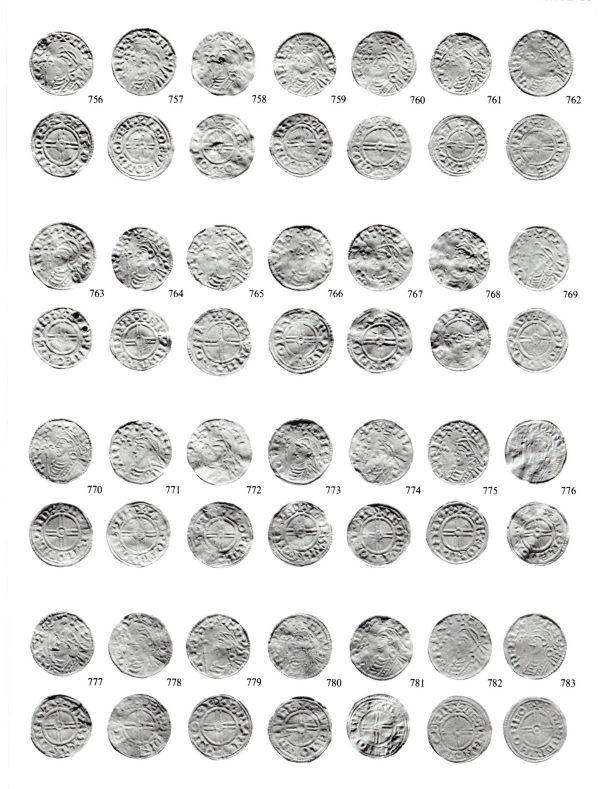

756   757   758   759   760   761   762

763   764   765   766   767   768   769

770   771   772   773   774   775   776

777   778   779   780   781   782   783

HAROLD I (*cont.*)

Fleur-de-lis (*cont.*)

	Weight		Die	Pecks	
	gm	gr	axis	o./r.	
812	1.04	16.0	90	1/2	*Norwich* (**NOR-Ð**), *Manna* (Man/Manna/Monna). *Obv.* **RCE**. 7/1897, ex Juura/Odenpäh find 1888. Menadier 1898c, no. 156.
813	0.93	14.3	90	0/0	*Stamford* (**STA**), *Brunwine*. *Obv.* **RE✚:**. Old collection.
814	0.93	14.3	270	0/0	*Stamford* (**STA**), *Godric*. 7/1897, ex Juura/Odenpäh find 1888. Menadier 1898c, no. 157.
815	1.14	17.6	180	0/2	*Winchester* (**ÞNC**), *Leofwine*. *Obv.* **REX:**. Same dies as *SCBI* Copenhagen iv 594. Adler coll. 1821.
816	1.11	17.1	90	6/1	*York* (**EOF**), *Grimulf* (Grimulfr). Gansauge coll. 1873.
817	1.06	16.4	0	0/0	*York* (**EOF**), *Swegen* (Sveinn). *Obv.* **RE**. Same *obv.* die as *SCBI* Copenhagen iv 113. 532/1897, bt. Weyl, ex unknown Polish find.

HARTHACNUT, joint king 1035-7, sole king 1040-2

Arm-and-Sceptre (BEH B and Cnut I, *BMC* ii and Cnut xvii, North 799 and 811)

818	1.18	18.2	180	1/0	*Lincoln* (**LINCOL**), *Othgrim* (Authgrimr). *Obv.* **CNVT REX AN**. Mossop LXV:2. 7/1897, ex Juura/Odenpäh find 1888. Menadier 1898c, no. 143 (as Cnut).
819	1.00	15.4	0	0/0	*London* (**LVNDE**), *Ælfred* (Ælfræd)[1] *Obv.* **CNVT REX AN**. Dannenberg coll. 1870, ex 'Berlin I' find 1856. Dannenberg 1857, p. 213, no. 151.
820	0.87 (fragment)	13.4	90	1/2	*Northampton* (**HÆMTV**), —*lfwine* (Ælfwine). *Obv.* **HARD—NVT R**. 265/1892, ex Hornikau/Horniki find 1890.
821	0.96	14.8	90	0/1	*Norwich* (**NR-ÐI**), *Leofwine*. *Obv.* **CNVD DRC**. 7/1897, ex Juura/Odenpäh find 1888. Menadier 1898c, no. 150 (as Cnut).
822	1.09	16.8	270	0/0	*York* (**EOFERÞI**), *Sculaa* (Skuli). *Obv.* **CNVT RECX ANGL**. Ruehle coll. 1842.
823	0.84 (pierced)	12.9	0	0/0	*York* (**EOCI**), *Ulccetel* (Ulfketill).[1] *Obv.* **CNVT RC✚ AN**. 740/1913, ex Seemark/Zakrzewko find 1913. Not recorded in Menadier 1924.

EDWARD THE CONFESSOR, 1042-66

Name and title of the king are variously spelt, so that the actual form on the coin is always indicated.

Pacx/Jewel Cross mule (BEH D/Harthacnut A, *BMC* iv/Harthacnut i, North 813/802)

| 824 | 0.75 (cracked) | 11.5 | 50 | 2/4 | *Exeter* (**EXCE**), *Wulnoth* (Wulfnoth). *Obv.* **✚EDÞERD REX**. 295/1892, ex Weyl auction 114 (1891), lot 1455, ex 'Berlin I' find 1856. Dannenberg 1857, p. 215, no. 167. A mule between these two issues has not been recorded before and might not be expected to occur. However, it is struck from the same reverse die as two Harthacnut *Jewel Cross* coins (Brettell sale, Glendining 28 October 1970, lot 187, wt. 1.10 g, and Sotheby 12 September 1981, lot 51, wt. 1.10 g, 180°) and, based on considerations of weight and style, the late Michael Dolley regarded all three coins as official English products (pers. comm.). |

Pacx (BEH D, *BMC* iv, North 813)

825	1.08 (cracked)	16.7	90	0/0	*Chester* (**LEG**), *Argrim* (Arngrimr). *Obv.* **EDÞARD RREC**. Cf. BEH 258. 76/1893, bt. Heyn.
826	1.09	16.8	80	0/0	*Lincoln* (**LINC**), *Godric*. *Obv.* **CDÞ—RE:C✚:**. Mossop LXVI:16. 531/1897, bt. Weyl, ex unknown Polish find.
827	1.13	17.4	0	3/4	*Northampton* (**HA**), *Lefwiine*. (Leofwine). *Obv.* **EDÞARD RCCX**. Ruehle coll. 1842.
828	1.10 (pierced)	17.0	180	5/4	*Oxford* (**OXAN**), *Ælwi* (Ælfwig). *Obv.* **EADÞARD RECX:**. Same dies as *SCBI* Oxford 767. Dannenberg coll. 1870, ex Simoitzel/Siemyśl find. Dannenberg 1865, p. 161, no. 67.
829	1.17	18.1	90	3/5	*Southwark* (**SVDGE**), *Bured* (Burhræd).[1] *Obv.* **EDÞARD RECX**. Dannenberg 1897, p. 24, no. 47. Dannenberg coll. 1892.

[1] Moneyer not in BEH, *BMC*, or Smart 1981 for type.

[*continued overleaf*]

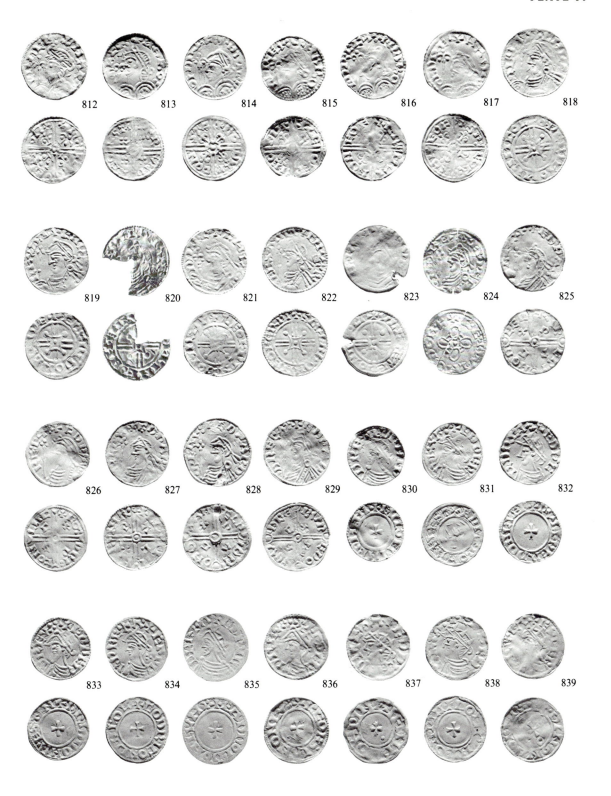

PLATE 30

812 813 814 815 816 817 818

819 820 821 822 823 824 825

826 827 828 829 830 831 832

833 834 835 836 837 838 839

Plate 30 (*cont.*)

Radiate Small Cross (BEH A, *BMC* i, North 816)

	Weight		Die	pecks	
	gm	gr	axis	o./r.	
830	1.02	15.7	90	2/1	*Canterbury* (**CTN**), *Guldewine* (Gyldwine). *Obv.* **EDꝸNFD DRE**. 531/1897, bt. Weyl, ex unknown Polish find.
831	1.14	17.6	180	2/9	*Exeter* (**EAXCEST**), *Edmær* (Eadmær). *Obv.* **EDꝸER REX A:**. *Rev.* double struck. Probably same dies as *SCBI* Copenhagen iv 805. Ruehle coll. 1842.
832	1.11	17.1	270	0/0	*Gloucester* (**GLER**), *Wulfwerd* (Wulfweard). *Obv.* **EDꝸERD REX**. Same *rev.* die as *SCBI* Copenhagen iv 877. Dannenberg coll. 1892.
833	1.04	16.0	0	0/1	*Hastings* (**HÆSTIN**), *Bridd* (Brid). *Obv.* **EDꝸERD REX**. Cf. BEH 208. Gansauge coll. 1873.
834	1.14	17.6	0	0/0	*Lincoln* (**LINCOL:**), *Godric*. *Obv.* **EDꝸERD REX A**. Three pellets behind bust. Mossop LXVIII: 17. 872/1905, bt. Hess.
835	1.06	16.4	90	0/0	*London* (**LVND**), *Eadwold* (Eadweald). *Obv.* **EDꝸNED REX A**. 1139/1892, bt. Hahlo.
836	1.05	16.2	90	1/2	*London* (**LV:**), *Leofstan*. *Obv.* **EDꝸERD REX**. 536/1872, ex Zaborowo find 1871. Cf. Menadier 1887, pp. 177–8.
837	0.90	13.9	0	0/1	*Winchester* (**ꝸINC**), *Ifincc* (Ifing). *Obv.* **EDꝸED RCEX A**. Pellet in field of rev. Same *obv.* die as *SCBI* Copenhagen iv 1252. 7/1897, ex Juura/Odenpäh find 1888. Menadier 1898c, no. 134 (as Æthelræd II).
838	1.06	16.4	90	0/0	*Winchester* (**ꝸIN**), *Lodwine* (Godwine). *Obv.* **EDꝸERD REX**. Same *obv.* die as *SCBI* Copenhagen iv 1268. 372/1895, ex Weyl auction 127 (1893), lot 1247.
839	0.86	13.2	270	0/1	*York* (**EOFER:**), *Othin* (Authunn). *Obv.* **EDꝸERD RE+ A**. Annulet in field of *rev.* 263/1892, ex Hornikau/Horniki find 1890.

Radiate Small Cross (*cont.*)

	Weight		Die	Pecks		
	gm	*gr*	*axis*	*o./r.*		
840	1.08	16.7	250	0/0	*York* (**EOC**), *Sæfuhel* (Sæfugl). *Obv.* Đ**ÞERD REX A**. Annulet in field of *rev.* Same *rev.* die as *SCBI* Cambridge 827. Ruehle coll. 1842.
841	1.07	16.5	180	0/0	*York* (**EOFI**), *Thurrim* (Thorgrimr). *Obv.* **EDÞARD REX**. Annulet in field of *rev.* Same dies as *SCBI* Copenhagen iv 863, *SCBI* Merseyside 716. Same *obv.* die as **842**. Ruehle coll. 1842.
842	1.06	16.4	180	0/0	*York* (**EOF**), *Thurrim* (Thorgrimr). *Obv.* **EDÞARD REX**. Annulet in field of *rev.* Same *obv.* die as **841**, probably same *rev.* die as *SCBI* Copenhagen iv 864 and *SCBI* Merseyside 717. Gansauge coll. 1873.

Trefoil Quadrilateral (BEH C, *BMC* iii, North 817)

843	1.04	16.0	0	0/0	*Colchester* (**COLI**), *Elfwine* (Ælfwine). *Obv.* **EDÞEI[D REX]**. Gansauge coll. 1873.
844	1.16	17.9	10	5/4	*Lincoln* (**LINCO**), *Brithrc* (Beorthric). *Obv.* **EDÞRD REX:**. Mossop LXIX : 30. Ruehle coll. 1842.
845	0.95	14.6	0	1/0	*London* (**LVNDE**), *Ælfwi* (Ælfwig). *Obv.* **EDÞNER RDE**. 565/1903, bt. Kube, ex Altranft find 1901.
846	0.90 (cracked)	13.9	270	0/0	*London* (**LVNDE**), *Ælfwi* (Ælfwig). *Obv.* **EDÞNRD E+ A**. 1138/1892, bt. Hahlo.
847	0.95	14.6	90	0/0	*London* (**LVNDE**), *Golsi* (Goldsige). *Obv.* **EDÞERD REX**. Gansauge coll. 1873.
848	0.94	14.5	270	0/0	*London* (**LVND**), *Wulcred* (Wulfræd). *Obv.* **EDÞNE—RDE+**. Dannenberg coll. 1870
849	1.14	17.6	90	0/0	*Uncertain mint* (**ROCCE**), *Tafere*.[1] *Obv.* **EDR — ÞDE⊢⊢⊢**. Ruehle coll. 1842.

Small Flan (BEH B, *BMC* ii, North 818)

850	1.11	17.1	270	1/0	*Bath* (**BA**Đ), *Ægelmær* (Æthelmær). *Obv.* **EDÞERD REX**. 872/1905, bt. Hess.
851	1.17	18.1	180	4/3	*Colchester* (**COL**), *Stanmæ* (Stanmær).[2] *Obv.* **EDÞARD RE**. Dannenberg coll. 1870, ex Simoitzel/ Siemyśl find. Dannenberg 1865, p. 160, no. 65.
852	0.99	15.3	270	0/0	*Hastings* (**HÆSTI**), *Brid. Obv.* **EDÞARD RE**. Cf. *BMC* 494. Grote coll. 1879.
853	1.10	17.0	0	0/1	*Lincoln* (**LIN**), *Alfnath* (Ælfnoth). *Obv.* **EDÞARD RE**. Mossop LXXII : 6. Ruehle coll. 1842.
854	1.10	17.0	90	0/0	*London* (**LVN**), *Ægelwi* (Æthelwig). *Obv.* **EDÞERD RC**. Grote coll. 1879.
855	0.87	13.4	90	0/0	*London* (**LD**), *Elfstan* (Ælfstan). *Obv.* **EDÞRD RE**. Gansauge coll. 1873.
856	0.99	15.3	180	0/0	*London* (**LVN**), *Liofred* (Leofræd). *Obv.* **EDÞERD RE**. Old collection.
857	0.64 (chipped)	9.8	90	0/2	*Uncertain mint and moneyer* (**+ITINICI LIO—NO**). *Obv.* **EDÞIRD R—**. 14/1851, ex Ploetzig/ Plocko find 1850.

Expanding Cross (BEH E, *BMC* vi, North 820–4)

(*a*) Light Coinage (small flans)

858	1.15	17.7	90	1/0	*Exeter* (**EXSCE:**), *Wulmær* (Wulfmær). *Obv.* **EDÞERD REY**. North 820. 522/1883, ex Borzecice find 1883. Cf. Menadier 1887, p. 175.
859	1.12	17.3	340	0/0	*York* (**EOFER**), *Arngrim* (Arngrimr). *Obv.* **EDÞARD RE**. Annulet in second quarter of *rev.* North-Eastern variety with 'Pacx' style bust. North 821. Same dies as *SCBI* Cambridge 864 and *SCBI* Merseyside 752. Ruehle coll. 1842.

(*b*) Heavy Coinage (large flans)

860	1.76	27.2	180	0/0	*Thetford* (**Đ**EOTF), *Leofric. Obv.* **EDÞERRD REX**. North 823. Dannenberg coll. 1892.
861	1.76	27.2	90	1/0	*York* (**EOFE:**), *Leofenoth* (Leofnoth). *Obv.* **EDÞERD REX:**. Annulet in first quarter of *rev.* Same dies as *SCBI* Oxford 857, *SCBI* Copenhagen iv 842, *SCBI* Merseyside 773. Ruehle coll. 1842.

Pointed Helmet (BEH F, *BMC* vii, North 825)

862	1.36	21.0	90	10/2	*Lewes* (**LÆÞE**), *Oswold* (Osweald). *Obv.* legend illegible. 295/1892, ex Weyl auction 114 (1891), lot 1456.
863	1.31	20.2	0	0/0	*Maldon* (**MEL**), *Godwine. Obv.* **EDÞERD REI**. 295/1892, ex Weyl auction 114 (1891), lot 1458.

[1] Mint-signature and moneyer are not recorded in BEH, *BMC*, or Smart 1981. Imitation?
[2] Moneyer not in BEH, *BMC*, or Smart 1981 for type.

[*continued overleaf*]

PLATE 31

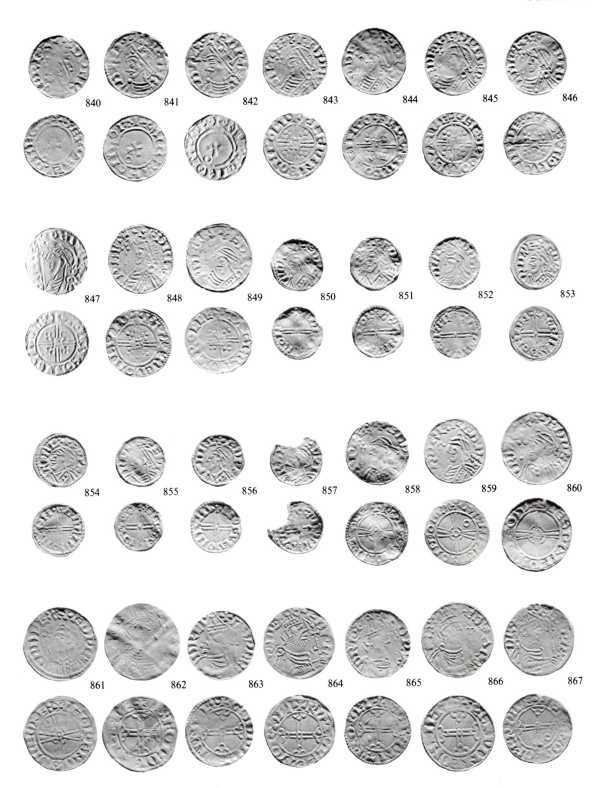

840   841   842   843   844   845   846

847   848   849   850   851   852   853

854   855   856   857   858   859   860

861   862   863   864   865   866   867

Plate 31 (*cont.*)

	Weight		*Die*	*Pecks*	
	gm	*gr*	*axis*	*o./r.*	
864	1.34	20.7	180	0/0	*Norwich* (**NOR-ÐPI**), *Rincolf* (Hringwulf). *Obv.* **EDPERD RX**. Old collection.
865	1.32	20.4	270	1/2	*Oxford* (**OXEI**), *Swetman. Obv.* **EDPERD REX**. Old collection.
866	1.24	19.1	180	0/1	*Wilton* (**PILTV**), *Ælfwine. Obv.* **EDPARD REX**. 295/1892, ex Weyl auction 114 (1891), lot 1459.
867	1.27	19.6	180	0/0	*York* (**EOFERPICE**), *Ræfen* (Hrafn). *Obv.* **EDPERD RX**. Same dies as *SCBI* Merseyside 782. Gansauge coll. 1873.

Pointed Helmet/Sovereign-Eagles mule (BEH F/H, *BMC* vii/ix, North 825/827)

	Weight		Die	Pecks	
	gm	gr	axis	o./r.	
868	1.31	20.2	50	0/0	*York* (**EOFER**), *Iocitel* (Ioketill). *Obv.* **EDꝜERD R**. Vollard. Another specimen occurred in the York (Bishophill I) hoard, *SCBI* Yorkshire collections 340.

Sovereign-Eagles (BEH H, *BMC* ix, North 827)

869	0.47	7.2	90	0/0	*London* (**LVN**), ——*nc* (Leofing/Lifing?). *Obv.* **EADꝜ——GLOX**. 531/1897, bt. Weyl, ex unknown Polish find.
	(two fragments)				
870	1.39	21.5	0	0/0	*Oxford* (**OXNE:**), *Eadwine*. *Obv.* **EADꝜARD REX ANGLO**. Same *rev.* die as *BMC* 1120. Vollard.
871	1.30	20.1	180	0/0	*Wilton* (**ꝜILTV**), *Swetric*. *Obv.* **EADꝜEARD REX ANGLO**. 531/1897, bt. Weyl, ex unknown Polish find.

Hammer Cross (BEH G, *BMC* xi, North 828)

872	1.02	15.7	90	0/0	*Canterbury* (**CÆNT**), *Lifstan* (Leofstan). *Obv.* **ADꝜARD REX**. 531/1897, bt. Weyl, ex unknown Polish find.
873	1.28	19.8	90	0/0	*Chester* (**LECCS**), *Alesige* (Ælfsige or Ealhsige). *Obv.* **EDꝜAR REX A**. Grote coll. 1879.
874	1.25	19.3	270	9/5	*Stamford* (**STANFO**), *Lefric* (Leofric).[1] *Obv.* **EDꝜARD RE**. 565/1903, bt. Kube, ex Altranft find 1901.
875	1.21	18.7	90	0/0	*Wilton* (**ꝜILTVN:**), *Swwine* (Sæwine). *Obv.* **EADꝜARRD RE**. 872/1905, bt. Hess.
876	1.32	20.4	90	0/0	*York* (**EOFRI**), *Iocitel* (Ioketill). *Obv.* **EDꝜARD DRE**. Annulet in second quarter of *rev.* Same dies as **877–8**. Same *obv.* die as *SCBI* Merseyside 801. Ruehle coll. 1842.
877	1.31	20.2	90	0/0	*York* (**EOFRI**), *Iocitel* (Ioketill). Same dies as **876, 878**. Grote coll. 1879.
878	1.30	20.1	90	0/0	*York* (**EOFRI**), *Iocitel* (Ioketill). Same dies as **876–7**. Grote coll. 1879.
879	1.10	17.0	270	0/0	*York* (**E**), *Swartcol* (Svartkollr). *Obv.* **EADꝜARD RE**. Annulet in fourth quarter of *rev.* Ruehle coll. 1842.

Facing Bust/Small Cross (BEH Ac, *BMC* xiii, North 830)

880	1.10	17.0	270	0/0	*Lincoln* (**LINC**), *Garfin* (Geirfinnr). *Obv.* **EADꝜARD REX**. Not in Mossop, *obv.* similar to Mossop LXXIX:23. Gansauge coll. 1873.
881	0.92	14.2	0	0/0	*Norwich* (**NOꝜ**), *Godeverd*.[2] *Obv.* **EADꝜARD**. 7/1897, ex Juura/Odenpäh find 1888. Menadier 1898c, no. 121 (as imitation), illustrated ibid., p. 229. Reading and attribution by the late Michael Dolley. For moneyer's name V. Smart suggests the normalized form Guthfrithr (pers. comm.).
882	1.04	16.0	160	0/0	*York* (**EOFR**), *Thorr*. *Obv.* **EADꝜAERD REX**. Annulet in field of *rev.* Same *obv.* die as *SCBI* Merseyside 826, same *rev.* die as *SCBI* Cambridge 958, *SCBI* Oxford 1060. Gansauge coll. 1873.

Pyramids (BEH I, *BMC* xv, North 831)

The York coins have an annulet instead of a pyramid in one of the quarters.

883	1.31	20.2	0	0/0	*Chester* (**LEGEEE:**), *Ælfs* (Ælfsige). *Obv.* **EADꝜARD RE**. Ruehle coll. 1842.
884	1.42	21.9	0	0/0	*York* (**EOF**), *Outhgrim* (Authgrimr). *Obv.* **EDRRDI REX**. Same dies as *SCBI* Merseyside 834. Gansauge coll. 1873.
885	1.42	21.9	0	0/0	*York* (**EOFRꝜIEC**), *Thorr*. *Obv.* **EADꝜARD REX**. Same *rev.* die as *SCBI* Merseyside 840. Ruehle coll. 1842.
886	1.48	22.8	270	0/0	*York* (**EOFE**), *Ulcetel* (Ulfketill). *Obv.* **EADꝜARD REX**. Same *obv.* die as *SCBI* Oxford 1087. Dannenberg coll. 1870.

[1] Moneyer not in BEH, *BMC*, or Smart 1981 for type.
[2] Moneyer not in BEH, *BMC*, or Smart 1981.

[*continued overleaf*]

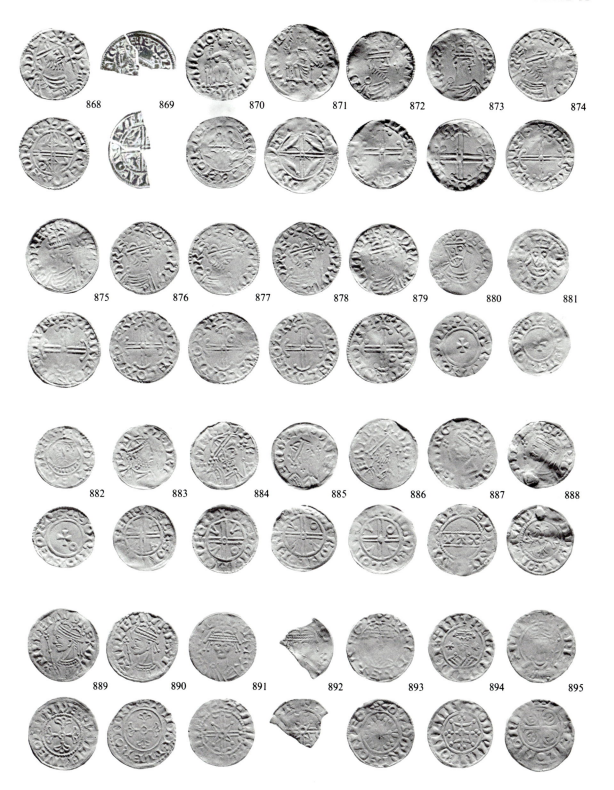

PLATE 32

868 869 870 871 872 873 874

875 876 877 878 879 880 881

882 883 884 885 886 887 888

889 890 891 892 893 894 895

Plate 32 (*cont.*)

HAROLD II, 1066

Pax (BEH A, *BMC* i, North 836)

	Weight		Die	Pecks	
	gm	gr	axis	o./r.	
887	1.25	19.3	0	0/0	*Wallingford* (Þ), *Burewine* (Burhwine). *Obv.* **HAROLD REX ANGL**. *Rev.* legend starts at 9 o'clock. Probably same *obv.* die as *SCBI* Oxford 1113. Ruehle coll. 1842. For mint-attribution cf. *BMC* 89 and *SCBI* Oxford 1113, both have ÞALIN.

NORMAN SERIES

WILLIAM I, 1066–87

The obverse legend reads +ÞILLELM REX unless otherwise indicated.

Profile/Cross Fleury (*BMC* i, North 839)

888	1.30	20.1	180	5/4	*London* (**LVNDE**). *Eadwine. Obv.* ÞI[LLEM]VS REX AI. Remains of suspension loop. 307/1890, bt. Weyl, ex Reval/Tallinn find.
889	1.39	21.5	0	0/0	*London* (**LVNDE**), *Wulfwine. Obv.* ÞILLEMVS REX AI. Grote coll. 1879.
890	1.31	20.2	270	0/0	*Romney* (**RV**), *Wulfmær. Obv.* ILLEMV REX I. Probably same dies as *SCBI* Copenhagen iv 1336 and *SCBI* Stockholm 9. 678/1872, bt. Webster.

Bonnet (*BMC* ii, North 842)

891	1.19	18.4	180	0/0	*York* (**EOFE**), *Autholf* (Authulfr). *Obv.* ÞILLEMV REX. Same dies as *SCBI* Merseyside 858 (*rev.* die uncertain). Gansauge coll. 1873.
892	0.62	9.5	270	3/0	*Uncertain mint* (——**OR**) *and moneyer* (*W*———). 576/1903, bt. Kube, ex Altranft find 1901.
(fragment)					

Two Sceptres (*BMC* iv, North 844)

893	1.32	20.4	0	0/0	*York* (**EOF**), *Outhgrim* (Authgrimr). *Obv.* ÞILLM REX ANGL. Same *rev.* die as *SCBI* Merseyside 873. Adler coll. 1821.

Two Stars (*BMC* v, North 845)

894	1.18	18.2	180	0/0	*London* (**LVN**), *Godwiine* (Godwine). *Obv.* ÞILLELM REX AI. Ruehle coll. 1842.

Paxs (*BMC* viii, North 848–50)

895	1.38	21.3	0	0/0	*Cambridge* (**GRANT**), *Ulfcil* (Ulfketill). Probably same dies as *SCBI* Copenhagen iv 1315 (*obv.* die uncertain). Grote coll. 1879.

WILLIAM I (*cont.*)

Paxs (*cont.*)

	Weight		Die	Pecks	
	gm	gr	axis	o./r.	
896	1.38	21.3	90	0/0	*Lincoln* (**LINCO**), *Sifreth* (Sigeferth). Mossop LXXXIII:21. Dannenberg coll. 1870.
897	1.41	21.8	180	0/0	*London* (**LVNDNE**), *Æwi* (Ælfwine or Eadwig). Friedlaender coll. 1861. On the identity of the moneyer see *BMC*, p. ccxx (Ælfwine) and *SCBI* Reading, p. 13 (Eadwig).
898	1.35	20.8	90	0/0	*London* (**LVNDI**), *Edric* (Eadric). 296/1892, ex Weyl auction 114 (1891), lot 1461.
899	1.36	21.0	90	0/0	*Southwark* (**SV-ÐI**), *Lifwword* (Leofweard). Same dies as *BMC* 967. 287/1845, Pfister exchange.
900	1.42	21.9	0	0/0	*Winchester* (**PNCE**), *Æstan* (Æthelstan). Same die as *SCBI* Stockholm 134. Dannenberg coll. 1870.
901	1.40	21.6	90	0/0	*Winchester* (**PINCE**), *Æstan* (Æthelstan). Same *rev.* die as *SCBI* Copenhagen iv 1359. Dannenberg coll. 1892.
902	1.39	21.5	90	0/0	*Winchester* (**PINC**), *Liefwold* (Leofweald). Same *obv.* die as *SCBI* Copenhagen iv 1366. Friedlaender coll. 1861.
903	1.39	21.5	270	0/0	*Winchester* (**PINCE**), *Lifinc* (Leofing/Lifing). Same dies as **904-5**. Same *obv.* die as *SCBI* Copenhagen iv 1363. Grote coll. 1879.
904	1.37	21.1	90	0/0	*Winchester* (**PINCE**), *Lifinc* (Leofing/Lifing). Same dies as **903, 905**. Grote coll. 1879.
905	1.37	21.1	90	0/0	*Winchester* (**PINCE**), *Lifinc* (Leofing/Lifing). Same dies as **903-4**. Dannenberg coll. 1870.
906	1.33	20.5	180	0/0	*Winchester* (**PINC**), *Liofwold* (Leofweald). Gansauge coll. 1873.
907	1.40	21.6	180	0/0	*Winchester* (**PIN**), *Spraclinc* (Spræcling). Grote coll. 1879.
908	1.40	21.6	90	0/0	*Winchester* (**PINC**), *Wimund* (Wigmund). 1336/1951, bt. Grabow.

WILLIAM I, 1066-87 or WILLIAM II, 1087-1100

Profile (*BMC* William II, i, North 851)

| 909 | 1.38 | 21.3 | 270 | 0/0 | *Salisbury* (**SAEREB**), *Esbrn* (Osbern). 7/1897, ex Juura/Odenpäh find 1888. Menadier 1898c, no. 166 (uncertain). *BMC*, p. ccxxxiii, cited from this. |

WILLIAM II, 1087-1100

The obverse legend reads **+PILLELM REX** unless otherwise indicated.

Cross Voided (*BMC* iii, North 853)

910	1.46	22.5	90	0/0	*Cambridge* (**GRANT**), *Wibrn* (Wigbern). *BMC*, p. cc, cited from this. 7/1897, ex Juura/Odenpäh find 1888. Menadier 1898c, no. 160.
911	1.34	20.7	0	0/0	*Canterbury* (**CANTI**), *Simier* (Sigemær). *BMC*, p. ccii, cited from this. 7/1897, ex Juura/Odenpäh find 1888. Menadier 1898c, no. 164.
912	1.32	20.4	90	0/0	*Chester?* (**LECEC?**), *uncertain moneyer*. Obv. **PILLELM RE**. 7/1897, ex Juura/Odenpäh find 1888. Menadier 1898c, no. 165 (as uncertain).
913	1.39	21.5	270	0/0	*Lewes* (**LIEP**), *Brihtmer* (Beorhtmær). 7/1897, ex Juura/Odenpäh find 1888. Menadier 1898c, no. 161 (as Brintwine).
914	1.35	20.8	90	0/0	*London* (**LV**), *Bruninc* (Bruning). 7/1897, ex Juura/Odenpäh find 1888. Menadier 1898c, no. 163 (as uncertain mint, Brintwine).
915	1.42	21.9	270	2/0	*London* (**LV**), *B—old*. 7/1897, ex Juura/Odenpäh find 1888. Menadier 1898c, no. 162 (as Lincoln, Ordgar).
916	1.41	21.8	90	0/0	*Norwich* (**NOC-ÐPIC**), *(Alf)ri* (Ælfric). Same dies as *BMC* 210, same *rev.* die as *SCBI* Stockholm 229. 7/1897, ex Juura/Odenpäh find 1888. Menadier 1898c, no. 165 (as uncertain).
917	1.27	19.6	90	0/0	*Steyning* (**S[T]EN**), *Thrben* (Thorbjorn). Same dies as *BMC* 224. 7/1897, ex Juura/Odenpäh find 1888. Menadier 1898c, no. 165 (as uncertain). Normalized form of moneyer's name by V. Smart (pers. comm.).

HENRY I, 1100-35

Double Inscription (*BMC* xi, North 867)

| 918 | 0.65 (fragment) | 10.1 | 90 | 0/0 | *Oxford* (**OXN—**), *uncertain moneyer*. Cf. *BMC*, p. ccxxxi. 372/1889, ex Londzyn/Ładzyn find 1887. |

[*continued overleaf*]

PLATE 33

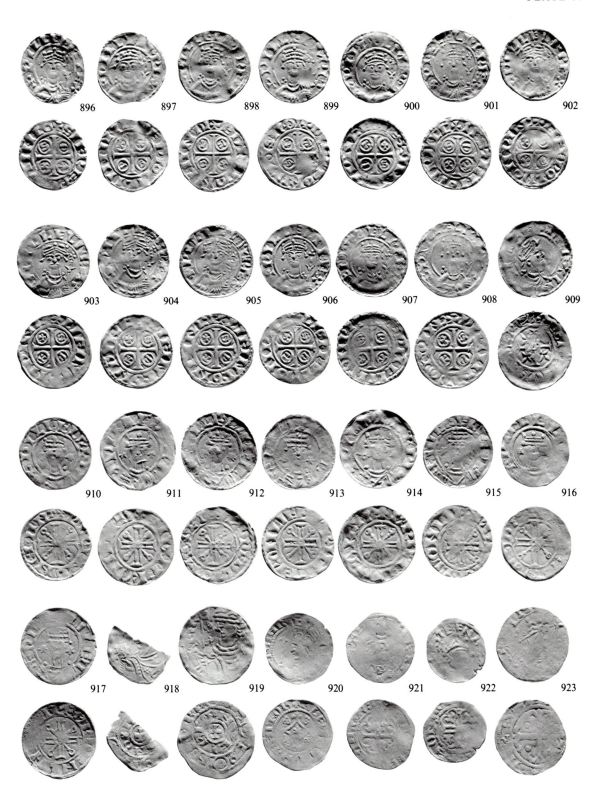

896   897   898   899   900   901   902

903   904   905   906   907   908   909

910   911   912   913   914   915   916

917   918   919   920   921   922   923

Plate 33 (*cont.*)

	Weight		Die	Pecks	
	gm	*gr*	*axis*	*o./r.*	
919	1.38	21.3	0	4/0	*Uncertain mint* (**VEIRE**, Warwick??) *and moneyer*. 306/1890, ex Reval/Tallinn find.

Star-in-Lozenge-Fleury (*BMC* xiii, North 869)

920	1.34	20.7	130	0/0	*Thetford* (**TETFOR**), *Alf*(*ward*) (Ælfweard). *Obv.* **HENRICVS**. *BMC*, p. ccxliii, cited from this. 679/1872, bt. Webster.

STEPHEN, 1135–54

Watford (*BMC* i, North 873–4)

921	1.37	21.1	0	0/0	*Uncertain mint and moneyer* (—E—**AN**). *Obv.* **STIFNE REX**. Dannenberg coll. 1892.
922	1.13	17.4	90	0/0	*Uncertain mint and moneyer*. *Obv.* **STEFN REX**. No inner circle on *obv.* (North 874). Cross voided and no punctuation on *rev.* 446/1871, ex Dannenberg coll. 1870.
923	1.36	21.0	?	0/0	*Uncertain mint and moneyer*. Contemporary forgery? English? 519/1920, Ball/Grunthal gift.

HIBERNO-NORSE SERIES

PHASE I, *c*.995–1020 (Contemporary imitations of English coins)

'*Crux*' imitation

With the name of Sihtric and the Dublin mint-signature

	Weight		Die	Pecks	
	gm	gr	axis	o./r.	
924	1.54	23.8	310	0/0	'*Eole*' (DIFLIME). *Obv*. +ZITIR DIFLI[M] MEO. Same dies as *SCBI* Copenhagen v 1 and *SCBI* Belfast ii 5. Grote coll. 1879.

'*Long Cross*' imitations

(*a*) With SIHTRC RE+ and the Dublin mint-signature

925	1.34	20.7	270	3/0	'*Fænemin*' (DYFLI). *Obv*. ÐYFLN. Same dies a *SCBI* Copenhagen v 10. Grote coll. 1879.
	(pierced)				
926	1.35	20.8	90	1/5	'*Færemin*' (DIFLI). *Obv*. DYFMN. Ruehle coll. 1842.
	(pierced)				
927	1.34	20.7	90	0/0	'*Færemin*' (DYFL). *Obv*. DYFLNN. 556/1872, ex Althoefchen/Starydworek find 1872. Friedlaender 1877, no. 197.
928	1.47	22.7	180	1/8	'*Færemin*' (DYFLI). *Obv*. +SIHTRC RED+ RDNN. Same *rev*. die as *SCBI* Belfast ii 20. Gansauge coll. 1873.
929	1.31	20.2	200	1/4	'*Færemin*' (DYFLI). *Obv*. DYFLNI. Ruehle coll. 1842.
930	1.35	20.8	220	0/11	'*Faerenim*' (DYMI). *Obv*. DIFLNII. Ruehle coll. 1842.
	(pierced twice)				
931	1.27	19.6	270	0/7	'*Faerenin*' (DYMI). *Obv*. DYFLM. Ruehle coll. 1842.
932	1.27	19.6	90	0/0	'*Siel*' (DYFLNIEIMTIV). *Obv*. DYFLNI. Same dies as *SCBI* BM H/N 22. Grote coll. 1879.

(*b*) With +DYMNROE+MNE-ÐI and the Dublin mint-signature

933	1.32	20.4	180	10/12	'*Fienemin*' (DYMI). Same dies as BEH Thymn 12, *SCBI* Copenhagen v 19, *SCBI* Helsinki 929. Ruehle coll. 1842.

(*c*) With +ÆÐELRÆD REX ANGO and the Dublin mint-signature

934	1.45	22.4	270	1/0	'*Færemin*' (DYFLI). Same dies as *SCBI* BM H/N 31–2, *SCBI* Belfast ii 29. Dannenberg coll. 1892, ex Plonsk find 1854. Dannenberg 1871, p. 262, no. 2.

For a *Helmet* coin of York probably struck from a Hiberno-Norse die, see **499**.

'*Last Small Cross*' imitations

(*a*) With SIHTRC REX and the Dublin mint-signature

935	1.12	17.3	90	0/0	'*Colbrand*' (DM). *Obv*. DYFLM. Same dies as *SCBI* BM H/N 51, same *obv*. die as *SCBI* Copenhagen v 43. Dannenberg coll. 1892, ex Plonsk find 1854. Dannenberg 1871, p. 262, no. 1.
936	1.28	19.8	0	0/6	'*Færemin*' (DYFLM). *Obv*. DYFLMMI. Same dies as **937** and *SCBI* Helsinki 937. Ruehle coll. 1842.
937	1.27	19.6	90	6/8	'*Færemin*' (DYFLM). *Obv*. DYFLMMI. Same dies as **936**. Ruehle coll. 1842.
938	1.49	23.0	90	3/11	'*Færemin*' (DYFLN). *Obv*. DYFLMNIO, legend starts at 6 o'clock. Ruehle coll. 1842.
939	0.95	14.7	180	1/1	'*Siy(r)bern*' (DYFLNMR). *Obv*. DYFLINMON, legend starts at 6 o'clock. 371/1895, ex Weyl auction 127 (1893), lot 1415.
	(pierced)				

(*b*) With SIHTRC REX and an 'English' mint-signature

940	1.16	17.9	250	0/2	'*London*' (LVNDI), '*Dgdoan*'. *Obv*. DYFLNMO. 795/1914, bt. Friedensburg, probably ex Zottwitz/Sobocisko find 1902.

(*c*) With ÆÐELRED REX ANGL and the Dublin mint-signature

941	1.11	17.1	70	0/2	'*Færemin*' (DIFLN). Ruehle coll. 1842.

[*continued overleaf*]

PLATE 34

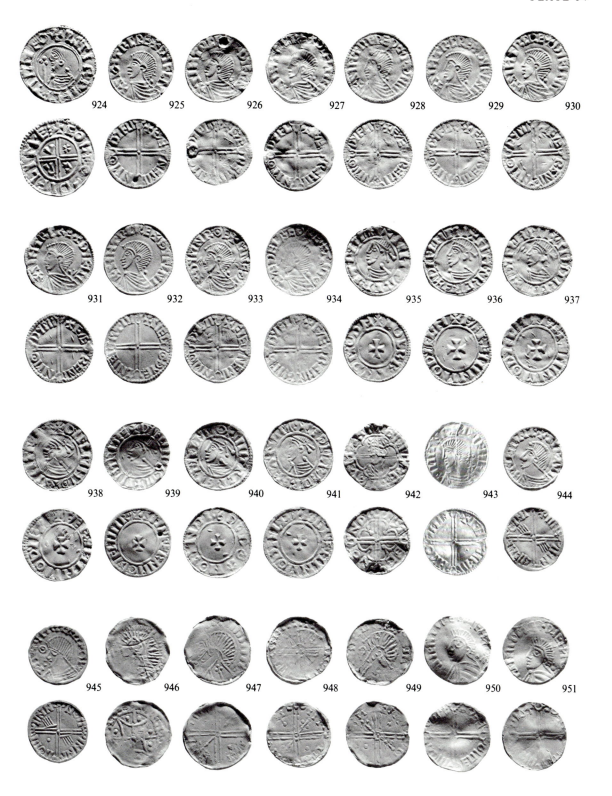

924 925 926 927 928 929 930

931 932 933 934 935 936 937

938 939 940 941 942 943 944

945 946 947 948 949 950 951

Plate 34 (*cont.*)

'Quatrefoil' imitation

With **SITERIC REX IRVM** and the Dublin mint-signature

	Weight		Die	Pecks	
	gm	gr	axis	o./r.	
942	0.83	12.8	180	0/0	*'Stegn'* (**DY**). *Obv.* legend starts at 10 o'clock. Same dies as BEH 101. Dannenberg coll. 1870. Dannenberg 1874, p. 368 (but this coin did not come from the Dobra find).

PHASE II, *c*.1020–35

Reduced-weight *'Long Cross'* imitations with blundered legends.

943	105	16.2	270	0/0	*Obv.* **+INITNRIN+IFHHC**. Small cross and two pellets behind bust. *Rev.* **+IFN / NFIN / HNO / IFMN**. Two pellets in each quarter. Ruehle coll. 1842.
	(cracked)				

PHASE III, *c*.1035–55

Further reduced-weight *'Long Cross'* imitations with blundered legends.

(*a*) With no additional emblem on *obv.* and two 'hands' on *rev.*

944	1.00	15.4	0	0/0	*Obv.* **+NHRNC+NPNI**. *Rev.* **+IIN / NIN / NFṄ / OINI**. Grote coll. 1879.

(*b*) With additional emblem on *obv.* and two 'hands' on *rev.*

945	0.98	15.1	110	0/0	*Rev.* **NOII / INNI / IOIII / NNN**. Ruehle coll. 1842.

PHASE IV, *c*.1055–65

'Scratched-die' imitations of *'Long cross'*

946	0.56	88.7	?	0/0	7/1897, ex Juura/Odenpäh find 1888. Menadier 1898c, no. 120 (as uncertain imitation). Attribution of this coin by M. Dolley.

PHASE VI, *c*. first half of 12th century

Very degraded imitations, ultimately from *'Long cross'*

947	0.55	8.5	180	0/0	Gansauge coll. 1873.
948	0.48	7.4	90	0/0	Gansauge coll. 1873.
949	0.48	7.4	340	0/0	Grote coll. 1879.

IMITATIONS OF HIBERNO-NORSE COINS

PHASE I

'Long Cross' imitations with blundered Sihtric legend

950	1.55	23.9	320	0/0	*Obv.* **+SIEIIDCIC+DYEHNOE**. *Rev.* legend retrograde **+NO / RDIII / EMIO / DEOD**. Same dies as **951**. 343/1874, ex Parlin find 1874. Cf. Menadier 1887, p. 177 (as barbarous Anglo-Saxon coin).
951	1.36	21.0	160	0/0	Same dies as **950**. Two notches. 261/1856, ex Wielowies find 1856. Cf. Menadier 1887, p. 176.

IMITATIVE SERIES

I. 'DIRECT IMITATIONS'. With both *obv.* and *rev.* imitating the same English type.

'Crux'

	Weight		Die	Pecks	
	gm	*gr*	*axis*	*o./r.*	
952	1.22	18.8	270	0/1	'Exeter' ([EA]XE), 'Elftan'. Obv. +EDELRÆD——. Same die as *SCBI* Copenhagen ii 1456, and Blackburn 1978, no. 175–7 (from Polish collections). 677/1901, ex Kinno find 1900 (not recorded in Menadier 1902).
953	1.87	28.8	90	3/12	'Southwark' (SV-ÐB), 'Byrhtric'. Obv. +ÆDELRÆD REX ANGLOX. Same *obv.* die as **954**. Blackburn 1985, no. 55(a). 1170/1898, ex Birglau/Bierzgłowo find 1898. Menadier 1898b, p. 302, no. 118 (as Brantring).
954	1.70	26.2	180	11/2	'York' (EOF), 'Alderth'. Same *obv.* die as **953**. Blackburn 1981b, p. 441, no. 10(b) but *obv.* not identical with 10(a); Blackburn 1985, no. 29(a). 1170/1898, ex Birglau/Bierzgłowo find 1898. Menadier 1898b, p. 302, no. 107.
955	1.56	24.1	320	3/2	'York' (EOFR), 'Oddaz'. Obv. Æ-ÐELRÆD REX ANGLORX. Same *rev.* die as *SCBI* Copenhagen ii 280, *SCBI* Reading 76. Blackburn 1985, no. 47(a). 1170/1898, ex Birglau/Bierzgłowo find 1898. Menadier 1898b, p. 106, no. 106 (as COLI, Colchester).
956	0.92	14.2	90	0/3	Blundered legends on *obv.* and *rev.* Right facing bust. 677/1901, ex Kinno find 1900 (not recorded in Menadier 1902).
957	1.30	20.1	320	0/0	Blundered legends on *obv.* and *rev.* Same dies as **958** and *SCBI* Copenhagen ii 1517–8. 944/1953, ex Reichsbank coll.
958	1.33	20.5	310	0/0	Same dies as **957**. 243/1978, bt. from a private collector.

'Long Cross'

A. Bust left

(a) With name 'Æthelræd'

959	1.81	28.0	340	1/2	'Chester' (LEC), 'Elewne'. Blackburn 1981a, p. 65, no. 102(f). Same dies as BEH 1515, *CNS* 1.1.9 : 468, *SCBI* Chester i 459, *SCBI* Glasgow 845. Dannenberg coll. 1870.
960	0.73	11.2	270	6/3	'Shaftesbury' ([S]CEFT), 'Goda'. Same dies as *SCBI* Copenhagen ii 1080. Square flan, cut quarter of a coin. No provenance, probably Old collection.
	(fragment)				
961	1.91	29.4	0	4/10	'Wallingford' (ÞELIG), 'Wulfnoth'. 556/1872, ex Althoefchen/Starydworek find 1872 (not recorded in Friedlaender 1877).
962	1.76	27.2	270	0/2	'York' (EO), 'Leofstan'. Pellet in first quarter. Blackburn 1981a, p. 71, no. 205(d). Same dies as BEH 758, *SCBI* Merseyside 1056. Dannenberg coll. 1892, probably ex Rummelsburg/Miastko find 1861. Dannenberg 1863, p. 41, no. 113.
963	1.72	26.5	180	2/6	Blundered *rev.* legend. Obv. +Æ-ÐELRÆD REX ANGLO. Same *obv.* die as BEH 194, *SCBI* Copenhagen ii 1662, *CNS* 16.1.8 : 1262, all linked with 'Last Small Cross' *rev.* (Lyon, van der Meer, and Dolley, die-chain K). 556/1872, ex Althoefchen/Starydworek find 1872 (not recorded in Friedlaender 1877).

(b) With name 'Cnut' (Cf. BEH Cnut B)

| 964 | 1.13 | 17.4 | 90 | 4/2 | 'Bath' (BA-ÐV), 'Elfrici'. Pellet in first quarter. Same dies as BEH 49. 677/1901, ex Kinno find 1900. Menadier 1902, p. 105, no. 98. |

(c) With blundered legends on *obv.* and *rev.*

965	1.69	26.1	180	0/8	Same dies as *CNS* 1.2.27 : 364, 1.3.34 : 756, same *obv.* die as **966** and *SCBI* Copenhagen ii 1621, *SCBI* Helsinki 957. Ruehle coll. 1842.
966	2.12	32.7	0	0/0	Same *obv.* die as **965** and *SCBI* Copenhagen ii 1612, *SCBI* Helsinki 957, *CNS* 1.2.27 : 364, 1.3.34 : 756. 1279/1905, acquired in 1905, details are unknown.
967	1.35	20.8	180	2/10	1279/1905, acquired in 1905, details unknown.
	(broken)				
968	1.90	29.3	0	0/3	Probably Old collection.
969	2.68	41.3	0	0/2	Square flan. 352/1874, bt. at Visby and probably from a Swedish hoard.

[*continued overleaf*]

PLATE 35

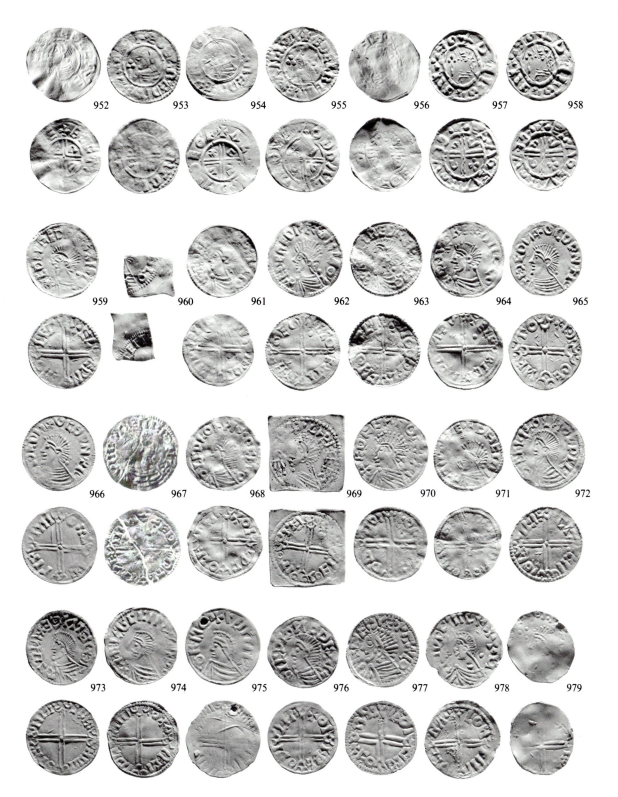

952   953   954   955   956   957   958

959   960   961   962   963   964   965

966   967   968   969   970   971   972

973   974   975   976   977   978   979

Plate 35 (*cont.*)

	Weight		Die	Pecks	
	gm	gr	axis	o./r.	
970	1.75	27.0	270	6/7	Same dies as *CNS* 1.1.9:666, same *obv.* die as *SCBI* Copenhagen ii 1567, 1581–2, *CNS* 1.4.18:2215. Ruehle coll. 1842.
971	1.44	22.2	90	4/10	Ruehle coll. 1842.
972	1.57	24.2	270	0/2	Same dies as *CNS* 16.1.5B:2. Ruehle coll. 1842.
973	1.26	19.4	230	0/1	Ruehle coll. 1842.
974	1.72	26.5	0	0/1	Same dies as *SCBI* Helsinki 965–6, same *obv.* die as *SCBI* Copenhagen ii 1475, 1605, *SCBI* Helsinki 967, *CNS* 1.4.24:154 (linked with '*Quatrefoil*' *rev.*). 121/1933, bt. Drachenfels.
975	1.50 (pierced)	23.1	0	0/4	Same dies as *SCBI* Copenhagen ii 1607. 121/1933, bt. Drachenfels.
976	1.69	26.1	40	1/3	Same dies as Blackburn and Chown, pl. 30, b (Evershof/Eversmuiza hoard, Latvia; Kluge 1981, L1). Ruehle coll. 1842.
977	1.97	30.4	270	0/2	121/1933, bt. Drachenfels.
978	1.79	27.6	90	3/0	Three pellets in front of bust and one behind. Same dies a *SCBI* Helsinki 975, same *obv.* die as *SCBI* Helsinki 976, 1021 (linked with '*Quatrefoil*' *rev.*), same *rev.* die as ibid. 1056 (linked with '*Last Small Cross*' *obv.*). Old collection.
979	1.22	18.8		1/2	Three pellets in front of bust. Provenance unrecorded, possibly ex Lupow/Łupawa find 1888.

IMITATIVE SERIES (*cont.*)

'Long Cross' (*cont.*)

B. Bust right

(*a*) With name 'Æthelræd'

	Weight		Die	Pecks	
	gm	*gr*	*axis*	*o./r.*	
980	1.36	21.0	70	0/2	'*Exeter*' (EAXE), '*Wynsige*'. *Obv.* +ÆÐELRÆD REX. *Obv.* and *rev.* legend retrograde. Same dies as **981–2** and *SCBI* Copenhagen ii 1457. Adler coll. 1821.
981	1.10	17.0	90	1/3	'*Exeter*' (EAXE), '*Wynsige*'. Same dies as **980, 982**. Dannenberg coll. 1892.
982	0.88	13.6	0	2/0	'*Exeter*' (EAXE), '*Wynsige*'. Same dies as **980–1**. 290/1897, acquired in 1897, details unknown.

(*b*) With blundered legend

983	1.99	30.7	290	0/0	Same dies as *SCBI* Copenhagen ii 1643, *SCBI* Helsinki 999. Same *obv.* die as *SCBI* Copenhagen ii 1644, *SCBI* Helsinki 1000, *CNS* 1.4.1:1598–1601. 74/1900, ex Denzin/Debczyno find 1889. Kluge 1985, no. 33.
984	1.67	25.8	70	6/1	Same dies as *SCBI* Helsinki 1001. Same *obv.* die as *CNS* 1.1.19:1765, 1.3.34:769, and 1.4.18:2236. Ruehle coll. 1842.
985	1.34	20.7	70	0/2	950/1953, ex Reichsbank coll.

C. Double reverses

986	2.11	32.5	180	5/6	Blundered legends. 40/1896, bt. Jungfer.

'Helmet'

987	1.49	22.9	180	0/5	'*London*' (LVND), '*Edwine*'. *Obv.* +EDELRED RX ANGLO. Same *obv.* die as Dolley 1981, p. 94, nos. 1–2, *SCBI* Copenhagen ii 1481, *SCBI* Helsinki 1024. 1270/1896, ex Leissow/Lisówek find 1894. Menadier 1898a, p. 176, no. 48.
988	1.55	23.9	180	1/10	+EL/MOV/DMP/LVIO. *Obv.* +EDELRED REX ANGL. 69/1893, bt. Loewenstimm, ex unknown Russian hoard.
989	1.81	27.9	180	2/0	+PO/IFSD/INIO/MIPI. *Obv.* +EDELRED REX ANGLO. Grote coll. 1879.

'Agnus Dei' (BEH Æthelræd G)

990	0.83	12.8	270	3/0	270/1892, ex Hornikau/Horniki find 1890.
	(fragment)				

'Last Small Cross'

(*a*) With name 'Æthelræd'

991	1.09	16.8	340	1/1	'*Exeter*' (EAXEN), '*Wuftiws*'. *Obv.* +[Æ]LRED RE+ ANEEO. Retrograde legend on *obv.*, R in REX inverted. Same dies as *SCBI* Copenhagen ii 1458–61, 1498. 40/1896, bt. Jungfer.
	(pierced ×3, cracked)				
992	0.95	14.7	240	1/2	'*Exeter*' (EAXEN), '*Wuftiws*'. Same retrograde *obv.* legend as before but R in REX not inverted. Same dies as **993–7**. 40/1896, bt. Jungfer.
993	0.92	14.2	250	0/0	'*Exeter*' (EAXEN), '*Wuftiws*'. Same dies as **992, 994–7**. 191/1894, ex Lodejnoe Pole find I 1875. Hess auction October 1891, lot 327 or 328.
994	0.90	13.9	180	5/12	'*Exeter*' (EAXEN), '*Wuftiws*'. Same dies as **992–3, 995–7**. 40/1896, bt. Jungfer.
995	0.88	13.6	300	2/3	'*Exeter*' (EAXEN), '*Wuftiws*'. Same dies as **992–4, 996–7**. 35/1895, bt. Jungfer.
	(cracked)				
996	0.83	12.8	210	4/7	'*Exeter*' (EAXEN), '*Wuftiws*'. Same dies as **992–5, 997**. 35/1895, bt. Jungfer.
997	0.74	11.4	90	10/2	'*Exeter*' (EAXEN), '*Wuftiws*'. Same dies as **992–6**. 354/1889, ex Londzyn/Łazyn find 1887.
	(fragment)				

Note. Nos. **991–7** were attributed by Dannenberg to the German mint Stade, Count Udo I (1034–57), on grounds of style (Dbg. 1611). For Stade two further imitations of '*Last Small Cross*' type are known with the name of Udo I (Dbg. 1610a, b) as well as '*Crux*' and '*Last Small Cross*' imitations with the name of Count Heinrich (976–1016), one of Udo's predecessors (Dbg. 1607, 1607a, 1608).

The present type is known from the Slav hoards of 'Berlin I' (Dannenberg 1857, p. 210, no. 138), Vossberg 1883 (Dannenberg 1884, p. 325, no. 472), Londzyn/Łazyn 1887 (cf. no. **997** above), Lodejnoe Pole I 1875 (cf. no. **993** above) and from the Scandinavian hoards of Munksjørup, Tørring, or Bonderup (cf. *SCBI* Copenhagen ii 1458). No. **991** is very similar to nos. **992–7** but from different dies. It seems possible that **991–2, 994–6** came from the Vossberg hoard 1883 which contained 6 specimens.

[continued overleaf]

PLATE 36

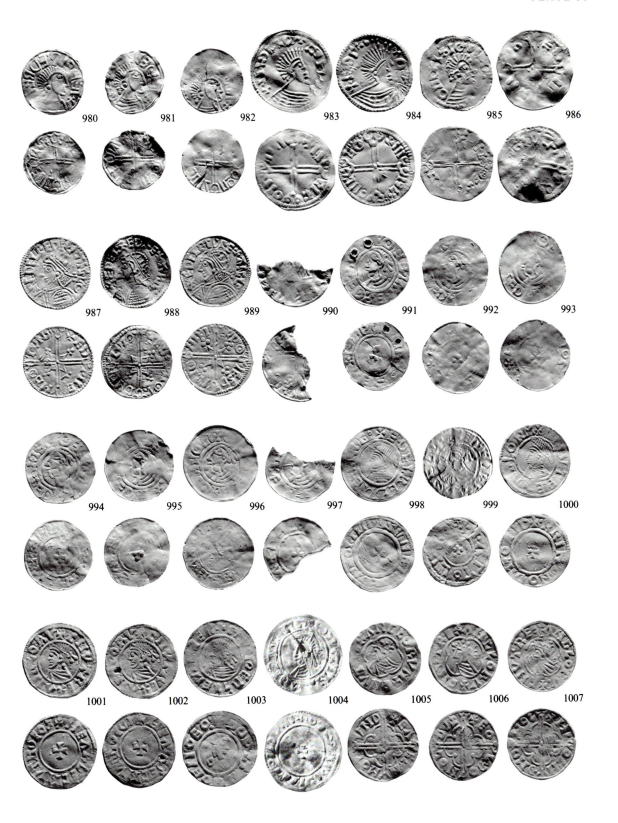

980 981 982 983 984 985 986

987 988 989 990 991 992 993

994 995 996 997 998 999 1000

1001 1002 1003 1004 1005 1006 1007

Plate 36 (*cont.*)

	Weight		Die	Pecks	
	gm	gr	axis	o./r.	
998	1.35	20.9	300	2/4	'Lincoln' (**LIIN**), 'Sumerled'. Obv. **+EÐELRÆD REX ANGO**. Same *obv.* die as *SCBI* Copenhagen ii 1473. Dannenberg coll. 1892.
999	1.02	15.7	90	6/7	'Fastolf'. Obv. **E-ÐED REX ANGLOR**. 69/1892, bt. Lange.

(*b*) With name 'Cnut' (BEH Cnut A)

1000	1.70	26.2	180	0/8	'London' (**LVD**), 'Brihtnoth'. Obv. **CNVT REX ANGLORM**. Pellet in each angle of the cross. Same dies as *SCBI* Helsinki 1045–6. Old collection.
1001	1.39	21.4	0	0/0	'York' (**EOF**), 'Heardecnut'. Obv. **CNVT REX ANGLORV**. Same dies as **1002** and BEH 639, *SCBI* Copenhagen iiia 706, *SCBI* Helsinki 1048–50 (Lyon, van der Meer, and Dolley, die-chain D). Same *obv.* die as **1034** below. Dannenberg coll. 1892, ex Plonsk find 1854. Dannenberg 1871, pp. 260–1.
1002	1.47	22.7	0	1/1	'York' (**EOF**), 'Heardecnut'. Same dies as **1001**. 589/1894, ex Mgowo find 1893.
	(pierced)				

(*c*) With blundered legends on *obv.* and *rev.*

1003	1.26	19.4	270	2/9	*Rev.* **+ÐORZTACXDEIIOEO:**, annulet and pellet in field. Same *rev.* die as *SCBI* Copenhagen ii 1466. 7/1897, ex Juura/Odenpäh find 1888. Menadier 1898c, p. 232, no. 136.
1004	1.38	21.3	270	0/4	Same dies as *CNS* 1.1.9:677 same *obv.* die as *SCBI* Copenhagen ii 1500, *SCBI* Helsinki 1052.
	(cracked)				Ruehle coll. 1842.

'Quatrefoil'

1005	1.39	21.5	270	1/0	'London' (**LVND**), 'Eaern'. Obv. **+CNVT REX ANGLORVM**. Same dies as *SCBI* Copenhagen iiib 2383, same *rev.* die as ibid. 2382. Adler coll. 1821.
1006	1.78	27.5	180	0/3	**+EOL-Ð ON OL-ÐVS**. Obv. **CNVT REX ANGLORV**. Same dies as *SCBI* Copenhagen iiic 4233, *SCBI* Helsinki 1064–5 and BEH 2998. 7/1897, ex Juura/Odenpäh find 1888. Menadier 1898c, p. 232, no. 151 (as 'Olthus', 'Eolth').
1007	1.32	20.4	90	7/11	**+HP/OLM/DMO/HOL**. Obv. **CNVT REX ANGLORV:** Ruehle coll. 1842.

'*Quatrefoil*' (*cont.*)

	Weight		Die	Pecks	
	gm	gr	axis	o./r.	
1008	1.06	16.4	340	3/5	Blundered legends. Old collection.
1009	1.73	26.7	90	0/0	+ÐVI/RLO/TOR/ENFI. *Obv.* +NTR-ÐETMXROEONI. Sceptre behind and sword in front of bust. Same dies as *SCBI* Copenhagen iiic 4290, *SCBI* Helsinki 1105. Same *obv.* die as *SCBI* Helsinki 1103–4 (linked with '*Long Cross*' *rev.*). Old collection.

'*Pointed Helmet*'

1010	1.01	15.6	240	1/3	+LEOFÞINE ON FONG. *Obv.* +CNVT REX A. 7/1897, ex Juura/Odenpäh find 1888. Menadier 1898c, p. 232, no. 154.
	(cracked)				
1011	0.89	13.7	0	0/0	+IEVSDEOFCRVEOMEI:. *Obv.* legend blundered. Same dies as *SCBI* Copenhagen iiic 4307. Adler coll. 1821.
1012	0.93	14.4	40	1/2	+EALDERER ON C+C. *Obv.* +CANLAF +CVNMLH. Ruehle coll. 1842.
	(cracked)				
1013	0.99	15.3	90	0/8	OLEICOMTERVCIENOEOCI. *Obv.* legend blundered. Same dies as *SCBI* Copenhagen iiic 4316. Adler coll. 1821.
1014	0.92	14.2	0	4/5	Same dies as *SCBI* Copenhagen iiic 4296. Old collection.
1015	0.62	9.5	90	0/3	+DVRGR——. *Obv.* Bust right, blundered legend. 926/1892, ex Runowo find 1892.
	(fragment)				

'*Short Cross*'

1016	0.97	15.0	90	5/3	Adler coll. 1821.
	(cracked)				
1017	1.01	15.6	0	10/5	Same *obv.* die as *SCBI* Copenhagen iiic 4395 (linked with '*Jewel Cross*' *rev.*). 7/1897, ex Juura/Odenpäh find 1888. Menadier 1898c, p. 232, no. 154.
1018	0.83	12.8	270	2/0	Same dies as *SCBI* Copenhagen iiic 4362. Ruehle coll. 1842.

'*Fleur-de-Lis*'

1019	1.08	16.7	0	2/0	'*Chester*' (LEIH), '*Mana*'. *Obv.* CNVT REX ANG. Dannenberg coll. 1870.

'*Pacx*'

1020	1.27	19.6	0	0/3	+ÞVLENIMODIIITS. *Obv.* +EDDO——DDHI+. Same dies as *SCBI* Midlands 362 (as Stamford?). Gansauge coll. 1873.

'*Trefoil Quadrilateral*'

1021	0.76	11.8	270	4/4	Blundered legends. Dannenberg coll. 1870, ex Simoitzel/Siemyśl find. Dannenberg 1865, p. 162, no. 77 (as *obv.* ARNGRIM, *rev.* ITIGILIEI).
	(cracked)				

II. '**IMITATIVE MULES**'. With *obv.* and *rev.* imitating different English types. Blundered legends on both sides unless otherwise indicated.

'*Crux*'/'*Intermediate Small Cross*' (Cf. BEH Æthelræd Ab)

1022	1.72	26.5	0	1/3	Blundered *rev.* legend. *Obv.* +E-ÐELRED REX ANGLOX. Same dies as *SCBI* Copenhagen ii 1522, *SCBI* Helsinki 944. Blackburn 1981a, p. 440, no. 8(l); Blackburn 1985, no. 8(l) (with further die-links). Grote coll. 1879.

'*Long Cross*'/'*Crux*'

1023	1.54	23.8	180	0/0	+[RFFENMO]NATNAI. *Obv.* +EDELRED [REX ANLO]. Square flan. Same dies as Malmer 1965, pl. 4, no. 8; Lagerquist 1970, p. 30, fig. 34 (Olof Skötkonung (*c.*995–1022), type J), *SCBI* Copenhagen ii 1677–8. 28853/1869, ex Farve find 1848. Friedlaender 1850, p. 51, no. 79. The style and legend of *rev.* and the square flan suggest that the coin was struck at Sigtuna although there is no die-link with Olof Skötkonung's coins.
	(fragment)				

'*Long Cross*'/'*Last Small Cross*' (Cf. BEH Æthelræd Ae)

1024	1.19	18.3	0	4/1	'*Canterbury*' (CNTRA), '*Leofric*'. Same dies as **1025** and *SCBI* Copenhagen ii 1452. Adler coll. 1821.
	(pierced)				

[*continued overleaf*]

PLATE 37

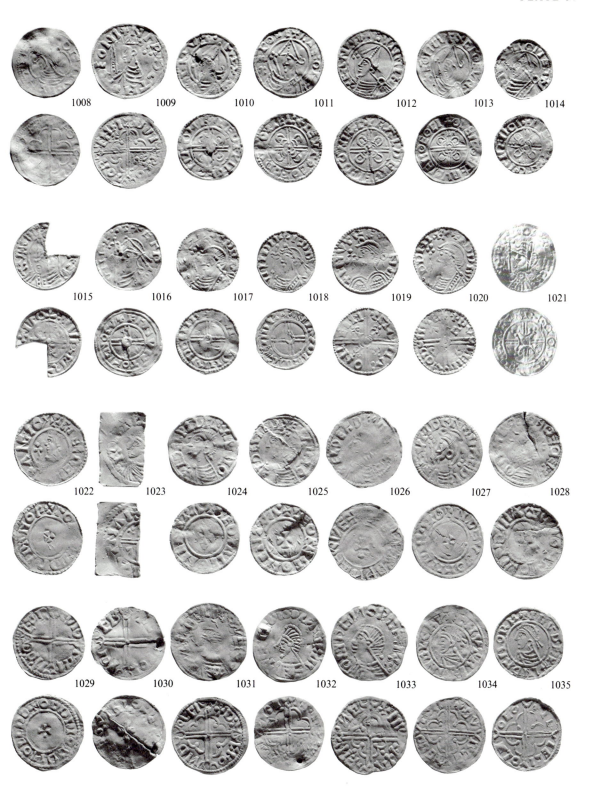

1008 1009 1010 1011 1012 1013 1014

1015 1016 1017 1018 1019 1020 1021

1022 1023 1024 1025 1026 1027 1028

1029 1030 1031 1032 1033 1034 1035

Plate 37 (*cont.*)

	Weight		Die	Pecks	
	gm	gr	axis	o./r.	
1025	1.16	17.9	0	8/21	'Canterbury' (**CNTRA**), 'Leofric'. Same dies as **1024**. Ruehle coll. 1842.
	(cracked)				
1026	1.54	23.8	270	2/0	Blundered *rev.* legend. *Obv.* **+ELDERD EX ANGLO**. Same *obv.* die as *SCBI* Copenhagen ii 1467. 75/1890, ex Denzin/Debczyno find 1889. Kluge 1985, no. 34.
1027	1.05	16.2	0	2/4	**+NOEVMOLNDCYHO**. *Obv.* **+CNMDLNOVRCDI**, sceptre in front of the bust. 170/1855, bt. Bruns, ex 'Posen' find.
1028	1.65	25.5	300	6/8	Right facing bust. Blundered legends, *obv.* legend retrograde. Same dies as *CNS* 1.1.19:1769. Same *obv.* die as *SCBI* Copenhagen ii 1642, 1676, *CNS* 1.3.34:775 (linked with 'Wilton', 'Leofwine'). 7/1897, ex Juura/Odenpäh find 1888. Menadier 1898c, p. 232, no. 136.
	(cracked)				
1029	1.41	21.8	0	0/0	Double reverses. Friedlaender coll. 1861, ex 'Frankfurt' find 1840. Friedlaender 1843, p. 160, no. 78.
1030	1.58	24.4	40	0/0	Double reverses. 40/1896, bt. Jungfer.
	(pierced and cracked)				

'*Long Cross*'/'*Quatrefoil*' (Cf. BEH Cnut Ef)

1031	1.73	26.7	180	3/1	Ruehle coll. 1842.
	(pierced)				
1032	1.37	21.1	270	9/7	Same dies as *SCBI* Helsinki 1019–20. Old collection.
	(pierced)				
1033	1.21	18.7	90	1/3	Same dies as *SCBI* Helsinki 1022–3, same *obv.* die as *CNS* 1.1.9:672 (linked with '*Long Cross*' *rev.*) and *CNS* 1.2.27:369, 1.4.24:155. Ruehle coll. 1842.

'*Last Small Cross*'/'*Quatrefoil*' (Cf. BEH Cnut Eg)

1034	1.41	21.8	180	1/0	'Torksey' (**TOR**), 'Thurcetel'. *Obv.* **+CNVT REX ANGLORV**. Same dies as *SCBI* Helsinki 1060–1. Same *obv.* die as **1001–2** above and *SCBI* Helsinki 1048–51, *SCBI* Copenhagen iiia 706, all linked with '*Last Small Cross*' *rev.* Same *rev.* die as *SCBI* Copenhagen iiic 3880–1, linked with '*Quatrefoil*' *obv.* 370/1895, ex Weyl auction 127 (1893), lot 1302.
1035	1.21	18.7	270	0/0	**+IC/IECI/OLM/OEO**. *Obv.* **CNVD REX IN DANORM**. This regular Danish *obv.* die is normally linked with *rev.* dies of '*Last Small Cross*' type with a Lund mint-signature (cf. Hauberg 1900, p. 190, no. 1), but it is unpublished with a '*Quatrefoil*' *rev.* Same *obv.* die as Friedlaender 1877, no. 191 (ex Althoefchen/Starydworek find 1872 with blundered '*Last Small Cross*' *rev.* from Lund). 166/1894, ex Lodejnoe Pole I find 1878. Hess auction October 1891, lot 1107.

IMITATIVE SERIES *(cont.)*

'Last Small Cross'/*'Quatrefoil'* *(cont.)*

	Weight		Die	Pecks	
	gm	gr	axis	o./r.	
1036	1.37	21.1	270	0/0	Blundered legends. Ruehle coll. 1842.

III. 'DERIVATIVE IMITATIONS'. Imitations of 11th-century English types in a degraded (or variant) form.

A. *'Lupow' types*

The 1888 hoard from Lupow/Łupawa (Poland) is the largest hoard of imitations of 11th-century coins in Europe. Unfortunately it was dispersed and has never been described (cf. pp. 27–8 above).

The following coins from that part of the hoard which is preserved in the Berlin coin-cabinet should give a first survey of the imitations of English types in this remarkable hoard. The 'mint' of these coins, we may anticipate, was probably in Pomerania. Coins of analogous types and of Slav workmanship from other Slav hoards or without hoard provenance are also included.

'Long Cross' derivatives

1037	1.04	16.0		0/0	Bust right. Hoffmann coll. 1930, ex Lupow/Łupawa find 1888.
	(fragment)				
1038	0.96	14.8		8/12	*'Long Cross'* obv./German *'Sachsenpfennig'* rev. Same obv. die as **1039**. 187/1888, ex Lupow/Łupawa find 1888.
1039	1.21	18.7	30	14/0	Same *'Long Cross'* obv. die as **1038**, and with *'Fleur-de-Lis'* obv. Old collection.
1040	1.29	19.9		2/2	Grote coll. 1879.
1041	1.55	23.9		3/0	*'Long Cross'* bust right with sceptre. Grote coll. 1879.
1042	1.28	19.8		6/3	*'Long Cross'* rev. Same dies as **1043**. Hoffmann coll. 1930, ex Lupow/Łupawa find 1888.
1043	0.83	12.8		0/2	*'Long Cross'* rev. Same dies as **1042**. Hoffmann coll. 1930, ex Lupow/Łupawa find 1888.
1044	0.88	13.6		2/0	*'Long Cross'* rev. The other side seems to be copied from the reverse of the *'Canopy'* type of William I. Hoffmann coll. 1930, ex Lupow/Łupawa find 1888.

'Last Small Cross' derivatives

1045	1.72	26.5	120	0/2	Same dies as **1046–7**. Same obv. die as Fiala 1916, pl. vi, 7 (ex Lupow/Łupawa find 1888, uniface). Friedlaender coll. 1861, ex 'Frankfurt' find 1840. Friedlaender 1843, no. 79.
1046	1.14	17.6		0/0	Same dies as **1045**, **1047**. Hoffmann coll. 1930, ex Lupow/Łupawa find 1888.
1047	0.94	14.5		0/0	Same dies as **1045–6**. Hoffmann coll. 1930, ex Lupow/Łupawa find 1888.
1048	1.11	17.1	0	3/1	Old collection.
1049	0.87	13.5		1/0	Hoffmann coll. 1930, ex Lupow/Łupawa find 1888.
1050	1.07	16.5		19/2	Hoffmann coll. 1930, ex Lupow/Łupawa find 1888.
1051	1.08	16.7		3/5	Bust right. Hoffmann coll. 1930, ex Lupow/Łupawa find 1888.
1052	0.86	13.3		0/0	*'Long Cross'* bust with cross behind. Same die as **1053**. Hoffmann coll. 1930, ex Lupow/Łupawa find 1888.
1053	1.05	16.2		3/6	Same dies as **1052**. Hoffmann coll. 1930, ex Lupow/Łupawa find 1888.
1054	1.18	18.2		3/0	Bust right. The rev. seems to be copied from *'Crux'* type. Dannenberg coll. 1892.
1055	1.79	27.6		2/4	Bust right. *'Short cross'* rev. Same dies as **1056**. Ruehle coll. 1842.
1056	1.36	21.0		1/5	Same dies as **1055**. 258/1892, ex Hornikau/Horniki find 1890.
1057	1.28	19.8		1/8	Bust left. *'Arm-and-Sceptre'* rev. Hoffmann coll. 1930, ex Lupow/Łupawa find 1888.
1058	1.00	15.5		3/0	Bust left and sceptre in front of bust. Non-English rev. Hoffmann coll. 1930, ex Lupow/Łupawa find 1888.
1059	1.26	19.4		7/7	Hoffmann coll. 1930, ex Lupow/Łupawa find 1888.
	(cracked)				

'Quatrefoil' derivatives

(a) With *'Quatrefoil'* obv.

1060	0.65	10.0		0/0	*'Helmet'* rev. Cf. rev. of **1128–9** (different die). Obv. copies the York *Quatrefoil* style. Hoffmann coll. 1930, ex Lupow/Łupawa find 1888.
	(fragment)				

(b) With *'Quatrefoil'* rev.

1061	1.99	30.7		0/0	*'Last Small Cross'* rev. Octagonal flan. 40/1896, bt. Jungfer.
1062	1.70	26.2		2/2	*'Last Small Cross'* obv., right facing bust. 14/1851, ex Ploetzig/Plocko find 1850.
1063	1.57	24.3		1/3	Hoffmann coll. 1930, ex Lupow/Łupawa find 1888.

PLATE 38

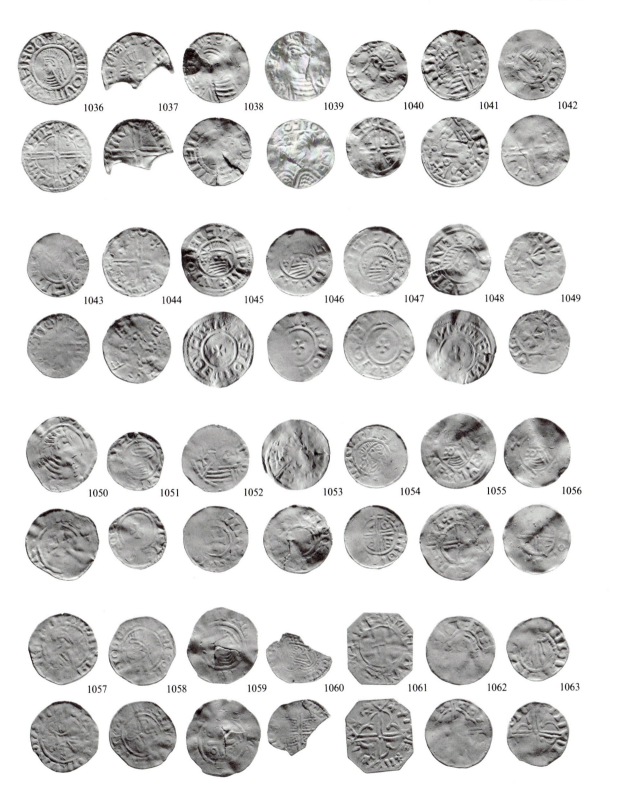

1036   1037   1038   1039   1040   1041   1042

1043   1044   1045   1046   1047   1048   1049

1050   1051   1052   1053   1054   1055   1056

1057   1058   1059   1060   1061   1062   1063

'*Quatrefoil*' derivatives (*cont.*)

	Weight		Pecks	
	gm	gr	o./r.	
1064	1.03	15.9	3/7	Same dies as **1065-6**. Hoffmann coll. 1930, ex Lupow/Łupawa find 1888.
1065	0.86	13.2	3/1	Same dies as **1064**, **1066**. Hoffmann coll. 1930, ex Lupow/Łupawa find 1888.
1066	0.87	13.5	2/0	Same dies as **1064-5**. Hoffmann coll. 1930, ex Lupow/Łupawa find 1888.
1067	0.93	14.4	4/4	Hoffmann coll. 1930, ex Lupow/Łupawa find 1888.
1068	0.75	11.6	4/5	Hoffmann coll. 1930, ex Lupow/Łupawa find 1888.
	(fragment)			
1069	1.55	23.9	5/0	Hoffmann coll. 1930, ex Lupow/Łupawa find 1888.
1070	1.42	21.9	8/4	Hoffmann coll. 1930, ex Lupow/Łupawa find 1888.
1071	0.81	12.5	0/2	Hoffmann coll. 1930, ex Lupow/Łupawa find 1888.

'*Pointed Helmet*' derivatives

(*a*) With '*Pointed Helmet*' *obv.* and *rev.*

1072	1.39	21.5	8/4	Same dies as **1073-5**. Hoffmann coll. 1930, ex Lupow/Łupawa find 1888.
1073	1.35	20.8	7/8	Same dies as **1072**, **1074-5**. Old collection.
1074	1.12	17.3	0/2	Same dies as **1072-3**, **1075**. 951/1953, ex Reichsbank coll.
1075	1.06	16.3	2/5	Same dies as **1072-4**. Hoffmann coll. 1930, ex Lupow/Łupawa find 1888.
1076	1.32	20.3	0/2	Hoffmann coll. 1930, ex Lupow/Łupawa find 1888.
1077	1.06	16.4	0/0	Same dies as **1078**. Hoffmann coll. 1930, ex Lupow/Łupawa find 1888.
1078	0.91	14.1	0/0	Same dies as **1077**. Ruehle coll. 1842.
1079	1.25	19.3	0/0	Same dies as **1080**. Hoffmann coll. 1930, ex Lupow/Łupawa find 1888.
1080	0.81	12.5	0/0	Same dies as **1079**. Hoffmann coll. 1930, ex Lupow/Łupawa find 1888.

(*b*) With '*Pointed Helmet*' *obv.*

1081	1.10	17.0	0/0	'*Short Cross*' *rev.* 390/1930, acquired in 1930, details unknown.
1082	1.25	19.3	0/4	'*Short Cross*' *rev.* 430/1894, ex Daber/Dobra find 1894.
1083	0.95	14.6	1/5	'*Short Cross*' *rev.* 953/1953, ex Reichsbank coll.
1084	1.26	19.4	3/2	'*Short Cross*' *rev.* Same dies as **1085**, same *obv.* die as **1086**. Hoffmann coll. 1930, ex Lupow/Łupawa find 1888.
1085	0.85	13.1	10/0	'*Short Cross*' *rev.* Same dies as **1084**, same *obv.* die as **1086**. Hoffmann coll. 1930, ex Lupow/Łupawa find 1888.
1086	1.38	21.3	1/1	'*Short Cross*' *rev.* Same *obv.* die as **1084-5**. Hoffmann coll. 1930, ex Lupow/Łupawa find 1888.
1087	0.89	13.8	0/2	'*Short Cross*' *rev.* Hoffmann coll. 1930, ex Lupow/Łupawa find 1888.
1088	1.08	16.7	2/3	'*Trefoil Quadrilateral*' *rev.* Same dies as **1089**. Cf. Hauberg 1900, p. 194, pl. iii, 27 where this coin is attributed to Cnut as king of Denmark, mint Roskilde (probably same dies). Old collection.
1089	1.06	16.4	7/6	'*Trefoil Quadrilateral*' *rev.* Same dies as **1088**. Hoffmann coll. 1930, ex Lupow/Łupawa find 1888.

(*c*) With '*Pointed Helmet*' *rev.*

1090	0.96	14.8	0/2	Hoffmann coll. 1930, ex Lupow/Łupawa find 1888.
1091	1.04	16.0	0/1	187/1888, ex Lupow/Łupawa find 1888.

PLATE 39

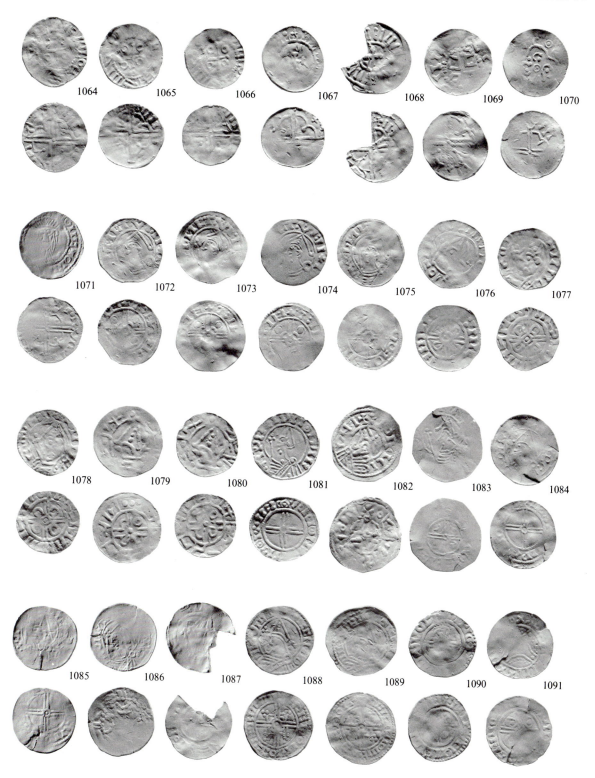

1064 1065 1066 1067 1068 1069 1070

1071 1072 1073 1074 1075 1076 1077

1078 1079 1080 1081 1082 1083 1084

1085 1086 1087 1088 1089 1090 1091

'*Pointed Helmet*' derivatives (*cont.*)

	Weight		Pecks	
	gm	gr	o./r.	
1092	0.84	13.0	2/1	Hoffmann coll. 1930, ex Lupow/Łupawa find 1888.
1093	1.12	17.3	0/0	Hoffmann coll. 1930, ex Lupow/Łupawa find 1888.
1094	1.07	11.9	3/7	Hoffmann coll. 1930, ex Lupow/Łupawa find 1888.

'*Short Cross*' derivatives

(*a*) With '*Short Cross*' *obv.* and *rev.*

1095	0.86	13.3	0/1	Same dies as **1096**. 535/1897, bt. Weyl, ex unknown Polish find.
1096	0.64	10.0	1/0	Same dies as **1095**. 952/1953, ex Reichsbank coll.
1097	0.97	15.0	1/0	Same dies as *SCBI* Copenhagen iiic 4370, 4383 (Lupow/Łupawa find 1888), and Fiala 1916, pl. vi, 5. Same *obv.* die as **1098**. Hoffmann coll. 1930, ex Lupow/Łupawa find 1888.
1098	0.83	12.8	3/1	Uniface. Same *obv.* die as **1097**. Old collection.

(*b*) With '*Short Cross*' *rev.*

1099	1.56	24.1	3/2	With blundered **S / COLONI / A**. Dbg. 1297; Hävernick 1935, p. 41, pl. 39, no. 121. Provenance uncertain, probably ex Lodejnoe Pole I find 1878. Hess auction October 1891, lot 566.
1100	0.85	13.1	0/0	Hoffmann coll. 1930, ex Lupow/Łupawa find 1888.
1101	1.08	16.7	1/0	Hoffmann coll. 1930, ex Lupow/Łupawa find 1888.
1102	1.02	15.7	1/0	Hoffmann coll. 1930, ex Lupow/Łupawa find 1888.
1103	1.43	22.1	2/2	Hoffmann coll. 1930, ex Lupow/Łupawa find 1888.
1104	0.57	8.8	2/1	Hoffmann coll. 1930, ex Lupow/Łupawa find 1888.
1105	0.88	13.6	0/0	Hoffmann coll. 1930, ex Lupow/Łupawa find 1888.

'*Fleur-de-Lis*' derivatives

(*a*) With '*Fleur-de-Lis*' *obv.*

1106	1.33	20.5	3/0	Cnut '*Short Cross*' *rev.* Same *obv.* die as **1107–8**. Hoffmann coll. 1930, ex Lupow/Łupawa find 1888.
1107	0.89	13.7	8/7	With *rev.* of Cologne (**S / COLONI / A**, blundered, cf. **1099**). Same dies as **1108**, same *obv.* die as **1106**.
(chipped)				Dbg. 1780; Hauberg 1900, pp. 124–5, pl. vii, 17; Hävernick 1935, p. 50, no. 176. 187/1888, ex Lupow/Łupawa find 1888.
1108	1.06	16.3	3/3	Same dies as **1107**, same *obv.* die as **1106–7**. 20/1894, bt. Jungfer, ex unknown Polish find.

(*b*) With '*Fleur-de-Lis*' *rev.*

1109	1.24	19.1	0/0	Same dies as *SCBI* Copenhagen iiic 4409. Same *rev.* die (head) as **1116–19** and Dbg. 1319 (linked with '*Sachsenpfennig*' *obv.*). 187/1888, ex Lupow/Łupawa find 1888.
1110	1.39	21.5	2/2	Same dies as **1111–12**. Hoffmann coll. 1930, ex Lupow/Łupawa find 1888.
1111	0.96	14.8	2/3	Same dies as **1110, 1112**. Hoffmann coll. 1930, ex Lupow/Łupaw find 1888.
1112	0.95	14.6	2/1	Same dies as **1110–11**. Hoffmann coll. 1930, ex Lupow/Łupawa find 1888.
1113	0.69	10.7	2/8	Hoffmann coll. 1930, ex Lupow/Łupawa find 1888.

'*Trefoil Quadrilateral*' derivatives

(*a*) With '*Trefoil Quadrilateral*' *obv.* and *rev.*

1114	1.03	15.9	3/3	Same dies as **1115**, same *obv.* die as **1116–19**. 40/1896, bt. Jungfer.
1115	0.76	11.8	5/0	Same dies as **1114**, same *obv.* die as **1116–19**. Hoffmann coll. 1930, ex Lupow/Łupawa find
(chipped)				1888.

(*b*) With '*Trefoil Quadrilateral*' *obv.*

1116	1.29	19.9	12/4	Same dies as **1117–19**, same *obv.* die as **1114–15**, same *rev.* die (head) as **1109**. 187/1888, ex Lupow/Łupawa find 1888.
1117	1.19	18.4	2/6	Same dies as **1116, 1118–19**. Hoffmann coll. 1930, ex Lupow/Łupawa find 1888.
1118	1.17	18.1	6/1	Same dies as **1116–17** and **1119**. 187/1888, ex Lupow/Łupawa find 1888.
1119	0.91	14.0	7/2	Same dies as **1116–18**. 187/1888, ex Lupow/Łupawa find 1888.

Note: The types of nos. **1114–19** also occurred in the 'Berlin I' find, Dannenberg 1857, pp. 208–9, nos. 134–5, pl. ix.

From the degraded '*Trefoil Quadrilateral*' *obv.* die a further die-link is known with an imitation of Cologne, **S / COLONI / A** type (Hävernick 1935, p. 62, pl. 42, 241 (Dresden)).

PLATE 40

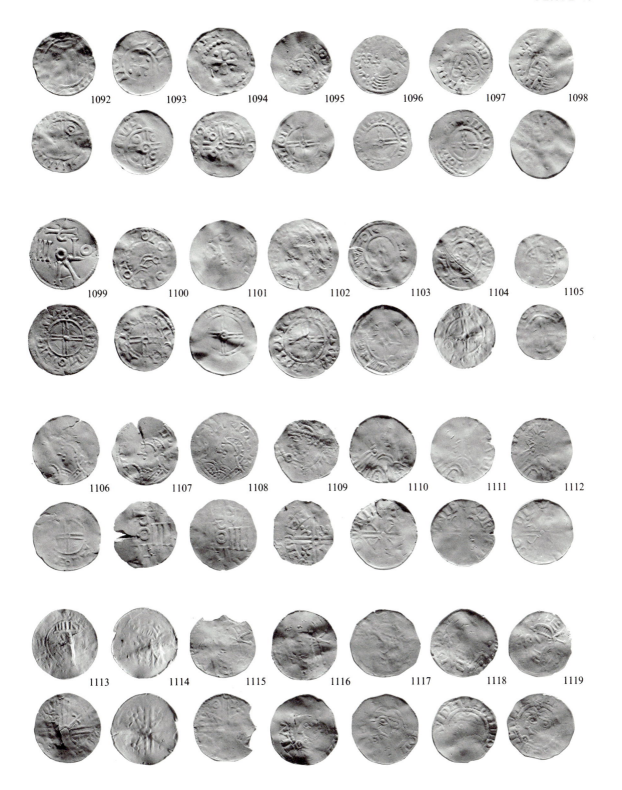

1092   1093   1094   1095   1096   1097   1098

1099   1100   1101   1102   1103   1104   1105

1106   1107   1108   1109   1110   1111   1112

1113   1114   1115   1116   1117   1118   1119

'*Trefoil Quadrilateral*' derivatives (*cont.*)

(*c*) With '*Trefoil Quadrilateral*' *rev.*

	Weight		Pecks	
	gm	*gr*	*o./r.*	
1120	1.57	24.2	2/0	187/1888, ex Lupow/Łupawa find 1888.
1121	1.05	16.2	0/0	187/1888, ex Lupow/Łupawa find 1888.
1122	1.31	20.2	1/1	187/1888, ex Lupow/Łupawa find 1888.
1123	0.98	15.1	4/1	Hoffmann coll. 1930, ex Lupow/Łupawa find 1888.
1124	1.21	18.7	0/0	Same '*Trefoil Quadrilateral*' *rev.* die as **1125**. Hoffmann coll. 1930, ex Lupow/Łupawa find 1930.
1125	1.11	17.1	0/0	Same '*Trefoil Quadrilateral*' *rev.* die as **1124**. Hoffmann coll. 1930, ex Lupow/Łupawa find 1888.

Derivatives with bust of types of Edward the Confessor

1126	0.84	13.0	2/0	✠ED////RE✠. Cross on *rev.* Old collection.
1127	1.02	15.7	3/4	Blundered legend. Cross with pellets in angles on *rev.* Hoffmann coll. 1930, ex Lupow/Łupawa find 1888.

B. Æthelræd II '*Long Cross*' derivatives of non-Lupow style, but probably of Slav origin.

'*Long Cross*' *obv.*/'*Helmet*' *rev.*

1128	1.36	21.0	0/3	Same dies as **1129** and *SCBI* Copenhagen iiic 4397 (Lupow/Łupawa find 1888). Cf. *rev.* of **1060**, different die. Ruehle coll. 1842.
1129	1.26	19.4	0/2	Same dies as **1128**. Old collection.

'*Long Cross*' *obv.*/'*Byzantine*' *rev.*

1130	1.47	22.7	0/0	'*Long Cross*' bust with sceptre. *Rev.* Standing figure with cross-banner in the right and cross in the left hand. Same dies as **1131–2** and Hauberg 1900, p. 213, pl. viii, 2. Old collection.
1131	1.37	21.1	1/3	Same dies as **1130, 1132**. Grote coll. 1879.
1132	1.35	20.8	0/0	Same dies as **1130–1**. No provenance, possibly ex Lupow/Łupawa find 1888.

Note. The type of nos. **1130–2** was attributed by Hauberg 1900, p. 213, no. 2 to Denmark, Svend Estridsen (1047–75) and the mint of Lund. The style is that of nos. **1128–9**.

FORGERIES

	Weight		Die	
	gm	*gr*	*axis*	
151	1.55	23.9	270	King Ecgberht of Wessex (802–39). Portrait/**DOROB C** monogram. *Svehe.* *Obv.* ✠ECGBEARHT REX. 926/1905, ex Murdoch 62, ex Nunn 72, ex Marsham 129, ex Wrighton 49. Emery forgery. Pagan 1971, p. 154, no. 3(b).

PLATE 41

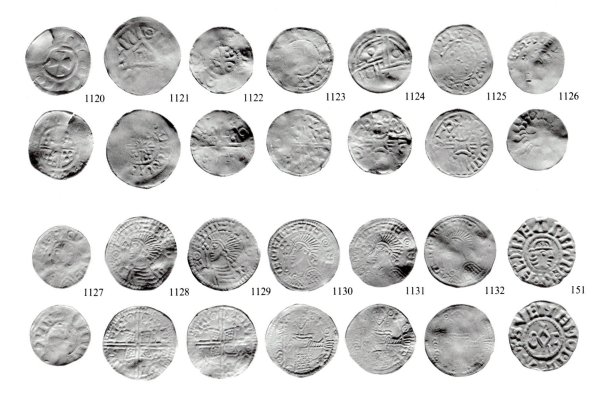

1120   1121   1122   1123   1124   1125   1126

1127   1128   1129   1130   1131   1132   151

INDEX OF MINTS

The arrangement follows *SCBI* Cumulative Index of vols. 1–20 (Smart 1981). The abbreviations of the rulers' names and types are set out in 'Abbreviations', p. 41 above.

AESDE see Hastings?

Barnstaple
[Cn E] 594
Bath
[Æth II C] 236
[Æth II D] 336–8
[Æth II E] 465
[Cn E] 595–6
[Edw III B] 850
imitation 964
Bedford
[Edwg ii] 185
[Æth II C] 237
Bristol
[Cn E (Ed)] 597–8
[Cn H] 749

Cadbury
[Æth II A] 501
Cambridge
[Æth II C] 238–43
[Æth II D] 339
[Cn E] 599
[Cn G] 677–8
[Cn H] 750
[Wm I viii] 895
[Wm II iii] 910
Canterbury
[Cn w] 73
[Ecgb Kent] 84
[Bldr] 85
[Abp Wfr] 86–7
[Abp Cln] 88
[Ecgb] 150, (151) forgery
[Æthst viii] 167
[Æth II B1] 199
[Æth II B2] 222–4
[Æth II B3] 232
[Æth II C] 245–8
[Æth II Ca] 324–6
[Æth II D] 340–2
[Æth II A] 502–4
[Cn E] 600–1
[Cn G] 679–80
[Cn H] 751–2
[Edw III A] 830
[Edw III G] 872
[Wm II iii] 911
imitations 1024–5

Chester
[Æthst vc] 175
[Æth II D] 343–5
[Æth II E] 466–7
[Æth II A] 505–9
[Cn E] 602–3
[Cn G] 681–2
[Har I A] 786
[Edw III D] 825
[Edw III G] 873
[Edw III I] 883
[Wm II iii] 912
imitations 959, 1019
Chichester
[Æth II D] 346–7
[Cn H] 753
Colchester
[Æth II C] 249–50
[Æth II Ca] 327
[Æth II D] 348
[Cn E] 604
[Cn H] 754
[Edw III C] 843
[Edw III B] 851
Crewkerne
[Cn H] 755
Cricklade
[Æth II D] 349
[Æth II A] 510
'Cuer'
[Æth II B1] 221

Dorchester
[Æth II C] 251
Dover
[Æth II Ca] 328
[Æth II D] 350–1
[Æth II A] 511
[Æth II Aa] 593
[Cn G] 683
[Cn H] 756–7
Dublin
[HibN phase I] 924–39, 941–2

Exeter
[Æth II B1] 200–2
[Æth II C] 252–4
[Æth II Ca] 329
[Æth II D] 352–7

Maldon
   [Æth II C] 290–1
   [Edw III F] 863
Milborne Port
   [Æth II D] 426
   [Cn G] 725

Northampton
   [Æth II A1] 197
   [Æth II B1] 209
   [Æth II D] 427–9
   [Har I B] 811
   [HCn B] 820
   [Edw III D] 827
Norwich
   [Æthst viii] 173
   [Æth II B1] 210
   [Æth II C] 292
   [Æth II D] 430–1
   [Æth II E] 493
   [Æth II A] 555
   [Cn E] 645–8
   [Cn G] 726–8
   [Har I A] 791
   [Har I B] 812
   [HCn = Cn I] 821
   [Edw III F] 864
   [Edw III Ac] 881
   [Wm II iii] 916

Oxford
   [Edg vi] 190
   [Æth II C] 293
   [Æth II D] 432–3
   [Æth II E] 494–5
   [Cn E] 649
   [Cn G] 729–30
   [Har I A] 792
   [Edw III D] 828
   [Edw III F] 865
   [Edw III H] 870
   [Hen I xi] 918

Peterborough
   [Cn E] 650

'Quentovic'
   [Vikings of Northumbria] 143

'Rocce'
   [Edw III C] 849
Rochester
   [Cnw] 72
   [Æth II B1] 211
   [Æth II C] 294
   [Æth II Ca] 333
   [Æth II A] 556
Romney
   [Wm I i] 890

Salisbury
   [Æth II A] 557
   [Cn E] 651
   [Cn G] 731
   [Cn H] 776
   [Wm II i] 909
Shaftesbury
   [Æth II C] 295–6
   [Æth II D] 434
   [Æth II A] 558
   [Har I A] 793
   imitation 960
Shrewsbury
   [Æth II D] 435
   [Æth II A] 559
   [Har I A] 794
Southampton
   [Æth II C] 297
   [Æth II E] 496
   [Cn E] 652
Southwark
   [Æth II C] 298–301
   [Æth II D] 436
   [Cn E] 653
   [Cn G] 732–3
   [Edw III D] 829
   [Wm I viii] 899
   imitation 953
Southwark/Sudbury
   [Æth II C] 302–5
   [Æth II D] 437
Stafford
   [Æth II C] 306
Stamford
   [Edg vi] 191–2
   [Edw II A] 195
   [Æth II B1] 212
   [Æth II C] 307
   [Æth II D] 438–40
   [Æth II E] 497
   [Æth II A] 560–5
   [Cn E] 654–5
   [Cn H] 777
   [Har I A] 795–6
   [Har I B] 813–14
   [Edw III G] 874
Steyning
   [Cn H] 778
   [Wm II iii] 917
Sudbury
   [Cn E] 656
   cf. Southwark/Sudbury

Tamworth
   [Æth II E] 498
Taunton
   [Cn E] 657
Thetford
   [Edg vi] 193
   [Edw II A] 196

INDEX OF MONEYERS

The names of the moneyers are recorded in the normalized form according to the Index of Personal Names in *SCBI Cumulative Index of vols.* 1–20 (Smart 1981). The actual spellings as they appear on the coins are specified only if they differ from the normalized form. Imitations are not indexed. The abbreviations of the rulers' names and types are set out in 'Abbreviations', p. 41 above.

Abba
  [Edw I] 159
  [Æthst i] 162
Abenel
  ABONEL [Æthst i] 163
  Hertford ABONEL [Æthst viii] 168
Ada
  Cambridge [Cn G] 677
Adalbert?
  AOLERII [St Edm] 97
Adrad
  ADRADVS [St Edm] 95
Ælfgar
  Lewes [Æth II D] 361
  London [Æth II C] 266
  Southwark [Cn G] 732
  Stamford [Æth II C] 307
  Tamworth [Æth II E] 498
  Thetford [Edg vi] 193
Ælfgeat
  Hereford ÆLFGET [Æth II D] 358
Ælfheah
  Winchester ÆLFEH [Cn H] 780
Ælfmær
  Exeter [Æth II E] 468
Ælfnoth
  Chester ELENOD [Æth II A] 507
  Exeter [Æth II E] 469
  Lincoln [Cn H] 758
    [Har I A] 787
    ALFNAD [Edw III B] 853
Ælfræd
  Canterbury ÆLERED [Æth II A] 502
    ÆLFRED [Æth II A] 503
    [Cn H] 751
    ÆLFRYD [Æth II D] 340
  London ÆLFRED [Cn I = HCn] 819
Ælfric
  Bath [Æth II D] 336
  Cambridge [Æth II C] 238
  London [Æth II A] 531
  Norwich [Æth II D] 430–1
    ALFRI [Wm II iii] 916
Ælfsige
  Chester ÆLFS [Edw III I] 883
    ALESIGE [Edw II G] 873 → Ealhsige?
    ELCSIGE [Æth II A] 506 → Ealhsige?

  Lincoln [Æth II D] 364–6
    ÆLFSI [Æth II D] 363
  Winchester (chipped) [Æth II C] 315
    [Cn E] 660
Ælfstan
  ELFSTAN [Abp Pl] 89
  Chester [Æth II D] 343–4
    [Æth II E] 466–7
  Exeter [Æth II B1] 200
    [Æth II C] 252
  London [Æth II Ca] 330
    ELFSTAN [Edw III B] 855
  Lydford [Æth II D] 425
  Totnes [Æth II D] 445–6
  Winchester [Cn E] 661
Ælfweald > -wald/-wold
  Bath ALFFALD [Cn E] 595
  Norwich ELFCFALD [Har I A] 791
  Stafford ALFFOLD [Æth II C] 306
  Thetford ALFFOLD [Har I A] 797
Ælfweard > -ward/-werd
  Lewes ÆLFFERD [Cn E] 614
  London ÆLFFERD [Cn G] 702
  Southampton ÆLFFERD [Cn E] 652
  Southwark ÆLFFERD [Cn E] 653
  Thetford ALF[FARD] [Hen xiii] 920
Ælfwig > -wi
  Cambridge [Cn H] 750
  London [Cn G] 703
    ÆLFFI [Æth II A] 532–3
    [Edw III C] 845–6
    ELEFFI [Cn E] 630 → Ælfwine
  Oxford ÆLFI [Edw III D] 828
  Southwark/Sudbury ÆLFFI [Æth II C] 303
Ælfwine
  Bristol [Cn Ed] 597
  Cadbury [Æth II A] 501
  Cambridge [Æth II C] 239
  Colchester ELFFINE [Edw III C] 843
  Dover [Cn H] 756
  Ilchester [Cn E] 612
  London [Æth II C] 267
    [Æth II Ca] 331
    [Æth II D] 380–1
    [Æth II A] 534
    [Cn H] 763
    ÆFI [Wm I viii] 897 → Eadwig

Dodda (*cont.*)
  Totnes (*cont.*)
    [Æth II B2] 231
    DODA [Æth II C] 310
Drengr
  Lincoln DRENG [Æth II D] 372–3
    [Æth II A] 518
Dropa
  Winchcombe [Cn G] 737
Dud/Dud(d)a
  Canterbury DVDA [Æth II B3] 232
    [Æth II C] 244
Dudwine
  [Bgr a] 77
Dunstan
  Exeter [Æth II D] 352–3
  London [Cn E] 625
Durand
  [Edg i] 187
  Worcester DVRANT [Æth II C] 320

Eadbeorht
  EADBERHT [Offa] 65
Eadgar
  Thetford [Æth II C] 308
    ÆADGAR [Æth II B1] 213
Eadmær
  Exeter EDMÆR [Edw III A] 831
Eadmund
  London [Æth II C] 271–2
    [Æth II D] 391
    [Cn H] 767
    EDMVND [Æth II D] 394
  Norwich EDMVND [Cn E] 645
Eadnoth
  Huntingdon [Cn E] 610
  London EADNOD [Cn E] 626
Eadric
  Cambridge EDRIC [Æth II C] 240
  Ipswich EDRIC [Cn E] 613
  Langport EDRIC [Cn G] 688
  London EDRIC [Wm I viii] 898
    EDRICC [Cn G] 707
  Taunton EDRIC [Cn E] 657
  Wallingford EDRIC [Æth II D] 447
  York [Æth II D] 458
Eadsige
  London EADSI [Cn E] 627
    EDSIGE [Æth II C] 274
    [Æth II D] 395
    [Æth II A] 539–40
  Rochester EDSIGE [Æth II C] 294
  Winchester EDSIGE [Æth II C] 318
Eadstan
  'Æsthe' [Æth II C] 255
  Bath EDSTAN [Æth II D] 337
  'Cuer' EATSTAN [Æth II B1] 221
Eadwacer
  Norwich EDFECÆR [Æth II A] 555

Eadweald
  Canterbury EADFOLD [Æth II B1] 199
    [Æth II B2] 223
    [Æth II Ca] 324
    [Æth II A] 504
  London EADFOLD [Æth II C] 273
    [Æth II D] 393
    [Cn H] 768
    [Edw III A] 835
    EDFOLD [Cn E] 629
Eadweard
  London EADFERD [Æth II A] 537
  Rochester EADFERD [Æth II A] 556
  Wallingford EDFERD [Cn G] 735
Eadwig
  Colchester EDFI [Æth II Ca] 327
  Hertford EDFI [Æth II C] 257
  London ÆFI [Wm I viii] 897 → Ælfwine?
    EDFI [Æth II E] 482
    EDFIG [Cn G] 708
Eadwine
  Cambridge EDFINE [Æth II C] 241–3
    [Æth II D] 339
  Exeter EDFINE [Æth II C] 253
  London [Æth II B2] 225
    [Æth II D] 392
    [Æth II A] 538
    [Wm I i] 888
    EADFN [Cn E] 628
    EDFINE [Æth II Cc] 235
    [Æth II C] 275
    [Æth II D] 396–7
    [Har I Ba] 807
  Oxford [Edw III H] 870
  Southwark [Æth II D] 436
  Thetford EDFINE [Æth II A] 566–7
    [Cn G] 734
Eadwulf
  EADVLF [Bgr a] 78
  EADVVLF [Abp Enb styca] 57
Ealhhere
  ALDHERE [Æth II Northumbria styca] 40
Ealhsige
  Chester ALESIGE [Edw III G] 873 → Ælfsige
    ELCSIGE [Æth II A] 506 → Ælfsige
Ealhstan
  EALHSTAN [Cnw] 72
Eanræd
  EANRED [Æth II Northumbria styca] 42–4
Eanwulf
  EANNLE [Osb styca] 54
  EANVLF [Edg i] 188
Eardnoth
  London ERDNOD [Cn E] 631
Eardwulf
  EARDVVLF [Æth II Northumbria styca] 51–3
Ed- → Ead-
Eoba
  [Cynethryth] 71

Eoda
　Wallingford [Æth II C] 311
Eoforheard
　FRARD [Edm i] 177
Eth- → Æth-

Fargrimr
　York FARGRIM [Cn E] 671
Farmann
　York FAREMAN [Æth II B1] 219
　　　FARMAN [Æth II B1] 220
Fordræd
　EORDRED [Eanr styca] 36
　　　[Rdw styca] 50
　FORDRED [Eanr styca] 37
　　　[Æth II Northumbria styca] 45–6
Frard → Eoforheard
Freothuwine
　London FREÐEƑINE [Cn E] 632
　Steyning FRÐƑINE [Cn H] 778
Frethi
　London [Cn E] 633–4

Garwulf
　Worcester GARVLF [Cn E] 668
Geirfinnr
　Lincoln GARFIN [Edw III Ac] 880
Gillacrist
　Chester GILACRIS [Har I A] 786
'Giodcic' [Godric?]
　Ipswich [Æth II E] 474
God/Goda
　Exeter GOD [Æth II D] 354
　　　[Cn E] 605
　　　GODA [Æth II Ca] 329
　Ilchester GOD [Æth II C] 259
　London GODGOD [Cn H] 769
　Lydford GODA [Æth II C] 288
　　　[Æth II A] 554
　Worcester GOD [Cn G] 739–40
Godhere
　London GODERÆ [Æth II A] 541–2
　　　GODERE [Cn E] 635
　　　[Cn G] 711
Godleof
　Huntingdon GODELEOF [Cn G] 684–5
　Stamford [Æth II D] 440
　　　GODELEOF [Æth II A] 563
　　　[Cn E] 654
Godman
　Bristol GODAMAN [Cn Ed] 598
　Canterbury [Cn G] 679
　Dover [Æth II Aa] 593
　Hertford [Har I B] 801
　Southampton [Æth II C] 297
　Winchester GODEMAN [Æth II D] 457
Godric
　Canterbury [Cn E] 600
　Colchester [Cn E] 604

Lincoln [Cn E] 617
　　　[Har I B] 805
　　　[Edw III D] 826
　　　[Edw III A] 834
London [Æth II C] 276–7
　　　[Æth II Ca] 332
　　　[Æth II D] 398
　　　[Æth II E] 483
　　　[Æth II A] 543
　　　[Cn G] 712–13
　　　[Cn H] 770
Northampton GODRICC [Har I B] 811
Southwark/Sudbury [Æth II D] 437
Stamford [Har I B] 814
Godwine
　Canterbury [Æth II C] 245
　　　[Æth II Ca] 325
　Chester [Cn E] 602
　Colchester [Æth II C] 249
　Dover [Æth II D] 350
　Gloucester [Cn E] 607
　Lincoln [Cn G] 691–2
　London [Æth II C] 278–9
　　　[Æth II D] 399–401
　　　[Æth II A] 544
　　　[Cn G] 714
　　　[Har I B] 808
　　　GODƑIINE [Wm I v] 894
　　　GODƑNE [Æth II E] 484
　Maldon [Edw III F] 863
　Milborne Port [Cn G] 725
　Norwich [Cn E] 646
　Oxford [Har I A] 792
　Salisbury GODPNE [Cn E] 651
　Stamford [Cn E] 655
　Warwick [Cn G] 736
　Winchester LODƑINE [Edw III A] 838
'Goinie' [Godwine?]
　Lincoln [Cn G] 693
Goldsige
　London GODSIGE [Har I A] 790
　　　GOLSI [Edw III C] 847
Goldwine
　London [Æth II C] 280
　　　[Æth II A] 545
Grimkell
　Lincoln GRIMCETEL [Cn G] 694
　　　GRIMCYTEL [Cn G] 695
Grimr
　Lincoln GRIM [Æth II D] 374
　Thetford GRIM [Æth II D] 441–2
Grimulfr
　York GRIMOLF [Cn G] 744
　　　GRIMVLF [Har I B] 816
Grimwald
　London [Æthst viii] 171
Gunnleifr
　Chester GVNLEOF [Cn G] 681

Guthfrithr
  Norwich GODEVERD [Edw III Ac] 881
Gyldwine
  Canterbury GVLDEϷINE [Edw III A] 830

Harthacnut
  Lincoln HERÐECNVT [Cn H] 761
Heahwulf
  HEAVVLF [Bgr a] 80
  London HEAϷVLF [Æth II D] 402–4
  Southwark HEAϷVLF [Æth II C] 299
Herebeorht
  Lewes HEREBYRHT [Æth II D] 362
Heremod
  [Edr i] 179
Hildulfr
  York HILDOLF [Æth II A] 585
        [Cn E] 672
        [Cn G] 745
    HILDVLF [Æth II E] 500
Hrafn
  York RÆFEN [Edw III F] 867
Hreitharr
  REGÐERES [Edr i] 182
Hringwulf
  Norwich RICNVLF [Cn G] 728
        RINCOLF [Edw III F] 864
Hunfrith
  HVNFRETH [Abp Pl] 90
Hunlaf
  NLADIR [Abp Wi styca] 64
Hunræd
  HVNRED [Edr i] 180–1
Hwætman
  Norwich HϷATEMAN [Æth II E] 493

Ifing
  Winchester IFINCC [Edw III A] 837
Ighar
  London IGERE [Æthst viii] 172
Ingalric
  Winchester INGLRI [Æth II B1] 218
Iohannes
  Lymne IOVNVS [Cn E] 644
Ioketill
  York IOCITEL [Edw III F/H] 868
        [Edw III G] 876–8
Iosteinn
  Lincoln GVSTAN [Cn G] 696–7
      IVSTAN [Æth II A] 519
        [Cn E] 618
Iri
  York IRA [Æth II D] 459
    IRE [Cn G] 746
Isengod
  Exeter ISEGOD [Cn E] 606

Kaupman
  COPMAN [Edg i] 186

Ketilbjorn?
  Lincoln CYTLERN [Æth II A] 517
Ketill
  York CETEL [Cn G] 743
Kolgrimr
  Lincoln COLGRIM [Æth II D] 370–1
      [Cn H] 760
      [Har I B] 804
  York COLGRIM [Æth II E] 499
Kolsveinn
  Lincoln COLSϷEIGN [Æth II A] 516

Leofdæg
  Peterborough LEOFDÆI [Cn E] 650
Leofgod
  Cricklade [Æth II D] 349
  Worcester [Æth II A] 584
Leofheah
  London LIOFHEH [Æth II A] 550
Leofing/Lifing
  LIABINCG [Abp Cln] 88
  Canterbury LIFINC [Æth II C] 246–7
  Ipswich LIFINC [Har I B] 803
      LIFINC [Cn G] 687
  Lincoln LEOFING [Cn E] 619
  London LIFINC [Æth II C] 281
      [Cn G] 715–16
      [Har I B] 809
    LYFINC [Æth II D] 414–15
    (fragment) [Edw III H] 869
  Northampton LIFING [Æth II B1] 209
  Norwich LIVINC [Æth II B1] 210
  Oxford LIFINCC [Cn G] 730
  Southwark LEOFINC [Cn G] 733
  Winchester LEIFINC [Cn E] 662 → Leofwine?
      LIFINC [Wm I viii] 903–5
Leofnoth
  Bedford [Æth II C] 237
  Canterbury [Cn G] 680
  Chester [Æth II A] 508
    LEONOÐ [Cn E] 603
  Lewes [Cn E] 615
  Shrewsbury [Æth II D] 435
  York LEOFENOÐ [Edw III E] 861
Leofræd
  London LEOFRED [Æth II D] 405
      [Cn H] 771
    LEOFRYD [Æth II D] 409–10
    LIFRED [Har I B] 810
    LIOFRED [Edw III B] 856
    LIOFRYD [Æth II E] 488
Leofric
  Canterbury [Æth II Ca] 326
  Chichester [Cn H] 753
  Ilchester [Æth II C] 260
  London [Æth II D] 406–8
    [Æth II E] 485–6
    [Cn H] 772
  Lymne [Æth II C] 289

LEFRIC [Æth II B3] 233
(fragment) [Æth II B2] 229
Stamford LEFRIC [Edw III G] 874
Thetford [Edw III E] 860
Leofsige
Ipswich [Æth II C] 261
[Æth II D] 359
Leofstan
Canterbury [Æth II B2] 224
[Æth II D] 341–2
LIFSTAN [Edw III G] 872
London [Æth II B2] 226
[Æth II D] 411
[Cn G] 717–19
[Cn H] 773
[Edw III A] 836
LEOFSTA [Æth II A] 546–7
Shrewsbury LEFSTAN [Har I A] 794
Winchester [Cn E] 663
Leofweald
Colchester LEOFⱯOLD [Æth II D] 348
Winchester LEOFⱯOLD [Æth II C] 319
[Cn E] 664
LIEFⱯOLD [Wm I viii] 902
LIOFⱯOLD [Wm I viii] 906
Leofweard
London LEOFⱯERD [Cn H] 774
Southwark LIFⱯFORD [Wm I viii] 899
Leofwig
London LIOEⱯI [Æth II A] 549
Leofwig?
Lincoln LEⱯⱯA [Har I A] 788
Leofwine
Bristol [Cn H] 749
Canterbury [Cn H] 752
Dover [Cn H] 757
LVFⱯINE [Cn G] 683
Lewes LEOFⱯNE [Æth II C] 262
LOFⱯNE [Æth II E] 476
Lincoln [Har I B] 806
London [Æth II B2] 227
[Æth II D] 413
[Æth II A] 548
[Cn E] 636
LEOFⱯNE [Æth II E] 487
LIOFⱯINE [Cn E] 637–8
LYOFⱯINE [Æth II A] 551
Northampton [Æth II D] 428–9
LEFⱯIINE [Edw III D] 827
Norwich [Cn I = HCn] 821
Southwark/Sudbury [Æth II C] 305
Stamford [Æth II A] 564
Winchester [Æth II A] 576–7
[Har I B] 815
LEIFINC [Cn E] 662 → Leofing?
York [Æth II C] 321
Lufa
Shaftesbury [Æth II C] 295–6
[Æth II D] 434

Lif- → Leof-
Lul/Lulla
LVLLA [Offa] 70

Man/Manna/Monna
MONN [Æthst I] 92
MONNE [Eanr styca] 38–9
[Osb styca] 55
Exeter MANNA [Æth II D] 355
Leicester MAN [Edg vi] 189
Norwich MANA [Cn G] 726–7
MANNA [Har I B] 812
Thetford MANA [Æth II A] 568
[Cn E] 658
Totnes MANNA [Æth II B1] 215
Mancrent
Northampton NANCRENT [Æth II A1] 197
Manning
Dover MANNINC [Æth II A] 511
Manticen
Norwich [Æthst viii] 173

'Nladir' → Hunlaf
Nother
[Æthst i] 164

Oban
York [Æth II D] 460
Oda
Winchester [Æth II A] 578–9
ODE [Cn E] 665
Oio
Stamford OGE [Edg vi] 191
OGEA [Edg vi] 192
Ordbeorht
Winchester ORDBRIHT [Æth II A] 580–1
[Cn E] 666
Orest/Ornost
Cambridge ORST [Cn E] 599
Os- → As-
Osbern
Salisbury ESBRN [Wm II i] 909
Thetford OSBER [Æth II C] 309
OSBRN [Æth II D] 443
Wilton [Æth II B1] 216
Oshere
[Æthbt i] 153
Osmund
[Æthwf] 152
Lincoln [Æth II E] 479
Osweald
Lewes OSⱯOLD [Edw III F] 862
Norwich OSⱯOLD [Cn E] 647
Oswulf → Asulfr
Oth- → Auth-

Pada
(runes) 1

R- see also Hr-

Ragnaldr or Reinald
    Lincoln RÆIENOLD [Æth II E] 480
    York REGNALD [Æthst v] 166
'Ryrlefa'
    [St Edm] 100

Sæfugl
    York SÆFVHEL [Edw III A] 840
Sæmann
    Salisbury SÆMAN [Æth II A] 557
Sæwine
    Wilton [Æth II C] 313–14
        [Æth II Intermed A] 335
        [Æth II D] 452–3
        (fragment) [Æth II B3] 234
        SƷINE [Edw III G] 875
Selakollr
    York SELECOL [Cn E] 673
Seolca
    Winchester [Æth II A] 572
Sibwine
    London [Æth II D] 417–18
Siduwine
    Rochester SIDEƷINE [Æth II B1] 211
          SIDƷINE [Æth II Ca] 333
Sigeboda
    Winchester SIBDOA [Cn E] 667
Sigeferth
    Lincoln SIFRED [Wm I viii] 896
Sigemær
    Canterbury SIMIER [Wm II iii] 911
Sigemund
    SIMVNDVS [St Edm] 101
Sigeræd
    Gloucester SIGERED [Æth II A] 512
    London SIRED [Cn G] 720
Sigestæf
    SIGESTEF [Cnw] 73
Sigewulf
    Wallingford SIGEVLF [Æth II C] 312
Skuli
    York SCVLÆ [Cn I = HCn] 822
Snell
    ISNEL [Æthst x] 174
Sperling
    Sudbury SPRLYNC [Cn E] 656
    Thetford SPYRELINC [Edw II] 196
         SPYRLING [Æth II B2] 230
Spileman
    Winchester [Æth II A] 583
        [Har I A] 798
Spræcling
    Winchester SPRACLINC [Wm I viii] 907
Stanmær
    Colchester STANMÆ [Edw III B] 851
Stefanus
    [Æthst i] 165

Steinbitr
    Lincoln STIGNBIT [Æth II C] 263
Styrkarr
    Leicester STYRCAR [Æth II B1] 204
    York STEORCER [Æth II D] 461
        STIRCER [Cn E] 674
Styrkollr
    York STIRCOL [Æth II A] 588
        [Cn E] 675
Sumarlithr
    Lincoln SVMERLÆÐ [Æth II A] 523
        SVMERLED [Æth II D] 376
          [Æth II A] 524
        SVMERLIDA [Har I A] 789
        SVMERLÐ [Cn E] 621–2
    York SVMERLEÐI [Æth II A] 589–90
        SVMRLEÐI [Æth II A] 591
Sunegod
    Lincoln [Cn E] 623
Sunnulfr
    York SVNOLF [Cn E] 676
        SVNVLF [Æth II D] 462
Svartbrandr
    Lincoln SƷARTBRAND [Cn G] 699
        SƷEARTABRAD [Cn G] 700
Svartgeirr
    Stamford SƷARTGAR [Æth II E] 497
        SƷERTGAR [Æth II A] 565
Svartkollr
    York SƷARTCOL [Edw III G] 879
Sveinn
    Chester SƷEGEN [Æth II D] 345
    London SƷAN [Cn H] 775
    York SƷEGEN [Har I B] 817
Svertingr
    Chester SƷARTINC [Æth II A] 509
    York SƷERTINC [Æth II C] 322
Swefheard
    Canterbury SVVEFHERD [Abp Wfr] 86
Sweting
    London SƷETINC [Æth II C] 283–5
        [Æth II D] 419–20
        SƷTINC [Æth II C] 286
Swetman
    Oxford [Edw III F] 865
Swetric
    Wilton [Edw III H] 871

'Tafere'
    'ROCCE' [Edw III C] 849
Theodgild
    Lincoln ÐEOTGELD [Æth II C] 264
Theodmær
    ÐEODMAER [Edr i] 183
Thorbjorn
    Steyning ÐRBEN [Wm II iii] 917
Thorfrithr
    Norwich ÐVRFERD [Cn E] 648

Wulfwine
  Colchester [Cn H] 754
  Huntingdon ᚱVLFINE [Har I B] 802
  London [Æth II C] 287
    [Æth II D] 424
    [Æth II E] 491
    [Wm I i] 889
  Oxford [Æth II D] 433
Wynsige
  Exeter [Æth II D] 356–7
  London [Cn G] 721

Wynstan
  Bath [Æth II D] 338
  London [Cn G] 722–4
  Salisbury ᚱINSTAN [Cn G] 731

Uncertain moneyer
  Chester? [Wm II iii] 912
  London [Wm II iii] 915
  Oxford [Hen I xi] 918
  [Wm I ii] 892
  [Ste] 921–3

INDEX OF HOARDS

Hoards are indexed under their original names, mostly German, and cross references are given, where appropriate, from their modern Polish forms. The contents of these hoards are summarised on pp. 12–36 above.

ENGLISH COIN TYPES AND THEIR CHRONOLOGIES, *c*.973–1100

The sequence of periodic coin types for the late Anglo-Saxon and early Anglo-Norman coinage is now securely settled. The dates used in the summary of finds (pp. 12–36 above) and set out below are those proposed by Dolley. These assume that at various periods the substantive issues were of broadly similar duration and, while greater refinement may be possible in the future, they provide an approximate chronology which is likely to be accurate to within a reasonable margin.

Edg	Eadgar (959–75)		A	*Radiate/Small Cross* (*c*.1044–6)
C	*Reform* (*c*.973–5)		C	*Trefoil Quadrilateral* (*c*.1046–8)
			B	*Small Flan* (*c*.1048–50)
Edw II	Edward the Martyr (975–8)		E	*Expanding Cross* (*c*.1050–3)
A	*Small Cross* (975–8)		F	*Pointed Helmet* (*c*.1053–6)
			H	*Sovereign/Eagles* (*c*.1056–9)
Æth II	Æthelred II (978–1016)		G	*Hammer Cross* (*c*.1059–62)
A1	*First Small Cross* (*c*.978–9)		Ac	*Facing Bust* (*c*.1062–5)
B1	*First Hand* (*c*.979–85)		I	*Pyramids* (*c*.1065–6)
B2	*Second Hand* (*c*.985–91)			
C	*Crux* (*c*.991–7)		Har II	Harold II (1066)
Intermed A	*Intermediate Small Cross* (*c*.997)		A	*Pax* (1066)
D	*Long Cross* (*c*.997–1003)			
E	*Helmet* (*c*.1003–9)		Wm I	William I (1066–87)
G	*Agnus Dei* (*c*.1009)		i	*Profile/Cross Fleury* (*c*.1066–8)
A	*Last Small Cross* (*c*.1009–18)		ii	*Bonnet* (*c*.1068–70)
			iii	*Canopy* (*c*.1070–2)
Cn	Cnut (1016–35)		iv	*Two Sceptres* (*c*.1072–4)
E	*Quatrefoil* (*c*.1017–23)		v	*Two Stars* (*c*.1074–7)
G	*Pointed Helmet* (*c*.1023–9)		vi	*Sword* (*c*.1077–80)
H	*Short Cross* (*c*.1029–35/6)		vii	*Profile/Cross and Trefoil* (*c*.1080–3)
			viii	*Paxs* (*c*.1083–6)
Har I	Harold I (1035–40)			
A	*Jewel Cross* (*c*.1036–8)		Wm II	William II (1087–1100)
B	*Fleur-de-Lis* (*c*.1038–40)		i	*Profile* (*c*.1086–9)
			ii	*Cross in Quatrefoil* (*c*.1089–92)
HCn	Harthacnut (1035–7, 40–2)		iii	*Cross Voided* (*c*.1092–5)
A	*Jewel Cross* (*c*.1036–7)		iv	*Cross Pattée and Fleury* (*c*.1095–8)
B	*Arm and Sceptre* (*c*.1040–2)		v	*Cross Fleury and Piles* (*c*.1098–1100)
Edw III	Edward the Confessor (1042–66)			
D	*Pacx* (*c*.1042–4)			